SHAMING MY RED LIPS

SHAGHAYEGH "POPPY" FARSIJANI

STORY MERCHANT BOOKS

STORY MERCHANT BOOKS • LOS ANGELES • 2018

Shaming My Red Lips

www.shfarsi.com

www.facebook.com/theburdenofmyredlipsintehran/

ISBN: 978-0-9991621-7-0

Story Merchant Books
400 S. Burnside Avenue #11B
Los Angeles, CA 90036

www.storymerchantbooks.com

Cover: Claire Moore
Interior Design: Lauren Michelle

To my parents, for showing me love in its rarest form.

SHAMING MY RED LIPS

1

Goodbye, Brooklyn

May 1996

DESPITE MUCH LABORED THOUGHT, I still couldn't figure out why my parents had decided to move back to Iran. Yes, I know it's my home country and I was born there but I'd had no affiliation with it since I was three years old. At seventeen, I definitely didn't have any connection with it! I hadn't heard anything fun about growing up in Iran, so why would I want to return there now, when I had all my friends, my hangouts, and a guy I kind-of liked here (although that didn't go far)? Maybe some punch ball in the playground followed with an iced gelato on a hot summer day. He sometimes took his shirt off, allowing me to admire his soon-to-be six-pack, but that was as far as our dates went. Robert was his name, and I had the hots for him.

Pardon me, I seem to have gotten off track.

My cousins all longed to come to the U.S. and here we were packing up our bags, headed for the country of burkas. I felt no lingering ties nor longing to return there. My mother's side of the family and some of my fathers still lived there, but I hardly ever spoke with them. What I most desired was to be free and near my friends right here in Brooklyn. Christina and Jennifer, my Italian buddies—what was life going to be without them? What were the Iranian girls going to be like? Would they be fun and exciting and go out on bike rides with me? Wait, would they know how to ride a bike since they were always wearing those long burkas and coats over their clothes? How can you ride a bike with a foot-long garment wrapped around your hips? Once you start pedaling, your foot might get stuck! That would be interesting. But again, why me? Why do I have to go to Iran?

Who could blame me? Even the slowest, bee-buzzing days in the neighborhood offered many charms: dog-walkers (each, like their pet, bearing unique quirks); lawn-tenders and their weekly rituals; or guys fixing and washing cars with scientific intensity, sometimes with their shirts off. A sight to see while eating gelato!

But I finally finished packing my bags and surged with dull nausea over the very idea of leaving Brooklyn. My mom and dad had no right to take me from my neighborhood, my life, my friends, and my way of living, to put me somewhere I had no idea about. The many unanswered questions about Iran frustrated me and they were topped with horror stories heard here and there from sources that never wanted to return to Iran. My dad had marvelously reached the conclusion that he wanted me to become acquainted with my Iranian roots. My theory was that he wanted to have better control over me. My mischievous ways were leaking out slowly and it must have frightened him and that's why he had finally decided to pack up. But shouldn't I have a say in this? When I asked why, I would get hit with, "This is the best route for you," and of course that was followed by a sentence I hated: "You will love Iran!"

Why would I love Iran when so many kids and their parents were migrating across the ocean and to the land of the free?

I just wanted to stay in Brooklyn, the place I called home. Now I had to decide on the best way to spend what little time remained, with the neighborhood that had given me so many valuable memories. God only knew what awaited me in another country, with new friends to be made, and a culture brimming with unfamiliar tastes, textures, sights and sounds. I knew I wasn't going to be able to ride my bike like I did here, or go out on a date with a guy. And prom? Forget about it. My cousins had told me the schools were separate, like Catholic school, and guys and girls weren't allowed on dates and there is nothing like a prom. Asking them about something like a prom had them LMAO-ing. And forget about reaching the legal drinking age! There was no age, alcohol was banned for all ages! I wasn't religious, and I would respect their religion, but who are they to tell me that because of worship, you can't go to parties, and forget about looking at someone's six-pack? How was a girl to have fun? This signaled me to take pictures of Robert and his body one time on the playground in case I needed some eye-candy.

If my parents loved Iran so much, why did they come here in the first place? I would eavesdrop on my mother's conversations with her friends at times and the conversation went something like, "*Va* it was the best decision to come here...that place is not made to live in anymore. Inflation kills!" Then at other times it went something like, "There is no opportunity *there* for children to grow, so I want her to grow up *here*, speak English fluently, and get a good education and job." This was all said with a deep Farsi accent and of course the *Va*, which was said with a slanted attitude most Iranian moms used to regulate conversation. In other words, it means "what'cha talkin' 'bout?"

3

But no, it was like I was in the twilight zone. They had brought me to the U.S. so I could have a good education, and suddenly at seventeen, they saw the devil sneaking out of me and thought, "Crap! Forget good job and education, let's split and head back to the mothership!" Again, no one thought to ask me, and when I asked, the response was always, "It's our decision as your parents to raise you in Iran. It's a *parental* decision." And then came my favorite part: "You will love Iran Shaghayegh Jan. Mami promises." Ugh.

So now that I was headed in a *parental* decision on the other side of the world, I might as well make some of my own decisions while I was still here. I wasn't allowed outside after sunset but asked my mom for permission to take one final bike ride and was granted this request.

With greater than normal anxiousness, I deftly pulled on my favorite sneakers, clumped none-too-slowly downstairs, and climbed on my bike—another piece of great memories I had to leave behind. This bike had gotten me out of trouble one too many times and was my ride to Coney Island, the playground we played punch ball on, watching Robert and closely observing his body while he was hanging out with his buddies, and quickly pedaling away once they started walking towards my hiding spot.

"Well, here I go. One last bike ride," I whispered to myself, thinking out loud.

Pedaling along the sidewalk, I caught isolated whiffs of grass-clippings, flowers, and phantoms of someone's backyard barbecue; the greasy smear of hamburgers.

"Hi! *Hey!*"

Here on the twilit sidewalk were Annie and Larry, out for an evening stroll with one of their four dogs. "Shaghayegh!" called Annie. "Don't run us over girl!" They all laughed.

I nearly wept over my love for them, our neighbors from two doors down. Tall debonair Larry was as handsome as they made men; Annie was a true Italian beauty, whose fashion sense and uniqueness often had her sporting a new pair of funky earrings and new toe rings, simply to walk the dog. Although I was considered young I knew their love-making had to be the tops. They showed lots of PDA but the way they talked to one another was so flirtatious, smoldering and intense; it had to get hot under the covers. I sometimes talked to Annie about having the hots for Robert, since I couldn't talk about it with my mom; she would probably become fearful that I might be having sex with him and pack up her bags and leave like, yesterday. Another issue with Iranian parents that bothered me! No worries, if I can't say it in front of you, I'll say it to someone else in back of you! I would have fun talks with Annie and it always ended with, "Remember pumpkin, you're the cream of the crop, so make those six-packs run for ya!" Good deal. Oh Annie and Larry...I'll miss you.

Before I came to tears I swallowed hard. Here was my favorite deli, with my favorite pastramis, and friendly faces inside eating and talking and laughing. Not much further away stood Ming's Golden Wok, exhaling garlic and stir-fried pork beneath the buzz of crimson neon. His pork was my favorite but again my parents never ate the pork; now that I'm heading to Iran I should probably forget about all things pork, along with prom nights. The "religious country" category and its storage would be in overload mode soon.

I coasted and rested my legs as I wheeled past the pizzeria and another symphony of aromas, a cozy heat swirling with molten mozzarella, spicy sausage, oregano and the holy promise of olive oil.

"Shaghayegh!" someone shouted through the bright doorway. I knew it was Mario from the pizzeria with his deep Sicilian accent. He had treated me to one too many slices on the house and had taught me how to make pizza dough the Italian way. This included understanding the physics of tossing the dough flattened into a CD and grabbing it at the right moment, while it still had momentum. Too much sophistication for just making dough in my opinion, but he made it fun by teasing me for not getting it right. I pedaled away, dreading tears but taking comfort in realizing nearly everyone who visited these happy establishments knew me.

I passed P.S. 200 Benson School and the park where I played a lot of punch-ball. My consciousness was swarming with smells of freshly made Italian tomato sauce and sights and sounds of all kinds, all markings of my sweet childhood. What was it about this place that filled me with potent feelings? Perhaps nothing more than a seventeen-year-old's mind contenting itself with what little I knew, and grasped, of the world.

As I pedaled up 21st Street, an occasional stranger I knew from some time or someplace favored me with a smile, and I recalled the ice cream truck that first acquainted me with its sugary cargo. Stuff I didn't really enjoy, but I loved asking my mom for money simply to relish in having a treat with the other kids on the block. Everyone *had to* do that, because the truck was besieged with an outer ring of parents surrounding jumping children jingling with coins, shouting, "I want a chocolate-sprinkle vanilla cone!" and "Gimme a chocolate-dipped almond-covered chocolate bar!" the last famous and famously heavy on calories. I had definitely gotten a bit fatter from my love for sweets, but it didn't matter, especially since I knew that now I had to cover up my body and trash my jean shorts too. Throw another item into the religious category of Islamic rules I had to obey.

Christina and Jennifer would always join when Mr. ice cream truck came along. They were *my girls*; it was the *2 Italians 'n a Persian* musketeer trio. We were inseparable in school and when the clock

6

hit three, we were already outside playing punch-ball. Jennifer had a crush on Robert's brother, Jason, so we would go out on imaginary double dates since her parents were just as strict as mine. Christina was the listener, the nerd, and brought in good food during lunchtime. My lunch would either be a simple bologna sandwich or something completely from the other end of the cultural spectrum called Kookoo. It was basically an herb soufflé with a strong herb smell that signaled whoever who was sitting next to me to ask, "What *is* that?" The answer, depending on how nice the question was asked, would either come with or without translation. Without translation it simply went by Kookoo, with a mind-your-own-beeswax tone and a twirling of my finger in a circular motion.

We had been friends for the longest time and now, right before prom year, right before the year we turned "the big eighteen," my parents were separating me from them. Christina would say we're "stretch worthy" and that our bond would never break. I knew it was true, but I would miss our days and evenings together. Forget about writing—the post office in Iran would probably throw out letters with an American address. Okay, I was exaggerating, but the time it took to exchange letters between two countries on two different continents would be a month! And my parents weren't up for a hefty phone bill either. I was scared I wouldn't find friends I liked, especially because my Farsi sucked. If I couldn't communicate how the hell was I going to establish relationships? I guess with a guy, sometimes communication didn't have to be with words. But on that note again, I couldn't date, so I'd have to make sure I brought some magazines with me so I could at least look.

Another issue was my dancing. I loved dancing, especially ballet, jazz, and hip-hop, and dreamt of being a choreographer after college. My hips and feet couldn't stand still; when the beat hit me my DNA was awakened. But I knew for a fact there were no dance

7

classes in Iran. If you had to cover yourself up when you walked around, then just moving the curves of your body—especially to the groove—was not classified as sophisticated or Islamic. But what if there *was* some underground dance studio offering secret services to attendees? It was a long shot, but I had to let these thoughts fly or else I would go nuts!

The girls kept telling me to chill out with these annoying thoughts, but they weren't in the hot seat. I knew I was headed toward big-time trouble.

The rushing emotions triggered my memories—the laughter, smiles, and faces that came during Christmases past and Hanukkahs celebrated with Jewish friends; snowball fights and birthday parties thrown by my parents. How could someone bear leaving behind the place that held such powerful memories? Why must the potential of more moments and days spent somewhere so close to my heart *end* because of a sudden urge to move to another continent? It wasn't fair...

No one asked if I would be bothered. Dad was an entrepreneur and had already closed his jewelry business here and was starting a curtain business in Tehran. Talk about jumpy. Mom was a hair stylist and would probably join my aunt in her females-only salon in Tehran. Easy breezy for her. And then came me—my job was to learn to adapt. "She is so talented and flexible, she will adapt within days," was what my counselor had told my mom. Oh Please!

One thing I knew was that this Shaghayegh was not the giving up type and I would find a way to cherish my delicate inner child, so sweet, playful, and vivacious. This inner child would be sustained (and sustain) its protector during the coming journey and whatever it held. That was a promise.

After pedaling through avenues and blocks of memories I finally made it home, finally ready to surrender and pack. I labeled some boxes "Not trash-worthy BUT valuable" so my mom didn't *accidentally* throw my things out with their junk. A special label was made for the box with all my precious books and diaries into which I'd spilled feelings, like paint spattered across a canvas. I had a restless spirit, a volcano of emotions, rolled onto a symbolic dance floor. Wasn't the most beautiful part of a human being their whirling dance of emotions? Even from my early teens I'd desired this dance…but now I had to obey my parents and move to a mysterious country where dancing was forbidden.

I called my folks Ziba and Kaveh, H₂O (water) and the Emperor, because it was funny and 90% of the time I would get what I wanted from both. They were flattered because one was the essence of life and the other a powerful king. But a little info regarding the two: total opposites. I don't even know how the powers of the universe brought them together. My mom was full of love, life, and fun. My dad was dry, his sense of humor drier, and he occasionally grinned. The rest of his head was basketball, baseball and occasional hikes. The Emperor was a great listener and an awesome poker and backgammon player. But I'm sure that wasn't what brought them together. Their "résumés" and my grandfather's firm, coupled with his angry eyebrows, were the cause of their marriage. I don't think they even went out on one date with each other. The differences formed mountains, but I felt my mom found a certain degree of security with my dad, and to this day they sometimes held hands and she used his shoulder as a pillow. A bit awkward when me and my little brother were in the room.

Oh, and my little brother, Saman. Well, he was too little to understand the big move. At ten years old, all he watched were reruns of Sylvester Stallone movies, followed Manchester United football games. He thought he was David Beckham, the George Clooney of football. He went wherever the ball went, and in this

9

situation the ball was kicked overseas. So he was following. He was in fourth grade, had his friends, and was too far from his teenage years to be worried about anything. We were good buddies, but I felt as if I would be his protector and shield since I was the clever fighter—at least that's what I thought of myself. He also helped me when I wanted to sneak out, and I would in return give him a buck or two. From early on, it worked out between us.

I knew my parents adored me and my love for life, dance, food, *Looney Tunes*, *MacGyver*, *Saved by the Bell*, *Melrose Place* and a good Scooby-Doo mystery. But even knowing all the American things I loved, they thought the best way for me to grow and understand life and my culture, would be to return to Iran, even if only for a couple of years. They were excited they were going home; I was fearful I was headed into an alternate reality I thought of as the twilight zone, even at its finest moments.

2

Hello, Tehran

June 1996

THE PILOT ANNOUNCED THAT OUR Iran Air flight would be landing shortly.

My mother, H$_2$O, regarded me with a serious gaze. "Put on your scarf before you get off the jet. You'll have to get used to this style of dressing from now on."

I realized then I had glued myself to my seat.

It wasn't that I minded donning my scarf, considering this just another aspect of my new mystery life. It was that the look in my mother's eyes shouted that I was heading into a deep culture shock, or coma. The good part was that I was aware I was headed into a coma, whereas other people do something to prevent this medical condition. The only action I could take now was to jump off the plane into the landing area. They would most likely catch me before I touched the exit door. Bad plan. With no money and no one I could trust to share my true feelings with, the backup plan was to suck it up. I already had a bad feeling about this, and all I could keep repeating in my mind was, "You're a warrior! Just do it!"

And so we landed and the passengers started cascading out of the plane. There was no line or order, everyone was on top of one another once they got out. Then there was a bus taking the passengers to the airport customs area. My parents waited until everyone got off. We were the last to exit, for fear of being run over.

With my scarf on, my mom had finally given me a carry-on, my brother two carry-ons, and my father was leading with the biggest carry-on since he was the strongest. Once we hopped off the bus, we had to step into the passport check line. These were my observations of Iran at first sight: everyone was complaining about how long the line was, even though they were the ones pushing the length of the line. It reminded me of Pac-Man. They were talking Farsi at lightning speed so I didn't even come close to understanding what they were saying. The security guards and passport officers, if male, had beards that covered their entire face except their eyes and nose; the females were wearing burkas, long coats, and just looked mean. If I knew or understood any Farsi I was hearing, I still kept my mouth shut and let my mamma do the talking.

My dad was pretty good at saying the right words with the right tone, so we got our Iranian passports stamped. That was when it really started to hit me. This was it, the game, the journey, the web, the Hunger Games had started. Now it was bag pick-up time and then seeing my mystery family. I didn't know what to expect— would they be the Addams family or the Brady Bunch?

The baggage check was fun. They basically dug through our bags to see if we had porn magazines, sex toys, Madonna CDs, or anything else of that nature that was illegal here. Maybe they were searching for a gun but no, this was much more than a security

12

search. I had to remember I had stepped into the religious hot tub and had to be a zombie to their wishes. At least in public. No more *People* magazine or *TV Guide* for checking out the latest steamy encounters in *Days of Our Lives*, and definitely no more *Baby-Sitters Club* books. I don't even know if they were imported to the mothership country!

After we put that mess behind us we headed into the greeting section and all I could see were big flower bouquets, people jumping into each other's' laps (men were throwing themselves at their "brothers"), people weeping as if someone pushed the cry button on their system, and a sea of scarves and black burkas—and *more* men with lots of facial hair! It's like the country was short on razors and shaving cream!

I didn't know what my mom or dad's family looked like but they seemed to know exactly what I looked like. When they approached me, I was surprised to see they weren't religious-looking at all, but totally groovy and hip. Diamonds in the rough!

Scarves and coats were mandatory, but they had made them into fashion statements! Their make-up was impeccable, everyone smelled of perfumes and colognes, and some let their blonde, brunette or highlighted hair hang out. My guy cousins were studs and they were kissing and hugging me! I thought that was illegal? I was ambushed by kisses and hugs from all directions without knowing any names or who these people were. If a stranger were to have kissed me I probably wouldn't have known the difference. And too bad, because my parents were so busy, so I could have gotten away with a kiss.

The family greeted us with warmth, hospitality and too many kisses. Some of which I even had to wash off my cheeks. But their love hit me like a warm wave, and I subconsciously returned every drop. It had been a while since I'd been the center of so much laughter and so many smiles. Everyone had ecstasy-like energy despite the pre-dawn hour, apparently oblivious to whatever duties lay waiting after sunrise.

My mother was in heaven and seemed the happiest, enjoying the massed presence of adored nieces, nephews, sisters, brothers, and of course her own mother, Aziz Joon. She was wearing a burka and was the only one that looked religious and when she came towards me I wanted to run because she was going to pull me under her burka. I couldn't escape, and eventually was pulled under her burka and got four juicy kisses smack on my cheeks—that's four per cheek. Then I was let go like a yo-yo into the crowd until another person grabbed me and put another three or four mushy kisses on me.

Personally, I couldn't stop grinning and had to constantly be aware of my scarf slipping off my head. This damn piece of garment that I had to wear...ugh! But I felt gleeful and everyone was smiling like it was taped to their faces!

After the mushy stuff I saw the men fighting for the suitcases to ensure the arrivals were properly taken care of. That was all right with me. I don't know if they wanted to spare us the back pain or if this was part of Iranian hospitality, but giving all my bags to someone and waiting for the car to pick me up was like an automatic and frequent-flyer valet service. Even my dad, considered powerful and muscular, was pushed away from any chance at lugging bags to the parking area.

My mother giggled helplessly. I think she was overwhelmed with family love because it definitely wasn't the smog and dirty air we walked into when stepping out of the airport. Man, the smoke was like the airport was built next to factories. So now, after the debate on who would take the luggage, a debate ensued regarding who would be sitting with whom and in whose car during the return to my grandmother's house. At least the destination was clear.

My first ride in this new life. What did this city look like? What types of cars roamed the streets—they could be Batmobiles for all I knew. The parking lot driveway was filled with ugly turtle-looking cars with the name "Peykan" engraved on the back. They looked like cheap frogs made with steel and four wheels. Looking through the windows the inside didn't even make it to a three-star interior. It was archaic for sure.

Surrounded by these ugly looking cars, a new Mercedes noticeably popped up in front of me. Nice! This must have been dropped down by God himself. I mean in the middle of all these animal-like cars we at least had a miracle from *Vogue* magazine! Whoa! Since we were the VIP arrivals, the best seats in the house were given to us in the Mercedes SUV. Everyone around the pick-up area was in an ugly Peykan while we were cruising high. It was strange. The difference was like an old run-down town in the middle of Kentucky vs. Monaco; the 99 Cents store vs. Rodeo Drive. The gap was getting bigger by the second.

So this is how it worked: my mother's side had my mother and me captive and my father's side had my dad and brother captive. My cousin sat next to me and started pouring out Farsi lingo. I sat there smiling, nodding, and agreeing with everything she said and when appropriate my mom dropped in a line or two to save me. What was up with all the talk anyway? And their smiles looked as if they were dripping down their faces. It was eerie. What type of fake communication was this crap?

The wheels started turning and with different conversations sprouting between the eight people squeezed into an SUV and someone's crutch stuck in between the manual shift gear, I zoned out to focus on the city's visuals. Tehran's weather in the summertime could get as hot as the Sahara Desert, but it was early morning and so I pulled down the window to breathe in the cool a.m. air. I needed it—I was going nuts with so many people talking on top of each other.

Cruising down the road I saw a billboard of a dude with a turban and white beard and automatically knew this was serious stuff and not just a gimmick for the cover page of a male magazine. I didn't know a lot of Iranian history, having come from the American Revolution and Civil War books, but knew this was the Islamic Leader. I could never remember his name, and afraid of mispronouncing the little bits and pieces in my head, I kept to myself. I'd ask eventually but didn't want to open my mouth for fear of hearing, "Oh, you are so cute," for the millionth time!

The ugly Peykans filled the streets and I saw they were used for not only cabs, but also commuter vehicles. Man, did they make the flowers lose their color. Cabs were parked in front of this square, which also looked famous, like from a war period. The drivers' legs were hanging out of their cars, indicating someone was having a little morning nap.

The square was more the shape of a sumo wrestler spreading his legs and trying to accomplish a split rather than a square. A strange, intuitive feeling told me this place was similar to our Statue of Liberty because of the size and its central location. My cousin looked at me as if reading my mind and said, "Shaghayegh Joon, this is Azadi Square, or as you call it, Freedom Square. It's a big deal and people always gather here for protests, especially during the revolution,' she spoke partly in Farsi and partly in English, knowing my Farsi was on special crutches. I noted her English was also on crutches.

The only revolutions I knew were the American and French Revolutions, so at the risk of sounding dumb I asked, with the

16

crappiest of verb and noun placement in Farsi, "Freedom from who, and why?"

Suddenly my mom looked at me as if I had to have known the answer to that question and must have been asking it rhetorically. "Shaghayegh *Jan*, you know about the Revolution *azizam*. You know the Shah leaving and the Ayatollah coming and the regime change, and that is why everyone has to wear the hijab. This was the famous square where they had all the protests and it's a true symbol of your country," she said firmly, as if the revolution rotated around her.

Jan and *azizam*, both terms of endearment in Farsi, should not be used in one sentence! It made me feel dumb but I didn't care what anyone thought and knew my mom was trying to do the famous Iranian *aberoo dari*—covering up my lack of knowledge in case of embarrassment. That happens a lot, because apparently you're supposed to be born an omniscient god if you're Iranian!

"Oh," I said, sounding surprised at both the historical fact and the realization that this country and the country I grew up in were such enemies. I loved the U.S., it had given me Brooklyn, good pizza, the Backstreet Boys and awesome memories. But here, next to the Freedom Tower, I didn't know how many years ago the threads of communication between the country where I was born and the country I grew up in were permanently disconnected. Sounds like a bad relationship ending. Even divorced parents communicate to keep the kids happy—so were the kids happy in Iran? I didn't think so, because many, including my parents, left during the Revolution to pursue better lives. But now we were back at square one. Pursuing a better life meant controlling me and helping me get in touch with my roots. By the way, I think I could have accomplished that in Brooklyn; going to an Iranian school in Queens had taught me the little Farsi I knew. What more did I need? But no…it had to be on a broader scale for my folks!

The streets were dirty with lots of construction zones and gutters on either side of the streets with little streams flowing through them. And whoa! The graffiti was like Picasso had stepped out of his grave and drawn a living dead skeleton, the famous Lady Liberty herself, and right down below her was a red-carpet arrival of the leader whose name I always mixed up with the President. About that, who was who and why the hell were there two people leading a country? It was like the Pres and his VP both in one position. One fact I knew from when the Emperor watched the news was that Iran had a leader like Khomenei—although I think he was dead now—and someone else was in his place, and the other was the President. Who picked who? What if they didn't like each other? Why was one wearing that turban all the time and the other wearing a beard? Oh, and the beard could never be a fashionable one, like a goatee or a special shave his girlfriend or wife gave him. It was always a traditional mullah one.

As we got further away from the airport, streets began looking more contemporary, clean, and the people's attire changed to tight pants (not the flammable type), more make-up, three or four-inch high heeled shoes, and the headscarves were worn far back as to cover up ponytails or enormous fake buns. Instead of the frog-looking Peykans, the cars transformed into Maseratis, BMWs, and lots of Mercedes Benzes. The guys were hot and the girls beat any *Vogue* or Versace model, hands down! It was easy to guess this was Northern Tehran and where the rich lived. So did that mean I could also dress like that, rather than having to focus all my energy on this piece of fabric falling off my head? My hair was already getting oily!

I thought the city would be more like Arabesque architecture with gold and turquoise popping out everywhere. Some buildings were tall, but not as tall as the Empire State Building; most were only two to four stories. Then we passed a hotel that looked like a burnt-out Hyatt or Four Seasons, like they had burst from the inside; maybe they had. The gutters expanded in width and some even had rocks and flowers growing in them. Trees lined the streets on both sides, but grass was a rarity. The sidewalk designs changed frequently, as if the task was left to every house or property owner to design their own sidewalk.

Drowned in thoughts, my cousin Arshia posed the golden question: "Do you guys want to get some *Halim* or *Kaleh Pacheh* for breakfast?"

My mom, and for that matter, everyone else in the car, favored *Kaleh Pacheh* over *Halim*, which was similar to oatmeal but with chunks of turkey meat and cinnamon. *Kaleh Pacheh,* or anything associated with sheep's head and hooves, disgusted me. I preferred a serving of good ol' wheat toast and feta cheese, accompanied by a glass of orange juice. In fact, the very smell of *Kaleh Pacheh* made me sick to my stomach. I didn't don't how my cousins could be even excited about it!

My Farsi wasn't the best, but I didn't fear making mistakes when speaking it, even though it sounded as if the words were literally plucked from old Farsi texts rotting in the basement of some old dusty library.

So I voiced objection—thankfully confirmed by my mom—to the breakfast suggestion.

"Why *Kaleh Pacheh*? It's gross!" I said with a moan.

My cousins grinned and Arshia said, "It's the best Shaghayegh! This place has the best and freshest. My stamp of guarantee!" he explained.

But I couldn't help wondering, "Who are you and how should I know your stamp is reliable?" How in any way eating the brain, tongue, and hooves of a sheep could be delightful was far from my understanding.

The morning was growing and now the buses, people going to school with the backpacks, and office people with their suitcases were popping out in the streets. "This is North Tehran called, *Fereshteh*, Shaghayegh Joon, and we live right down the street," my female cousin Ghazaleh pointed out as we parked in front of the "sheep's brain and hooves place." That made it sound more disgusting, which I was in favor of at this point, so I decided to use that rather than saying *Kaleh Pacheh*.

Everyone got out, with Arshia and Ghazaleh being the leaders. They were hungry for the food—I was just hungry to see whatever it was I was going to witness.

North Tehran meant fancy-schmancy in everything. Brains and Hooves was covered in marble tiles and designed with calligraphy and fancy metal work. My cousins' saliva output was quadrupling as we went inside. A summary of my thoughts: what was french toast or smoked salmon in the morning for me was brains and hooves for them. Great.

At the corner there was a big pot the size of my body, similar to the ones our Italian neighbors made tomato sauce in. The chef was guarding its side and slowly stroking it.

The chef was a piece of work, a burly man with a thick gold necklace over his hairy chest. Nothing like someone you would find on the Food Channel. The sous chef was busy filling baskets with special bread baked in a wood oven. Pots of tea were perpetually boiling. We sat down on the table Ghazaleh took and waited until the waiter saw us.

While waiting, Arshia asked, "Do you want anything specific Shaghayegh?" dropping the latter half of my name, trying to become friendly.

I looked past him and was going to barf as I saw the chef hold the sheep's head in the air with a long fork. "This is exactly the same as a human head, only we eat it until we reach the skull," he explained loudly while chuckling. That was enough to make me vomit but I held firm until my visual curiosity was sustained.

"Relax, it's really tasty. Put some lemon and cinnamon over it and it'll be a very tasty start to any morning. But it's high in cholesterol so having it every day may kill you," he laughed calmly.

Customers started to come in and drivers started parking their cabs. "One brain soup please," a man carrying a suitcase said.

"Can I have hooves and tongue this morning, Hassan Jan?" another dude asked. Like a favorite local diner, the place was flooded and business was in full swing for this dude, whose name was Hassan. The next order reminded me of the movie *Return of the Living Dead*: "Can I have an eye sandwich?" What the hell did that mean? Now we're extracting eyes from animals and making hearty sandwiches? If Christina or Jennifer were here they would get a kick out of this. And not just from the hooves.

Having sprinkled the remains of the sheep's eye with salt and drops of lemon juice, Hassan stuck it between a piece of bread and offered it to a customer. The eye was crushed, and the lemon and salt added to the oily flavor. Oh lord.... I hope the sheep had 20/20 vision.

Arshia ordered a couple of eyes, some tongues, three brains and some hooves. Once the order came to the table I suddenly longed for a simple everything bagel with cream cheese. My mom saw the direction my brows were sinking and said, "You will like it, even if it's gross at the beginning. Come on, you are a good sport, give it a shot! It's full of calories...very meaningful and refined."

Well, the only piece I was willing to give a shot to was the tongue. It looked like roast beef and I could actually eat it with my eyes open.

"*Kaleh Pacheh* has been passed on for centuries Shaghayegh, like old notes or songs passed along for generations," continued Ghazaleh. She was right, and it was helpful to have a wing-man to explain the weirdness to me.

So this is the gist of the hairy dude, Hassan, and how this place was run: he ran the place with his four brothers, all named after the prophets; typical to the David, Daniel and Jonathan of our Jewish brothers. After preparing 100 sheep heads every morning, one brother named Saeed would bring them all to the restaurant to cook. Saeed was in the cave room downstairs, but his appearance was anything but Islamic or ritzy. This guy had long hair in a ponytail, wore John Lennon shades, and had a tattoo of a cross on his upper arm. A Brooklyn heat wave came over me and I felt at home seeing someone that was just himself and not mummified.

"People think these guys are rich," said my aunt Elahe, Arshia's mom, "but only the elder brother owns a house." I still had my gaze on the tattooed guy, so my aunt added, "If you want to marry a *Kaleh Pacheh* guy, I will forbid it!" Ok...so I was attracted to the tattooed guy but he was hot and the tattoo was very sexy on his arm. That said, he also looked ghetto...but who's judging?

"Doctors say *Kaleh Pacheh* has major health issues because it's fatty, but I will take one spoon of this over forty plates of *chelo kebab*!" said my aunt, who was obviously the happiest among us to be here. *Chelo kebab* was rice and kebabs, my favorite in the Iranian dishes!

"But I would want the opposite," I told her. And I also wanted Mr. Tattoo guy, who was now outside having a smoke.

The tongue had a powdery texture and was surprisingly yummy. "I want another," I told H_2O, but instead got a brain. "Taste this, you will be hooked!" she said.

Slowly and carefully I put lemon juice on the brain and slipped it on my tongue, closed my eyes, and told myself this is NOT a brain. The piece of meat melted like a Hershey's bar on my tongue. For my first time, I stuck with the tongue and brain, but still passed on the eye and hooves. Could I be hooked on sheep's eyes? No way! I would have to have it with lots of lemon juice, if ever!

We finished breakfast and got some on-the-go for the peeps who had already made it to my grandmother's place. In my mind the whole table would probably be $100 plus a good tip, so $140 in all. It came out to $10, and forget the tip. No one paid tips in Iran. Well, the waiter was one of the owners and the chefs, so understanding the no-tips concept was easy breezy.

When the first rush of customers left, Hassan stepped from behind the giant pot and lit a small bunch of herbs. He blew the sweet-smelling smoke to disperse it throughout the restaurant. "Against the evil eye," he explained, referring to an Iranian custom to prevent misfortune. "We might be complaining but many people are jealous of us," he said. "I don't know why but it's God who gives us this food. *Shokr!*" The last word meant *thanks*. The prayer was like what the pilgrims would say at the Thanksgiving table. The Mayflower was nowhere to be found though!

The family walked out happier than when we had arrived and we were on the road again, hopefully with no more stops on the way to my grandmother's place. My folks planned to stay at her house until we bought a place of our own. In the Iranian culture it was rude to get a room in a hotel when your family was there to help. Hotels were mainly for tourists, and with the religious rules sprinkled in this country, hotels weren't the best hangouts for *Pretty Woman* and Richard Gere types of relationships…something to stay away from!

My grandmother's street had flowers lined up on every side and the homes were made of three-inch bricks three or four floors tall with big black parking doors that opened automatically when my cousin punched the jackpot numbers in.

Inside the parking lot looked like a car show; BMWs to the German Opel cars to a black Lexus. Man, who said Iranians were poor? There was also a BMW motorbike so I suspected a hot guy might live in one of the condos. To the right of the parking lots there were stairs leading to her backyard. Zombie-ing my way to the backyard I found a garden planted with herbs and another garden with every kind of fruit you can find in the fruit market. I titled my shades to see figs, permissions, mulberries, peaches, and even a walnut tree. Who said Persians can't plant? A big barbeque lay to the left and a fire pit was smack in the middle. I could only imagine how cool it would be at night reading my favorite *Baby Sitter's Club* book while under the stars. I never saw one of these homes in Brooklyn!

"Shaghayegh, come on!" my mother shouted. "You are holding us up!"

I ran toward the parking garage again and saw everyone waiting for me to get on the elevator.

"Don't worry cuz," Ghazaleh said. "Later in the evening when the sun is setting we will go eat our hearts out in the yard. That's the time to go!"

"Uh…ok," I replied anxiously with a smile. Food in Iran was becoming the #1 hit with me…so far.

My grandma was on the first floor and had a nice pad to her one-person self. The house was huge with four gigantic bedrooms, three bathrooms, a huge kitchen, and the list kept going. There was enough room for two more families to room with us.

I didn't know everyone could function without sleep. The sun was fully out now and everyone was wide awake and happy. Could they actually function on this little sleep? It seemed as if the *Kaleh Pacheh* was fortifying their blood!

Jet lag was the one thing keeping me awake and this allowed me to observe the others, their incredible energy more than sleep could have provided. I wonder what sort of work they did. Obviously no one was clocking in right now.

"Are you going to the bazaar?" my aunt Elahe, the same who was forbidding me to date a *Kaleh Pacheh* restaurant owner, asked.

"Ya, but later on. I want to chill with Aunt Ziba for a bit," said Arshia as he tossed his car keys on the console table by the door.

My grandmother, who was the silent one all throughout the car ride and restaurant, quickly went into the kitchen and her first words were, "Welcome, welcome! My house is your house. All these rooms are yours. You can even use my room. Whatever you want," she told my mom with enthusiasm that reflected someone who just guessed Double Jeopardy.

The first course of action after the welcome: turning on the tea kettle. We never turned on our coffee brewer when we had guests. Then I remembered that Brains and Hooves had an ever-boiling teapot. Tea was THE drink.

Arshia, Ghazaleh, Aunt Elahe, my grandmother, my other cousin Bahareh, who was Ghazaleh's older sister, and I sat in the living room to have another chat. God, what could they want to talk about now?

"Are you guys still hanging out? Don't these people have lives?" I asked my mother.

"Yes they do, but we have just arrived and this is part of being hospitable. They are all going to head out for work soon. Stop complaining," she answered, turning her head. We drank tea, snacked on pastries—Danish ones that were far better than any peanut butter and chocolate chip cookie I had ever eaten—told jokes (irrelevant because I didn't get them), and my mom told them everything about my life that was impressive and hid the bad stuff until the clock hit 11 a.m. and Arshia trooped out to go to work. Who goes to work at 11 a.m.?

"See you tonight Aunt Ziba. I love you!" he said as he kissed her.

Gay flag. Surely he was gay. The way he said, "I love you," and kissed her was totally gay-ish. Dude, just say "Later," and shut the door, like the boys I knew back home did.

Then he kissed me and said, "Can't wait to hang out!" Yep, the tone was definitely gay-ish. Thank god he left quickly, not waiting for an answer, because my answer would have been, "Dude...please go home after work."

Everyone else cleared out and I finally had some privacy. I lay down on the couch and found the TV remote. I sat in a dreamy haze, watching a riot of brightly-colored censored cartoons. The channels were:

1: News

2: More news

3: Sports news

4: A cartoon with Japanese logos in the upper right corner

5: Cooking with female wimple-wearing chefs

6: International news

7, 8, 9 and 10: No signal

But suddenly I hit gold: MTV videos! My eyes weren't playing tricks on me because the next channel was a soap opera, *The Bold and the Beautiful!* Where were the mullahs and burkas in these? Not to be found! Suddenly I craved watching some good drama like *Melrose Place*, or would even surrender to watching *Dynasty*. But the lingo in the other channels turned to Turkish and I even hit a Bollywood movie where the main actor and his lover were running around in a garden and swinging on branches until the dude grabbed her. Ugh, where was HBO or Showtime when you craved it?

More interested in the cartoon channel than the Islamic channels, I decided to chill with some non-*Scooby-Doo* and *ThunderCats* cartoons. These cartoons, the "imports," had no action scenes, no funny lines like Scooby or Shaggy or Lionel had, but instead were more inspirational and heartwarming and—at this hour, in this state—kind of surreal. They didn't fascinate my Iran-born cousins as much as they did me, but regardless I focused on and genuinely enjoyed them. One of my basic joys, whether early in the morning or at three in the afternoon when I came home from school, were my cartoon cravings. But man, I hoped all of them here weren't as inspirational as these because after a while, that could transform to BORING!

Suddenly a thought rose in my mind while watching the Asian characters on Iranian TV: How else would my life change here? This thought eclipsed even the blaring TV; it possessed certain gravity, like some huge, beckoning challenge. Whatever it might be, I told myself, I'd be meeting it soon, whether I was ready or not.

•••

I got the second-biggest room at Aziz Joon's; by the way, that was my grandma's nickname, even though both words meant "dear," so "dear dear." I think "the dearest' is a far better translation! The room was isolated so I had privacy. There was a full-blown king size bed, an armoire, and a huge closet that could fit however many guys I chose to bring home. Right, as if I could even think those thoughts here!

My windows were huge and received plenty of sunlight and the curtains were absolutely gorgeous, like something straight out of the Shah's castle. They were designed with such elegance and made with lace satin champagne colored fabric. I didn't dare open the window because I was frightened I might ruin the design. Half of the room was wallpapered and the other half was green paint.

"You like your room," I heard behind me. It was Aziz Joon.

"It's awesome. Was it anybody's room or is it just the guest room?"

"It was your mom's room before she got married. The armoire she picked out and bought with her own allowance!" she said, grinning.

"Must have been some allowance!" The French design was classic grey with gold lines running vertically down the sides.

"She has good taste, and now it's all yours!" Her energy surprised me. I felt Christina and Jennifer living inside her; the feeling of an old friend that I could tell my darkest secrets to, and wouldn't have to worry about her spreading word around town. She wore the burka, was religious, but her heart was soulful. I didn't understand why she wore the burka outside, but in the house she took it off in front of my dad and other the dudes. What was the difference?

"Why do you cover your face? And now, why it that burka off?" I asked, hoping I didn't step too far.

"Weird, eh? I have my beliefs about God. But in Islam, you can take your burka off in front of your son-in-law and grandsons. So I do."

"What about in front of me?" I asked, baffled.

"You are not a man! This is only in front of guys...you know...like the tattoo-man you were gazing at in the *Kaleh Pacheh* place!"

28

Ha! She saw that. Old, clever and wears a burka! Accepted in my book!

"Wasn't he cute?" I asked, excited.

But then she dashed my excitement.

"No! And you better be careful. Your dad is a strict one!" she said smiling and walking toward the back room. "Unpack. I made kebabs for lunch and tea for afterwards."

I sighed. "Another round of tea? With the amount of tea you consume you should have a hose attached to your privates and just forget about bathroom trips!" I said, giggling.

"Maybe we will soon! *Yallah*!" she said. *Yalla*h meant "hurry up," and later on I found out it's really an Arabic word meaning "Oh God." But here, metaphorically it meant "hurry up mamma!"

My brother and I started to love staying at Aziz Joon's—we were sometimes The Three Stooges and sometimes we shifted into being The Three Musketeers. It was like staying at a bed-and-breakfast place in the Upper East Side. Gracious and welcoming, she cooked and served up huge meals. The house was old but fully renovated and charming, with great views of Tehran at night because it was on a slightly-elevated hill. But like every hill has a side going up, it also has a side going down.

•••

Soon the time came to register for school, and I dreaded the very fact of this. Perhaps this fear came from knowing that the academic level of schools in Tehran was so different than those in America. Or maybe it was my own perception.

I was starting my senior year, turning eighteen, and here I was, alien to the local language, had no friends, and had to wear a wicked burka—mandatory in school!

Initially, my dad and I went to the regular Iranian schools to register; public ones filled with "regular" students—and *boy* did I feel lost. I stayed in the morning and temporarily sat in on a class. Not too much time had to pass before I decided to check-out. Let's start at the beginning, when they were singing their national anthem; Well, I guess now it was my national anthem too. Anyways, it was like the turtle and the hare, and I was the turtle, trying to slowly and linguistically interpret the non-groovy, opera-like anthem. I could sing "The Star-Spangled Banner" in my sleep. But this had a complete different feel to it. Even if I had known the song, it would have been difficult for me to chime in. I felt disloyal to the "The Star-Spangled Banner." Or was I just being stubborn? Most likely the latter! Anthems aren't meant to be danced to, but this was depressing. Okay I confess, I was being stubborn.

Thank god the anthem wrapped up. I stood in a line, following the other girls upstairs. My dad wasn't really allowed inside so he stood in the yard smoking a cigarette.

I noted some more differences between my old school and this Iranian School:

1) A wimple and a coat had to be worn at all times for girls, with the front root portion of the hair completely covered. I didn't understand why this had to be worn at *all* times if the purpose was to cover up in front of the dudes? To elaborate, the wimple is like wrapping one big scarf around your head covering the north, south, east and west part of it. The only openings were for breathing purposes and seeing directly in front of you.

2) One dudette, since everyone was a girl, would get up first then all the girls would get up after her once the teacher walked in. Getting on your feet was some sort of sign of respect. Like we were in the army and a higher-ranking officer would walk in and everyone had to stand at attention. "On your feet soldier!" I couldn't help

thinking. But I totally ignored it and kept cozy on my chair with a nice smile glued to my face until the green burka-wearing teacher came in with her purse and a book in her hand.

3) She then lined up ten girls in front of the class, like a police lineup. A question was zapped at each student, and depending on how complete and right or wrong each answer was, they would get a positive or negative sign. Some girls cared while some straight up answered, "I haven't studied!" I wanted to clap my hands for the signs of bravery and courage the "non-kiss-asses" displayed.

4) I noticed one of the girls had a picture of a football player she was totally checking out. "Oh, he is so hot!" she said to her friend.

"I would kiss him up and down until my lips were dry," said the other.

"*Khak bar saret!*" said the girl with the picture. "He is mine, only mine!" she answered and they both giggled. *Khak bar saret* literally means "soil on your head" but metaphorically means "go die in a hole or gutter or bury yourself alive." But I think she meant something more along the lines of "get lost chick, he's all mine for the taking!" Wowzers! Nice to know Iranian public school girls were human! Sweet!

Finally my dad and I left the school both implicitly knowing there had to be an alternate means of education for "aliens" like me. Culturally I felt like an outsider, but I even felt like the content was different. For example, it was like the biology was begin taught in a different language, and one I couldn't make out! It was like nothing we had studied...it sounded more like content and lingo you would study in med school! I wondered if everything was this advanced...and how I would keep up with it.

• • •

After calling around to every friend or neighbor they could reach out to, my parents finally found a place for me to get my diploma. They would never just let me go uneducated—god forbid, my father would rather be hanged!

They finally decided to send me to Tatbighi, the international school for children of families unfamiliar with Farsi or Iranian culture. Convenient. Maybe it would be a good cushion for culture shock—or maybe it would intensify it—who knew? Students from all around the world would register here and the fees were off the charts. Here, the attire was similar to what would have been worn in a strict Catholic school…except I still had to wear a wimple. Still mandatory. Grrr! I felt like I was being partially mummified around my head.

But the school was much more laid back than the public school tragedy I went through. The teachers even let us take our wimples off in class and dump them in our bag to wrinkle up. Sometimes it even seemed like the teachers were scared of the students. We had all kinds of girls that came from all over. The ones from Sweden were super open minded and constantly talked about sex in class and showed me the condoms they had exported from Sweden to use here. I wondered if they supplied condoms in the pharmacy in this country. Probably not to any seventeen-year-old!

Then there was the girl from Germany, who was a tomboy and talked about cars, sports, the Bundesliga, and her crush on Michael Ballack. He was what Pele was to Brazil, but the German version. I have to admit she did have good taste.

Then we had the U.K. crowd, which was about four or five girls, and they frequently changed channels to "Brit English" to talk to one another. No fish and chips here, but some were more traditional than the public school girls, in my view.

The rest of the girls were from Canada and my home. My home, which was the U.S…I couldn't call Iran my home yet! There was no connection! Ah!

But this was soothing. They looked "normal" to me and we hung out frequently. Sometimes while we were in the yard it was as if the FIFA games were underway in the yard, with Team U.S. vs. Team U.K. vs. the remainder of the European countries. Oh there was one girl from Spain that got completely on my nerves. Her lunch was always tapas-style, really small portions, so then she would leech off our lunches. I wanted to smack Spain sometimes!

The classes were more like my classes at P.S. 200 in Brooklyn, and it was like they were slowly training or hypnotizing us towards their study methods. Since we were the aliens, our classes also included learning the Farsi alphabet and pronouncing the letters correctly. It was like starting from scratch, you know, the way toddlers learn how to read. But at least I had teeth and I could walk, so I guess it wasn't all from scratch.

Then we had six or seven subjects we were required to learn— they were similar to the books in the public schools but the teachers were more chill with us. I mean super-duper chill—extra patient!

Farsi and Arabic language and literature were replacing Spanish as my second language. No more *como estas* or *por favor* or *tambien* for me. I had to read the Koran, even though I had no idea what I was reading—I was just trying to make out the alphabet.

Among history, geography, and math, Islamic education included the "arts," which was something! We had to knit, sew, learn to wash stains off fabric (washing blood off silk was the most difficult). It also somehow consisted of learning where milk came from and how to make yogurt out of it. They were turning us in the housewives!

Since the peeps were all from my alien side of the world, we connected quickly. They were almost Christina and Jennifer exactly. I mean, turn Italian to Persian, light brown and blonde hair to dark brown, and take the meatball sandwiches and replace them with *Joojeh kebabs*. Come to think of it, it was much healthier! I needed to lose a couple of pounds anyways!

I missed my girls but these *mammas* had lots to offer and there was a familiarity between us that set us apart. It was as if they knew my secrets and I knew their secrets, and we had both been to the "other side" and seen it all. Well, now that I put it that way I probably had seen more, coming from the streets of Bensonhurst, Brooklyn. And I wouldn't change it for anything, not the cops coming around the corner, the FBI at some a door arresting some drug dealer, or even the Italian godfather who was said to have lived in our hood. These California girls never would have survived where I was from!

Oh, I forgot to mention I was the sole New Yorker among the Californians, Oklahomans, and—somehow—one Idahoan. The Persians' primary starch resource was rice, so I'm not sure how her family survived in the Potato State!

Whether you liked the school subjects, or were slow in the subjects, or didn't understand the subjects at all, was irrelevant. You still had to memorize all paragraphs word for word and get a good grade, because that led to a good reputation. This is what kept the ego fuel going—the unleaded type!

For me, the annoying subject was Islamic history. "Why do I have to study this nonsense? It's not like I'll be applying any of it!" I complained to my mom.

"You won't lose anything by becoming familiar with it. It's your religion after all," she would answer.

"My religion? I haven't picked one yet!" I would fire back.

"You are Muslim, even though we don't practice it."

"Leave the determining what I am to me, mom. I may want to choose to be a Jew or become a Buddhist," I said, chuckling.

"A Buddhist?"

"Just sayin.' You push me, I fly to extremes!" I answered back, turning my head to indicate the conversation was over.

"Relax. No one is pushing you. In your own words, take a chill pill," she said, knowing that my knee-jerk reaction would be to get into tackle mode, yet again. I can wear a wimple on the outside, pretending to be okay with it. Studying and wasting my time over crap I would never use in order to get an "A," I could still pretend. But force a religion down my soul in the comfort of our home, and I will punch you out with brass knuckles—accompanied by a charming smile.

I sensed the general pace of the education was to turn you into a big nationalist, to know Iran's position in the region and the Islamic world, to understand how their democracy came about and how it worked, and everything about Jihad and martyrdom. Jihad: the fight a Muslim puts up to defend their beliefs. Whoa! Slow down! It reminded me of a chick flick, when the girl was dating a guy and then one day they just showed up at her door with a dozen red roses and she was suddenly labeled "The Girlfriend." Slow down! This relationship is moving too fast!

So yeah, the studies were heavy, but my friends were dope! We had lots of fun, which took away some of the pain of studying. I looked forward to seeing them and exchanging gossip with them day to day. The staff at school wasn't restrictive of our friendships, and us peeps weren't *followers* either. Everyone behaved like a leader or representative of the culture they flew out of, and we grew in that way with each other.

Initially, the studies felt as painful as pregnancy, but I was determined, so I sat at the front of the class and became a straight-A student. It was a real mission but I banged out the books with lots of overnight study and coffee. Eventually, my grades weren't far from my Brooklyn scores. Competitiveness ran in my blood and I was hungry to learn—the difference was, I wanted to do it passionately, and not with anyone pushing me. I completed this with satisfaction, and couldn't admire my teachers, who I envisioned as females stuck in a world where they'd lost the key to freedom.

Okay, so let me clarify. I didn't want to be like my teachers or anyone similar to my teachers because I felt they were zombies who had forever surrendered to their circumstance and led very boring lives. Ambitions crushed, goals not achieved, hobbies ignored. Some due to traditional families, some culture, some the country. They were rotting pieces of flesh, but had so much flavor. By flavor I mean potential. For example, my math teacher had an edge, which I liked. I enjoyed talking with her. She didn't like living in Iran and wanted a way out, so she was applying for an education visa. That girl was smart and I could easily think of her as the next Nobel Peace Prize Winner! Smarts and edge went far for a girl...at least in my opinion. But in this country you had to stop at the fence and look over it at the pond. The diver was prohibited! The frustration of it made me want to strangle somebody until they choked!

I felt some teachers had lost the ambition to even *want* to feel the rush of freedom, or worse, some never wanted it at all. They were followers with an unclear destination. I couldn't summon the will to interact with all of them, instead gearing that energy toward my girls in class.

Friendships slowly blossomed with mostly the U.S. and Canada crowd, and we carefully nurtured the blossoms. There was an escape path behind the school leading to a forest and one day me and Neda, the girl from Idaho, found a short wall leading to this forest, and we decided to ditch school. She had a date, and I was searching for Tarzan! An English speaking one *por favor*!

Anyway, we jumped over that wall and came back three hours later, at which time the principal escorted us right into detention. I wonder what the look of surprise and dismay on their faces was like when they found out we had been gone that long, and wished I could have been there to immortalize their faces with a photograph. Disobeying all school authorities, causing trouble, and at times feigning ignorance, were all becoming daily routines, designed to prove to my parents they had erred in bringing their daughter back to Iran.

My rebelliousness was due to more than anger; I was also disappointed they had brought me here. I didn't even like being told what to do by my own parents, and now I had to obey the religious government restrictions put upon me. I missed Brooklyn, I missed Annie and Larry, and I missed freely admiring Robert's six-pack with fantasies about touching them countless times! Here, I was afraid to even dream about it!

But detention wasn't all that bad because I had Neda. She was going through everything I was going through, the religion and burka suffocation...but lucky for her, her parents were planning on leaving the country by the time she was nineteen. Her father loved the U.S. and wanted to return because his mom was dying of cancer. What a good son. Although now that I think about it, that plan sounded like he was waiting for his mom to die in a couple of years...who sets a time for their mom to die?

Naghmeh, one of the girls from Cali, was the other girl I got close with. Her dad was going bankrupt so he had done some illegal shit in the U.S. and ran away to Iran with his family. I didn't know much more than that.

"So, you guys aren't returning anytime soon?" I asked curiously.

"Well, my dad isn't for sure. He also has a school loan that he hasn't paid back yet!" she said without thinking that I might go report her dad's whereabouts.

"Do you like it here?"

"It sucks girl! I can't wait to turn eighteen and get the hell out!" she said.

That made me sad...if I got out, I would have preferred it be with the folks. But it looked like her family was a broken one: her parents were divorced and her brother was a pothead that had refused to come to Iran with them. She was trying to keep it together.

"Sometimes, I just want to give in!" she said.

"Give in, to what?" I asked, completely confused.

"Disasterville! This place is a horror story, you can't find a place to dance or have fun, and I miss wearing my ripped denim jean shorts!"

"Sorry to be blunt—you're not thinking suicidal thoughts, are you?" I asked, a bit fearful for her mental issues.

"No...well, sometimes...okay *no*...not really..." she said in beats. "So what about you? Which one is it? Kill or save?" she asked me.

"Let's just save your life for now. I may need a friend to talk to!" I said sarcastically.

"Deal!"

"That's my girl!" I said, giving her a high-five.

Whoa! I told myself. This one was on the verge of collapse. Maybe those thoughts ran through all the girls' heads around here. Our friendships all went through their own collective path of twilight zones, but we all, in our own unique way—understood each other. It probably sounds like a mental asylum! But no, we were not insane, just completely and near-insanely confused!!

One the thing cementing our bond was the jumping back and forth between Farsi and English. Everybody knew how to speak Farsi at different levels. Thanks to the Emperor and H$_2$O speaking Farsi back and forth at home and on the telephone, I was able to pick up a lot, even though I was below negative when it came to speaking it. Others had it black and white, with one parent being American and the other Iranian, so the Iranian was forced to speak English in the house. As a result, their child was last place in our communication competition! Poor thing, she always got skipped over in conversation. I was glad that wasn't me.

No matter what we knew in English and Farsi, we sprinkled our girlish accents onto the words and spoke with one another almost in our own code. Five words English to one word Farsi...or five-and-a-half words English and a preposition in Farsi, and we were at the finish line. To those fluent only in Farsi, we probably came across as nonsensical. Occasionally, in a bind, hand gestures were used, as if we'd here moved directly from Italy! And sometimes when the last technique failed, I simply gave up on the conversation!

Although only one year away from graduating and we were considered adults, our motto was "girls just wanna have fun!" So sometimes when the teachers hadn't come into the classroom yet, or when we had a break, one of the girls would shut the door and we started shakin' it! God bless to both Vanilla Ice's "Ice Ice Baby," and M.C. Hammer's "Hammer Time"!

"Shake that ass, girl!" Neda would say to one of the U.K. girls.

"Shakin' every little part of it I can!" she'd reply with her Elton John-type accent. She also wore the same glasses Sir John always wears, so she could have passed for his Iranian cousin.

Then suddenly the teacher would come in and see a music video in production, frown, and command us to take our seats. What would she do? Punish us? We were in school and there were no men to be sexually aroused by our dance moves. And the whole lesbian thing wasn't a concern—Islam strictly prohibited homosexuality! Besides, our wimples had turned into a blazer wrapped around our hips, covering any small (or big) butt issues.

It's not like we would say, "Yes ma'am, as you wish," to her anyway—that's the type of backwards control we had in the international school. In my eyes, if they didn't have the willpower to go after their dreams, I wouldn't let them dash mine.

Although this was no big deal to the girls—just plain fun—they would quickly take their seats instead of choreographing the song to completion. With my wimple hanging to my hips, I would elegantly take my seat and wonder whether the "regular" Iranian schools would haul us off to the principal's office. But this being *Tatbighi*, they let it slide—mostly. Once in a while the teacher would raise her voice and yell, "*Khanoom*, take your seat fast! Stop these moves and steps!" *Khanoom* meant "missy" or "young lady," but had an imaginary pointed finger attached to it.

When this happened, the students still shrugged it off. "Okay," they'd say, without hostility or desire to carry on. It was what it was. Weird, confusing, but fun, especially when you knew it wasn't allowed. Lots of stuff didn't sink in for me. And thank god for having accomplices in my mystery boat with me. The empathy and understanding and acceptance I'd developed with Neda, Saloomeh and the rest of the crowd was comforting.

Each morning we would talk to one another in English, and say goodbye in English. Start and end the day with English. It was a forming habit, and it brought Brooklyn back to my heart. For me, Arabic and Farsi grammar were real killers. "Study these," advised my mom, "by memorizing them. It'll stay with you when you memorize."

"I don't *want* to memorize this, I want to understand it."

This conversation often replayed, expanding to include science, social studies, and Islamic studies. What was the point? Competitiveness and curiosity ran in my blood, and also ran in my parents' blood, but they primarily thought success carried a label. Perhaps to them the label was gold; perhaps to me, nothing but evaporated air. Thrust into this new situation, I obeyed simply because I understood so little!

Sweet days rolled by in *Tatbighi* and at my grandmother's home. Boring studies and memorization highlighted by great times with friends sharing the same lingo. My energy was bouncing everywhere; mischievous, spontaneous behavior at school was key to driving everyone crazy. There was a Swedish girl who was having unprotected sex because she ran out of condoms and was too scared to purchase more for fear of getting caught and then disgraced. Neda, Saloomeh and I got closer as the days passed—I was getting closer with them than I was with Christina and Jennifer. Since I lived at grandma's I couldn't really bring any guys home, but both Neda and Saloomeh would talk about having guys over and making out until their parents got home and threw the guy out the window. Yikes!

For me, at least for now, it was all about getting tight with grandma, finding new friends, and exploring this undiscovered sense of whatever I felt was coming over me. I had to take a stake in my position. I grew certain I'd succeeded in this role, despite the subtle melancholy of knowing these times were the most important of my teenage years. I scattered my energy into school, basking in my security without the necessity of too many words with teachers or the principal.

But now the truly difficult part approached.

My parents started searching for a different school in which to enroll me, which was customary. Goodbye *Tatbighi*. After a couple of months of being there and getting into the academic process, parents were required to put their child in a "regular" school. You either had to be very dumb or stubborn to stay in that school— otherwise, you had to find a new home. I had to leave mid-school year and was to be transferred to an "outside" public school.

This really burned me. What if culturally I wasn't ready for the crap outside? But I told myself no; this girl has smarts and she *should* be flexible to external adaptations! But the Outside included speaking completely in Farsi, understanding where to say what, how the culture operated. And how is all this religious crap going to fit into my new pretentious Outside life? And this may seem trivial...but who would I go bike riding with? On the "absolute Iranian side," there'd be no more joking around and no more wimple freebies! No more "Hammer Time" or crush talks!

I was scared to the bone, but I had come this far—maybe it wouldn't be so bad.

"I'm a warrior," I told myself. But I would soon find out if that were true.

3

Strange New World

July–September 1996

SOME MONTHS PASSED AND WE moved into the condo on the top floor of my grandmother's building. My father had bought the place so my mom could be near her mom. I also liked it because whenever I had to do something private or needed space, I would just come to the first floor, my grandmother's. The problem was all my cousins also had the keys to her place and would do the same! If you wanted to bring a chick home or call a boyfriend, where did you go? Grandma's!

It was a nice condo. My mom had decorated it and spent every last penny doing so. The latest refrigerators and stylish cabinets filled the kitchen. My bedroom was twice the size of my bedroom in Brooklyn, and I decided to paint it blue on one side and green on the other. My mom knew when it came to decorating *my* room, she had to take her hands off and move her opinions out of my way. Styling my room like the latest Italian photo shoots was not my "thang." My furniture was white, the walls were different sassy colors, and I had posters of New Kids, Madonna, and Guns N' Roses on the wall. I had my own stereo, which blasted Ace of Base whenever I felt like it. Now *this* was home.

Coming home from school was not the happiest time of my day though.

There was nothing to watch on TV, no bike rides or walking down to the pier with friends, and definitely no pizzeria to hang out in, nor parks where we could play punch-ball. I didn't know how people survived here…it was so boring!

Girls couldn't ride bikes in the streets because it wasn't "normal"—but I had heard from my cousin that there was a park called *Cheetgar* that had a secret area where girls could bike!

Dear strict rules, please be nice to the girls….

My dad (not the most liberated of parents) allowed me no access to recreation or nearby green spaces. This off-limits policy came from his awareness that soldiers, or *Sarbaz* in Farsi, upon release from their designated stations, hung out in these areas. Ugh! Another roadblock. I wondered who these soldiers were.

"Can I just take a walk, dad?" I would sometimes ask.

"No, walking alone in the park is not suitable for girl," he would answer back.

"Dad! It's just a walk! What, you don't trust me?" I was furious and annoyed.

"Of course I trust you Shaghayegh Jan—it's them I don't trust!" he would always say with finality, as if we had just settled a case in court.

What was that supposed to mean? He had never said that stuff to me when we were in Brooklyn, but then again my mom had me home before he came home from work every night. But even she was behind him on this one!

"Your father knows best, listen to him beautiful," she would say.

I almost said, "Why don't you stop going around with your sisters and friends to coffee shops and see how that feels!" But I bit my tongue. I knew I would regret saying it.

So apparently the problem wasn't me, but was irresponsible teenaged boys trying to hit on every girl brave or stupid enough to walk through the park. And when they weren't doing that, they were making prank calls from the public yellow telephone booths. It seemed strange to me, so out of curiosity, I found a more complete answer.

At eighteen years old, all Iranian boys were required to do military service. Some did full service, while others found ways out, like through employed government connections, "disability," or the ever-reliable money to merit exemption. Clearly this was a duty many preferred to run away from.

So what was the point of all this nonsense anyway?

Couldn't these guys just go to work, or get married? I knew things weren't that simple, though, especially considering Iran's economic woes, which were worsening every month. I mean, I never bought a piece of Bazooka bubblegum for more than five cents in Brooklyn; here, there were days you could buy a piece of gum for five cents one hour, and the next hour, you would buy it for twice as much! Eventually you'd have to stop chewing gum! It was crazy, and it definitely affected the poorer social class in Tehran. I don't know if it was because of bad businessmen, or the crazy political situation, or something else I wasn't even aware of.

Okay, back to the *Sarbaz* dudes—I mean the soldiers. So all eighteen-year-old guys had to join and learn how to handle military weaponry, and learn how to kill; how to react and cope without completely losing it. Their duty extended six months, sometimes more for some.

Oh-Em-Gee! Seeing these somewhat pointless packages of humanity lingering in the park, I couldn't help my downward feelings. What a waste of energy! Of life! Some of these young men were quite handsome; some gave off a foul odor; others appeared ignorant, perhaps trying to escape their station for a better bite to eat. A few even climbed the walls to escape service, but were nearly always caught, and thus earning another punitive six-month stretch. No wonder many weren't accepted into university after service. Use your brains people!

Then again, I realized some behaved like typical eighteen-year-olds, who just don't know what to do with life. I knew plenty of dudes like that back home. All things considered, I wasn't allowed to walk the park unless accompanied by another family member.

So what *was* a girl to do after school? All things I was used to doing were not allowed for girls in the Islamic state, or in my parents' perspective, which had suddenly changed drastically now that we lived in this environment. I wondered if all fathers who came back here experienced such a changed perspective. It was hard to imagine.

So my life was study, study, study, or learn to knit...how fun! From bike riding to learning how to knit? Please.

Well, let's see: loop yarn through needle-hole, thus creating a stitch...pull it through with yarn, and you have created the classic purl stitch! Then do it again a thousand times. Ugh.

But for lack of other activities, that was my after school ritual. My parents were still diligently researching where they should place me and I didn't interfere. Not that I knew any facts to interfere with...nor did I want to know. The Outside world still was scary for me.

I managed to endure roughly ten minutes of knitting on my own at a time, interrupted often by the presence of my grandmother who, with utmost kindness, demonstrated the basic steps and how to be coherent with it. It was like cheating, only in the house, with your grandma. So not really cheating. Go Aziz Joon! Her efforts of affection often evolved after ten minutes into loud music and dancing because I would get bored. I'd take the yarn and needles from her, take her glasses off her face, and put on some Madonna! She would always shake it—sometimes better than the queen herself! She had more soul than me, and even though she wore a scarf and burka, she had energy like she too was on a world tour!

But back to reality: to pass a school course, we were charged with knitting a small sweater for a baby. Blue or pink was irrelevant—I sure wasn't going to have a baby! My hard work extended as far as purchasing my favorite colored yarn and needles, then smothering Aziz Joon with lots of love and kisses. I did eventually learn knitting, but the results little resembled an actual piece of clothing. Aziz Joon did 90% of the work—I put in the passion. Whether my teacher noticed this or not didn't matter: the combination of whatever I'd learned and Aziz Joon's time earned me a nice fat passing grade. Sometimes you only have to give a little to get a lot, right?

The days passed slowly, bit by bit, moment to moment. I gradually adapted to my new settings, although still complained about having been moved to this boring, dark country. "This is your country now," H_2O would declare. "Try to understand it, because you have the same inside yourself." Whatever that meant.

Okay so I was Iranian, a brunette, had exotic almond shaped eyes, olive colored skin, had two passports, and spoke Farsi like a five-year-old. This was the Iranian side I had to understand? Oh, I forgot to mention that now I was learning about wearing mandatory clothing, having a pretentious look while walking out in the streets, and knowing what color the taxis were and what the drivers looked like. What was there to understand? The culture was vague for me and now at seventeen, I was suddenly supposed to understand.

But they didn't understand I would always be a Brooklyn gal more than an upper-Tehran kinda girl. That wasn't going to change. Walking in my neighborhood in Tehran, I had the least amount of make-up on and wasn't trying to be someone else. All the other girls were make-up artists and designed different hair-dos under their scarves. Sometimes the front of their hair would be split in two, sometimes slanted and sometimes it would come up as if they had a big bump in front of their hair. It seemed so *fake* to me. I always had a ponytail and honestly I think I looked hotter than all of them combined! I tried to understand them but had difficulty accepting all their disguises! They acted like they were hiding the truth beneath their blue eyeshadow or the latest model BMW!

Frankly, I felt and acted bored. No one understood me, except for maybe Neda and Saloomeh. But even my hobbies were different from them. The sun came up, the moon rose, and my days after school were filled either with studying (fine as long as I wasn't knitting!), watching taped music videos of my favorite American artists (from the satellite dish my dad had put on the roof, thank god), or spending time downstairs with my grandma or any family that randomly decided to drop in. This was quite frequent. Labeling these activities bad or uncomfortable wasn't entirely fair or accurate, but I sensed yet more change and challenge coming for me.

•••

September loomed. The school transfer was getting closer. My parents were eager to send me to a private school called *Geyre*

Entefaii, with regular students, teachers, a principal, and the requisite over-the-top religious clothing. All good things come to an end and now *Tatbighi* was becoming like a dream I was letting go of. Why couldn't I just stay there? Maybe if I pretended I hadn't progressed in my Farsi or adapted in the slightest to my surroundings, they would keep me here...but I couldn't pretend. It just wasn't in me!

Finally, the new school became reality.

The class was still all female, round twenty girls. Twenty privileged girls who had the bucks to come here. So I guess it was better than a public school, but the girls seemed snobby and most of them had actually been to the other side for vacation to places like England or France, common countries that would give Iranians visas to visit.

Some knew English and some spoke it to me like they knew I had first talked Farsi four months ago and was in progression-mode. Smart girls for sure. Neda and Saloomeh had also been taken to other schools, but mine was a class of its own.

We were served kebab lunches and had different courses like French, which was not usually taught in the public schools. My school attire changed from a grey manto and black long wimple at *Tatbighi,* to a green manto and a black burka. Thank god we didn't have to wear rainbow colored burkas or wimples!

The green trench-like coat was made of cotton and polyester. The heavy outfit was guaranteed to sweep up all dust and hair it encountered, thus reducing janitorial fees!

Collectively, the class looked like a rain forest, and any girl who objected to this attire would find themselves in the principal's office.

I noticed the place was furnished better than most public schools, with new desks and whiteboards instead of blackboards. They said chalk was bad for our lungs, which I laughed at—they must forget to look at the air pollution in Tehran!

All told, I didn't quite know what to make of this novel atmosphere, which felt odd and weird. The girls were warm and well-humored, a definite plus. Not exactly the type of dry Jewish and Italian humor I was used to, but nonetheless pleasing. I don't know if it was a cultural connection, but I was surprised to find they didn't look at me like I was an alien from outer space, even though simply coming from America was enough to draw heavy attention. Upon learning I hailed from the U.S.A., girls would besiege me with questions and comments:

"Could you please speak some English?"

"She has no accent, that's so cool!"

It was like I had stepped out of a movie and I was a celebrity they were meeting! Some took the easy way and just stared at me with intensity; enough to be classified as creepy. Afterwards they would remark, "She is so cute!"

The girls came from educated families and they were all sophisticated in their own seventeen-year-old worlds. But were still edgy, and although they were forced to do lots of stuff, like me, underneath I learned they had their own little world.

Whether from some obscure inner perception or simply because the other girls were genuinely easygoing, I felt secure and had fun with them. The principal had given the approval that we were allowed to remove our wimples while in class. There were no guys around, so I still don't understand why we had to get this approval, but I'd stopped asking that question.

But a few kiss-ups would keep those bad boys on! Don't know if leaving it on would help in getting the A, or if they had a phobia that some man might be peering at them from a secret window. Whatever the case, I think the wimple wearing kiss-ups in class were looking for approval. But the rest of the girls were laid back and some actually had pretty nice hair when the wimple was removed.

Nice hair accessories too—ones I could relate to over the crazy up-dos I had seen on the street.

My friend Ghazaleh's parents also wanted her to attend a private school, so they had registered her here with me. Our parents thought we would get closer and be like sisters going to school together. How beautiful (that's sarcasm)! I didn't trust her with my secrets. I felt like if I told her anything, the next thing I know, the whole family would be talking about my secret because of her big mouth! But I will say that at the beginning, my Farsi was not that strong, so Ghazaleh often came to the rescue and completed my sentences. Or she would utter a string of slang words, and I would end up staring at her and trying to catch the meaning. But amazingly this worked! I slowly, deliberately, picked up local slang and, the rest from books, proper usage of certain terms.

Recesses resembled a college schedule, with fifteen-minute breaks between classes. We had five courses throughout the day, an hour-long lunch, four fifteen-minute breaks, and as if school wasn't long enough, this school also had PRAYER TIME! OMG! No way was I going to pray Islamic-style. I refused! At the beginning I said I had "girl issues," but of course that could only last for about ten days. Then I started getting "stomach aches," and then I was given a big lecture that I *had* to pray. So then I started pretending to pray, but instead was singing Madonna's "Borderline" while doing the up and down movements of the *Namaz*. That was my prayer.

I liked the study-recess system though. It allowed time to devour a Mortadella sandwich or chicken kebab, which the school usually ordered for our lunch. If someone didn't like it they would head down to the cafe and grab a sandwich. The good part was that it didn't matter if you were overweight: the manto uniform concealed it. No more cheap pizza bagels or mac-and-cheese or ravioli with an apple for lunch. This food was way yummier! It was delicacy sandwiches and sometimes *koobideh* (beef) kebab with grilled tomatoes. The kind of stuff you would need an afternoon nap for after consuming.

I surely missed Sloppy Joes, but that soon faded into the deep end of my memory.

During lunch the girls sat circled on the ground discussing daily events, making jokes, or having water fights. Everything looked good to the principal unless—god forbid— someone got caught dancing, or wearing her wimple slanted or cut from the chin-piece to make it loose, or holding an unlawful item such as a CD or a troll doll, or daring to pluck her eyebrows. That last one was strictly forbidden. It made no sense to me; they were your own brows! If your *parents* allowed this and you weren't doing it on school time— well, so what? Show up plucked, get suspended—that's what!

So this new school was quite the maze, but it did give me a good laugh. The girls were different, but in some ways the same. And in a (for lack of a better word) *foreign* way—they were *fun*. As I grew closer to them, they welcomed me into their circles by way of birthday parties, pizza parties, and even study parties. Too bad all the parties were always all-female gatherings—they *had* to be all girls, otherwise I was banned from going! Emperor's rules!

Only after a while did I realize many of the girls had strict families too. I knew my father's attitude toward going out and partying with dudes could be boiled down to three words: no way José.

There were three girls who had become real good friends with Ghazaleh, and by way of her I had also become good friends with them. Mina, Azin, Nooshin, Ghazaleh and I hung out during breaks and slowly I got to know them.

Mina's mom was a firm Shah-defender who hated the current regime, and her dad was an American-educated electrical engineer from Stanford University that didn't like the current government either. But he had his own company and made lots of money. They both lived in Iran because they wanted to be near their parents. Her mom still looked at Iran as if the Shah was still around: in a backwards way. They had their own set of rules under their roof: no scarves, plenty of alcohol, and they allowed her to date, as long as they knew the guy. It was similar to my mom throwing a party in Brooklyn; the only difference was that the guests entered the house with a scarf and manto. The family was not religious at all and totally ranked in the upper-Tehran class.

Azin's mom and dad met at Northwestern University near Chicago, fell in love, and during the Shah's rule, came back to Iran to get married and establish a family, when the regime went sour on them. She was a psychologist but preferred to continue painting, and her paintings sold like crazy. She put Van Gogh to shame! Her dad had an MBA and was into real estate. His focus was building high rises in the northern end of Tehran. Again, I thought Azin had it easy. No scarves while at parties, she could talk to guys without being chaperoned, and her dad drank and smoke. Not too religious either!

Then we had Nooshin. Her dad had gone to Columbia in New York, was a bad-boy-turned-good-boy at age forty, returned to Iran to find a good wife, got married, and loved Iran so much that under no condition would he move back to the U.S. Something he had brought back from his college days were tattoos all over his arms— only to be seen inside the house. He wouldn't expose them out in the streets. Tattoos were not approved in Iran, and if some men had them, they wouldn't be put in the highly-educated or sophisticated categories. I wondered if he and his frat buddies had decided to hop on their motorcycles one night and head to Williamsburg! It definitely wasn't the type of design or art found in an Islamic country.

"In my country, no one can tell me to leave!" he would say when I asked him why he decided to stay in Iran. My guess was that he must have had some traumatic experience with racism back in America.

He was a mechanical engineer and her mom was an antique dealer. Too much money and sitting in the house had led to her mother traveling all around the world and buying old stuff. Her mom, Mana Joon, was also an American citizen and watching *The Addams Family* was her fondest memory of living in New York. Mana was cool and the same went for the whole family—well, almost. Nooshin wasn't allowed to have any boyfriends because her dad was super protective, like the Emperor, and only allowed her to go to girl sauna parties. But at least with no scarves, and plenty of wine. They even had a wine cellar!

Since Ghazaleh was friends with my family, the Emperor considered her family legit and let me go to their home, but never to spend the night. He never allowed slumber parties with Christina or Jennifer either for some reason. I was Cinderella in both worlds, always dashing away at midnight!

Their parties were similar to the ones with the *Tatbighi* and Brooklyn girls but they were warmer and friendlier. They were into guys and were dating here and there. My Farsi had gotten better and I could converse with them easier and of course, when in need, Ghazaleh always kicked in. Their families were super hospitable and I found a certain kind of cultural proximity and openness with them I had never found before. They had so much soul, love, and life, even though they were living in such closed boundaries.

Let me now take you to a night in school called *Shabe Ahya* night. It was a religious night, being the first night of the holy month of

Rajab. Those nights were the most fun with the girls, even though the rest of Iran's population was supposed to feel sad and display extreme emotion, even including fainting at times. These Nights of Awakening were a way to attempt to "revive the heart" during the month of *Rajab*—the entire month!

I loved these nights! People prayed (not me), recited *Duas* (verses from the Quran), ate, drank lots of tea, and we communed with the other school kids until dawn. School authorities pushed us to obey the religious practices of these nights, but since Ghazaleh and the girls were around, the nights were always super fun for reasons Rajab wasn't meant to be fun. Usually the events were taken seriously, with all the gravity one might expect, and *Duas* are considered weapons of the believer, affirming belief in One God, and shunning all else. Serious stuff.

Before I open up about *our* type of nights, let me tell you a little about these nights and their agendas. The upstairs café area would be covered with expensive rugs, and a type of tough fabric cushion would be leaned on the walls. Corner to corner the room would be filled with pretentious religious students sitting on the rugs cross-legged, leaning on the cushions, in an attempt to listen to the *Duas*. Sometimes it would reach extremes: the girls or the school principal and her staff would start shouting prophets' names, striking themselves in ecstatic empathy with the sufferings of the diviners, and I would ponder if they were crazy. I mean, c'mon! Shedding tears and showing compassionate understanding for the harsh deaths of the holy ones, I get. But the rest? Some of them looked like overheated fans passing out at a Michael Jackson concert!

After being introduced to what in my perception was like a depressing movie, I soon found other activities in which to invest my time during these *Ahya* nights, with the support of my newly found, warm-hearted girls.

55

On one of the *Ahya* nights, we gathered in one of the empty classrooms on the second floor. I imagined I was at a slumber party, under the covers, in a tent in my bedroom in Brooklyn, but with lots of mothership-produced goodies. My heart forever belonged to Oreos and Doritos, but I'll admit, I couldn't take my hands off the mothership pastries! Mina, Azin, and Nooshin would share their awe and slight fear of the rituals while I devoured pastries. This, and awareness of how the symbols and protocols connected them to religious mysteries, thrummed with magic. Occasionally, due to harsh restrictions imposed by the more traditional families of the other girls in class, they would use these nights to go on furtive dates.

The process would be simple: their boyfriends would arrange a pick-up at the school and, with their date's complicity, pose as a family member taking the girl home. Everyone knew and exploited the Nights as cover for meeting with "dates." The school doorman was laid back, cool and usually snoring by the door, so he never objected.

The following day would be a half-day, due to the previous late and active night. Everyone was sleepy (or acting sleepy in order to withstand even those few hours of school). I couldn't comprehend why attending the various rituals was mandatory. Sure, my parents are Muslim and they pray. But why was it necessary for *me* to pray? My parents were never practicing Muslims before. Why did we have to start now?

Often during these mandatory school prayer times, called *Namaze Jama-at,* meaning group prayers, I got caught singing Madonna's "Like a Virgin" while ritualizing the movements of sitting, standing and putting your head on the ground. I giggled because I thought it was similar to child's pose in yoga.

"Who do you think you are?" growled the principal, straightening her burka and wiping her mouth after she took a sip of boiling tea from her cup.

"Someone that doesn't like prayer," I said some hesitation, but mostly lots of determination.

"Start liking it *azizam*. This is your religion, and if we don't teach you when and how to pray, when will you ever start?"

"How about I start by learning what we're actually saying in the prayer?" I said back. "It's bad enough I don't understand Farsi regulary, but it's even worse praying in it!" I snapped.

"Don't you raise your voice on me *Khanoom*," she said, containing her cool. Maybe the tea was helping balance it out, because I could see the steam resting on the tip of her nose. "You will learn it, but this allows you to *feel* it, especially in the *Jama-at* style."

"I'd rather be doing it solo, but I can't win in this conversation, can I?" I asked.

"We have rules that you need to respect, and you will respect them!" she said. This time I think the steam was coming out of her nostrils.

"So I have to blindly respect what you are respecting, right?"

"No, not blindly, not with the smarts that you have."

I wanted to throw in the towel and just play dumb, because she just went back to square one.

The phone rang and she was summoned on a call. I blasted out of her office, but not soon enough. I was given a warning and next time the school cops caught me, I would be suspended. Since my honesty mattered more, I made a mental note to learn all the words to another Madonna song, or maybe do a remix.

There came times—one in a million—when I did feel content to recite from the Quran, but of my own will—even though the

Arabic was still a mess. Soon I was mixing up Arabic, Farsi, English, and Spanish and the result was, *no comprende* to anyone who was listening but me.

Another strategy I developed was taking a nap while in the prayer child's pose. After seven or eight minutes it was over, then I was off to class and doing whatever else might be required.

Though disrespecting the Islamic duties was not my style or intent, I would absolutely have no one dictate how I must worship, nor what I must say. No way. I would still be me. No matter what.

•••

A new friend, Leila, daughter of our downstairs neighbor, had invited me on a mountain climbing excursion along with some other friends. We first met while in the building's elevator and slowly bonded while sitting in the backyard. Some evenings we'd have barbecued *balal*, or barbecued corn cob, Persian style. So when she invited me I gleefully accepted, though I could hardly wait to hear my father's opinion on the matter. If he asked who the other people going were, the best answer was: Leila's cousins. Or something blood-related to Leila.

"Horseback riding and mountain climbing," said the Emperor, "with friends I know nothing about? That's out of the question!"

"But why? You haven't even seen my friends! They're our neighbors!"

"Out of the question. Completely." He sipped his cardamom tea, its sharp aroma perfuming the room.

"You won't let me go outside and you make no effort to come with me. I want to go out! It wasn't like this in Brooklyn you know," I said.

"It's different here *azizam*," he said softly.

"So what am I to do? Go back in time and change things?"

"Everything is so different here and it will take time for you to see this, but I guarantee you will love it here," he said with a smile.

"Love what, may I ask? Honestly, other than the pastries and good food, there is nothing that I enjoy!"

"Okay, okay. Enough." He nodded and sighed deeply, as if defeated. But he was strategizing. "We will go. Yes. Let's set something up with your aunt, uncle and cousins. Hmmm…we could make a day of activities out of it."

Of course, he was referring to his own sister. There were two sides of the family I had to get used to here: the mamma's side *and* the papa's side. Mamma would prefer to hang out with her side, and papa with his side, so I was split in the middle. The whole debate for me was: whose family is cooler? My mom said my dad's side gossiped a lot, and vice versa. My mom's family was a bit more into fashion and new cars and throwing lavish parties. My dad's was into more homey stuff like playing pool and poker in the house while ordering from some of Tehran's finest kebab places. Both sides were fun, but it was almost impossible to compare the two.

My dad had taken the conversation off track, but I knew his plan of getting the families together wouldn't likely happen before the day my hair was the color of my teeth! It was just a ploy to change the subject. This realization stung; what was he so afraid of?

4

The View from Darakeh

September 1996

PLEADING WITH MY DAD DIDN'T work. And my mom—forget it! Despite exerting considerable influence over her husband, I would have still hit another dead end.

Finally, I played the whole "why did you bring me here in the first place?" card—a winning gambit!

Designed to evoke parental guilt, this worked without flaw. "You turned my whole world upside down, and now you're opposed to my exploring it because you fear what's waiting for me in it?"

But the Emperor would not come all the way down from his "no" temple, so I had to bring Leila over, introduce her, and after extensive talking and asking her questions regarding what she does in life (mind you, she's seventeen years old), about her goals and ambitions, what her parents do for a living and their ideologies, he finally surrendered and told me to be back home in not more than three hours. Poor Leila—she left with a dry mouth! But we had finally succeeded because I told her to stay focused and just imagine she was next in line to be nominated for a Nobel Peace Prize. After that interrogation, and managing to keep the Emperor calm, she certainly deserved one! It also helped that my dad met her parents in the elevator, and they had proved they were well-mannered and capable parents!

Leila was the neighbor's daughter, so getting to know her family was not that difficult. It was nice to have a friend living so close, and yet I wasn't crazy about hanging out with her. She was way more into makeup and fixing herself up than I could stomach. What really annoyed me about her was that she laughed about everything, even stuff that wasn't funny. I called this disease "approval identity crisis." As they say in the land of the free: nothing succeeds like success!

My covert strategizing put me in the driver's seat (not literally) for our journey up a mountain. The weather couldn't have been much better as I (still basking in glory) prepared to go mountain climbing in Darakeh.

Leila had told me Darakeh had beautiful vistas, access to hiking and climbing, a selection of awesome places to eat, and was hugely popular on Friday mornings for getting away from Tehran's traffic, pollution, and smoke. From Leila's standpoint, it was also very expensive, but nothing seemed cheap to her—because she didn't do cheap. She was generous and stacked a fairly good allowance from her folks, but was stingy with me when it came to spraying on her perfume or borrowing her purse. Geez!

Regardless, I was pumped for a new journey. It was practically guaranteed we would have a blast up there, and first and foremost on everyone's mind: food. Leila had narrowed down one place for an excellent breakfast, where we could get fresh eggs taken directly from Mrs. Mother Hen. I had to see it to believe it though!

"Hey, you ready to go and have some fun?" said Leila over the phone, impatient with my ponderous prep. "Shahriyar is going to be there, you know!" Shahriyar was Leila's model-looking "friend," and the heartthrob of Tehran. We called him The Charmer. She wanted to introduce him to me, which was all good as long as the Emperor didn't find out. If we liked each other and decided to date, it would be my first boyfriend and I don't know how the Emperor would handle it, especially now that we were in Tehran.

I wasn't permitted to date, but I might be able to mingle with Shahriyar during the climb. No telling where it might lead. Perhaps the mountains would become the location for all future dates—who knew?

Vogue-ing before the mirror, I thought about which scarf to wear. "That one," Leila said sarcastically. She had come upstairs to push me through the difficult task of the scarf-manto match-up. The manto, the long trench coat, was usually matched up with a nice scarf, as if you were doing a blouse-and-pants or dress-and-stocking match-up. After you match them up, you also have to remember to match with your pants and shoes and bag! Some put on a burka and called it a day because the black sheet covered them from head to toe; others chose the less religious version and went with the scarf n' manto look.

Layers upon layers just to live out the religious dreams of your country! I thought it was a lot to sacrifice for someone's selfishness.

I was such an amateur when it came to choosing scarves and was still getting into having a closet filled with scarves and mantos. My Aunt Elahe had the most expensive mantos sewn for her because she didn't approve of the mass-sold ones. Hers either had to be from a boutique or made by her seamstress. It had become a fashion world of its own and people would pay good money for having the best!

"Let me take two scarves just in case anyone in the family sees me and I need to switch to change face!" I said laughing. I recalled another tense exchange with my dad earlier:

"Who are you going with again?" he had asked.

"Dad, remember? Leila, she came over!" I said defensively. Why on earth would he ask this ridiculous question?

"Who else is joining you? You know exactly what my question is."

Suddenly H_2O came into the room and asked the same question. Crap...two against one. But I had to hold my ground.

"Answer your father," she said, as if he needed backup.

"You guys already know! Leila and her cousins," I said biting my tongue. They could easily find out if they were really Leila's cousins by just going downstairs, but they put their trust in my firm voice.

"And who are the cousins?" asked my mom.

"Don't know, I've never met them, but the apple can't fall too far from the tree!" I said smiling.

"Okay. Have fun, but don't come back too late. Take my cell in case anything happens," said my dad. "Remember, I have to know everyone you go out with. I don't want you going out with this cousin and that cousin when I haven't met them."

"Sure dad, no problemo!" I said, looking away and hoping he wouldn't ask any more questions. How can you possibly know *everyone* I know? Was this the goal of this over-protectiveness? Lord help me!

The reality of the situation was that Leila, her boyfriend, one of his pals and I were going to Darakeh. I imagined we'd be a tight group, as we'd all recently been abducted by the same spaceship. We were contemporary versions, non-religious versions of citizens, and would be ourselves. They even seemed free from all the mandatory

Islamic stuff I was forced to abide by in school. They were far from mainstream, and I was excited to join them and see what they were all about.

Leila huffed and shook her head. "Oh my god! Just bring two, then hide somewhere, change, and walk down the mountain on a different path. You know, the same way you approach life."

I glared at her in the mirror. "Very not funny."

"Get over it. You know I've got your back," she said as she stood up to straighten her manto and retie her scarf.

Being with unknown males that weren't your husband, brother, or legal cousin was not considered admirable on the streets of Tehran. I don't know if it was taboo, but it wasn't on par with being a "good girl" in society's eyes. If my cousin or my dad saw me with this Shahriyar dude, first they would know he's not my brother. Second, they would probably assume the dude wanted me for one thing: sex. The saying went: "girls and boys are like cotton and fire; once the cotton is touched by the fire, we have to call 911!"

To eliminate myself from such assumptions, I took two scarves. The first and original scarf would be "me" and the second scarf would be "another girl they mistook for me." This strategy was good for places with lots of traffic where you could get yourself lost in a crowd.

I was admittedly nervous about meeting Shahriyar. If he liked me, would it be for my dual citizenship? Everyone in Iran wanted to dip their toes into the U.S. pool, so marrying someone with access to a green card would be their lotto ticket out of this place!

From Leila's explanations to get my hyped, Shahriyar was young, a macho boxer, and super smart, topped with lots of confidence. I just hoped he could stop liking himself for a few minutes so he could like me.

We were ready to leave so we strolled into the kitchen with feigned casualness and each plucked a tall glass from the cupboard, avoiding any eye contact with my parents. This was to avoid being assaulted with questions again. We both gulped water, clunked the glasses onto the counter, and I said, 'We're headed out. Love you! Will be back for lunch!"

"Be careful…this is Tehran!" my dad shouted as we turned and padded toward the door, and I swore I felt two pairs of eyes beaming into my back! I slammed the door.

Outside, I released an anxious breath. We climbed downstairs, and I paused at a row of plants growing in artful clay pots to excavate from the soil my freshly-dug makeup kit. Good thing no one watered these today! Now it was time to prettify my face in the cab.

This was another obstacle: hailing a cab carrying no perverts in the front, or—god forbid—in the back. Taxi drivers allowed a maximum two occupants in front and three in the back. Sometimes four were permitted in the back if one was a child. Or sometimes it was all thrown out the window and however many people could be stuffed in the car without the tires deflating was encouraged. No car rules, no regulations, anything could go!

A bunch of cabs passed right by Leila and me as if we were invisible. Well, at least Leila was (she was the one actually hailing the cab). Finally one stopped, bearing one dudette in the back, so we hopped in, hoping we'd be the first off. They usually locked and broke one door handle so if you sat next to the locked door, all remaining passengers had to get off before you got off. This was to make sure no one ran off without paying!

The mountains were located on the far north of the city, so we'd probably have to climb out or move around if there was any dropping off or picking up. Good thing was I was wearing pants and sneakers.

The whole payment process was a pain in my bootie! Why did some taxi drivers-annoyingly not have change for whole bills, and credit cards weren't an option at all? We didn't have exact change so we didn't get our fare returned, and we glared at him for the obvious display of rudeness. He response was a cynical shrug that implied it was time to get out! We gladly did and hoped he would spend the additional dough on some deodorant—he and his car smelled like dead fish heads marinated in garlic. Ugh!

Trotting toward the planned meeting place, I caught the sweet scent of black cherries and mulberry. A gathering crowd soon became visible, faces flushed even though there was cool, crisp air; some still shuffled along in sleep-mode. Others (the real troopers) lugged kettles, rugs, portable barbecues, and *ghelyoons* (hookahs) in their backpacks and were heading up the mountain at Olympic gold-medal speed.

"Look at these people! How can they hike up the mountain carrying all that extra weight?" I asked.

"For them it's just a Friday picnic. They're used to it...warriors of the light!" said Leila with satisfaction. In Iran, Friday was the entire weekend. So much for Saturday and Sunday.

After saying hello to Leila's boyfriend, Shahriyar, and their friend Ali, we started walking toward a path. Ali was a photographer in art school and wanted to just dig a hole to France or England and become a professional photographer. He said in Iran photography really doesn't pay much. Not surprising.

Shahriyar was definitely a boxer and from the looks of it...he had a six-pack. Move over Robert!

Not knowing where we were headed and trying to find a path less crowded, we continued movin' on up as they guys led. They were good company and we laughed and mocked each minor mishap and absurdity we came across. Leila was sweating bullets and turning red. I was doing okay because my manto was thin and unbuttoned and my scarf was about to fall off. I was deciding to take it easy, even though Leila kept telling me I better button up—the religious cops were always around. I ignored it.

Unfortunately Leila's sweating attracted bees, and then bursts of laughter from all of us. "Hey, Queen Bee!" I cried. "Look out! Remember the *Candyman* movie? Don't get stung!" I continued giggling, knowing that probably no one knew the movie reference. I didn't find Leila all that sweet, but the bees did! A thick cloud of pungent hookah smoke scattered the buzzing menaces, saving Leila (and everyone nearby) from potential pain.

We all continued to playfully shove each other and told silly stories. Being out of the so-called public eye was great. There was less traffic in the part we were climbing but it was steeper—because it wasn't supposed to be hiked on!

I started singing my favorite songs, as if I'd forgotten I stood in an Islamic country. Right now, I was free to be whoever I desired, to behave again like I had in my hood, BK. Funny, after several months here I still considered Jay-Z's hometown my hood!

After a while we stopped at an ideal spot: the riverbank, where burning feet could be soothed in icy rushing water, and out racing playful minds could be cleared by amazingly fresh air. One of the guys found mint and Persian watercress growing among tangled weeds, and we all plucked enough to eat. I was delighted by the clean green tang, so unlike the commercial herbs back home. Back home, everything would be labeled, packed, sealed with approval, and here we were eating from and with Mother Nature herself! It actually tasted better than the supermarket labels that shouted "Organic!"

Shahriyar stooped to wash his hands, and I tried pushing him into the river. "What are you doing?" he said, joking and trying to keep his balance.

"Having fun! What are *you* doing?" I flirted.

Standing straight, blotting his hands on his pants, he said, "Staying dry—or at least trying to! I can't show up back home with sopping we clothes, can I?"

"Okay, soooo, take'em off," I joked.

Shocked, then tickled by my dare, he smiled and hugged me, savoring my scent. A thrill of fear and pleasure surged through me. Oh wow, I can't believe this! What if the authorities saw us?

The "religious cops," as I liked to call them, were the famous bearded, gun-carrying, green-suited *Komitehs*. These guys were merciless and in the name of god, *Allah*, would take you down to their headquarters, *pedeghan*, and lock you for a couple of hours or interrogate you for good measure.

In this scenario, a sample interrogation question would be: "Who is this man?"

In this sample interrogation answer, my best choice would be: "My fiancé."

Sample interrogation reply: "Release them—they are *halal.*" That meant okay to touch each other by Islamic standards.

Any other answers would risk imprisonment. Sure, you could bail yourself out, but the bail was set upon your status and under-the-table cash. The more you had the faster the process! Azin, had told me about them and warned me to be careful not to be caught by them. If they were the wrong kind and wanted lots of money, they could sentence you to whippings or other punishments they implemented during the Middle Ages for crimes.

But hiding in the mountains and hugging Shahriyar made me feel like I was in a James Bond movie. Was I supposed to be scared?

Was it all really true? Should I be cautious? I preferred none of the above and just not giving a shit.

My stomach was beginning to growl and we were all getting hungry, so we decided to head to the breakfast place. Shahriyar put his arms around my neck, and for a few minutes we walked like that, until he stopped short.

"What's the matter?" I said, hearing his sharp intake of breath.

"It's the *Komiteh*. Let's put some space in between us. And quickly button and knot your scarf tightly around your neck," he whispered softly.

Now in "as soon as yesterday" mode, I redid my attire and looked in the direction opposite to Shahriyar. Trouble was surely coming right at us. I just had to act like I've never seen him before and we'd be all right...

Abruptly Shahriyar turned and began gesturing, asking directions as if he were some lost tourist. So much for being in a fantasy movie! The entire adventure had been muted by this unforeseen hand. The charade had to be played until the green-coats wandered off to browbeat other "innocent" hikers.

Leila and the others started making their way back down the mountain's rugged face, discouraged from going to breakfast. Everyone but Shahriyar might as well have been invisible, because all my attention was on him. I was upset. How had the *Komiteh* found us? I thought this place was hidden? Azin had told me they would fly down from the sky itself—now I understood why. What a challenge! All in the name of hiking! The *Komiteh* had smelled us out, even though I must admit my acting was impeccable! One of them had looked straight at me and I just continued walking.

And that was our short morning. My only goodbye was to Leila, who oddly returned a dry response, as if totally disinterested. Talk about an awkward girl...

The green coats loitered, casting what looked like sinister glances at departing hikers and picnickers. I wondered if going out was always this hard and fruitless! I mean, I could have made out with Shahriyar, my first make-out in the Islamic mountains of Tehran! I watched him and the guys walk away. Driving out my hormonal thoughts after several tense, lonely minutes, Leila and I finally got a cab.

5

SATs on Steroids

November 1996–June 1997

LIKE ALL POTENTIAL COLLEGE STUDENTS, I dreaded taking the *Konkoor*, Iran's version of the American SATs. There were referred to—with no trace of humor or irony—as "SATs on steroids."

How could I survive this? I had been here a total of eight months, and now I had to get ready for college. I wanted to study dance, choreography, and have a career in the arts. I despised becoming a doctor, lawyer, or engineer—the three jobs most respected in Iranian culture. If you were a doctor, you would be highly respected and definitely the number one pick on anyone's list of "people considered suitable for marriage." The other two careers were both highly sophisticated, but if you told anyone your son or daughter was a doctor, you automatically sat on their VIP list. You didn't even have to *be* the doctor!

There wasn't a dance major offered here, but even if there was, my dad would have strongly opposed it. He said "shaking my ass" was not a career, and my answer was that it was more than my ass that would shake. That was the wrong answer.

I taped music videos from our illegal satellite TV (made possible by well-greased bribes, the same way 70% of the country also have satellites), and after school I would push all the living room furniture to one side and make the space in my own private dance studio. Once the videos started playing, I acted like I was a paid dancer and learned all the choreography by heart. My parents would pass by, shake their heads, and say, "May God help her! She has to get this out of her system!"

But it wasn't some type of steam or sweat I could extract from my body. It was in me, and that never registered with them. They thought it was a teenager thing that would pass. But the "teenager thing" had made a solid home within me and every day it was my routine to dance it out, even if I had people walking from the front door towards the kitchen, which meant passing the living room. Hey, I was open to selling tickets too!

Dance was a dead-end in this country. In fact, any discipline involving extreme physical movement, especially by a female in the presence of a male, was forbidden unless you were *halal!*

But I had an idea: if we weren't allowed to shake dat booty in front of all males, then what about creating classes and a major with all females? The Islamic rules didn't apply to females and you could take your scarf off in front of the other females in the room; so that meant you could also dance in front of them, right? Why didn't they do something like that? Gender separation was applied on buses, in classrooms, and in prayer rooms, so why not here? Separate us so we can dance! Yeah right...

I was living in a society I couldn't completely understand, but one that was clearly un-accepting of my desires. And my parents were no help, they were set in their ways like concrete.

So I had to work on picking a "real" major and get into the exams. I agreed, but my primary reason was to escape staying home and doing nothing (watching the walls, anyone?). Home was utterly unproductive, meaningless, and no fun. Who wanted *that?* I had to explore—in fact, I was driven to do so. What better way than pursuing a higher education?

I noticed that most women in lower classes were expected to be excellent housewives, and if they happened to also pursue an education, it was a big plus. The combo of housewife and education was a great one, but most women were passive and usually stuck with being a housewife, even though they had knowledge to work with. Even when the kids were grown up, they still stayed at home.

But there were women who had education and actually worked with it. They were the tops and I loved them! I felt they knew their worth and acknowledged they were equals with their hubbies. Class issues led to different perspectives, which led to different actions and different ways of thinking. All I knew was that I would not be fulfilling my destiny if I just sat at home. But I had no idea where I was going, no idea what to declare on the soon-to-be-reckoned-with with university forms, but it didn't take long to figure out an answer (in 105% opposition to my parents' wishes, of course).

Biology, math, medical studies, and law were scratched immediately. That didn't leave me with much, but I always like learning Italian. So I had come up with an answer. Instead of going to a language institute and learning Italian, I told my parents I would be declaring it as a major! I was ready for the debate that came post-announcement—my dad had his eyes on me becoming a doctor!)

To clarify, in Iran, specifically Tehran, everyone was trying to teach a language and create a language institute. And the funny thing was, some didn't even have a certificate or degree to teach—they would just spend a couple of years in the U.S. or whatever country as a good citizen of society, learn the language, then return to the mothership to create a language institute. Instead of going the easy route and teaching English, I chose to learn a new language in college, where the professors had to have some sort of degree. This was how I got my parents on board:

"But you are so talented! And wouldn't you like your name on a nametag as Doctor Farsijani, MS?" my dad pleaded.

"Dad, I could care less about what's printed on a name tag. The best nametag would be "Shaghayegh the Beautiful and Great!" I said teasingly.

"I am serious. We are talking about your future," he answered firmly.

"I am too dad. I want to do what I like to do, not what your Iranian standards and society dictate to me. What if that won't make me happy?"

"But you have to think about it. If you were to dance, how would you make money?"

"With difficulty, but at least it's what I like doing."

"That is what you'll think the first couple of months, and then you will say 'my father was right!'" he said with a smile.

"Let's negotiate then! Let me study Italian literature, which I think I like, but I'm not so sure yet. Let's see what happens."

"I don't know why you are so stubborn, but I don't want to push you *azizam*. The more I push you, the more stubborn you are," he said with such a disappointed tone that I wanted to sink into the ground. But I went over and laid a big kiss on his cheek to let him know his wish would at least be considered...one-tenth of a percent. He cared, and despite his firm views and way of thinking, he would do this for me. But we both knew I got my stubbornness from him!

My dad was an engineer, so he naturally pushed me towards a non-art major. Doctors, engineers, and lawyers all ended up in my psychological Dumpster, not because I didn't appreciate their value, but simply because there I had no intellectual or emotional interest in them. My dad was a firm believer in education, and about 90% of Iranian fathers had the same beliefs as him. The other 10% thought their daughters were safer at home learning how to cook, knit, sew, and get pregnant. At least I was spared that.

I wasn't about to be a young, uneducated girl sitting at home waiting for some young, well-established guy to come *khasteghari*. That was when the guy and his parents visited to see if both ends approved of marriage. Sometimes it was decided within a month of visits, sometimes within an hour of the first visit. Super traditional! How dull would that be? And how dull must both the girl and boy be to tolerate such conditions?

I'd already told my parents that the last thing I wanted was to be *stuck* with someone. They weren't sure. So I think we were at least on one page, but still had two different mind-frames on *why* I wanted to attend university.

From the privacy of my bedroom, I mulled it over. There had to be a way out! The entire affair roiled its chaos through my head and heart. Damn I wished I was back in Brooklyn studying for my SATs. I was ready to live my freshman and sophomore years, the years that no one really studied, but primarily focuses on dating, having sex, and in general living it up. At least that was my perception of American college. In Iran, that thought had to stay hidden in the basement of my thoughts. God I missed Brooklyn!

All these pressures were pushing the rebel parts of me to light up and come out of hiding. It was a fight between being me and being what Iran and my parents were expecting of me...and it wasn't expressing itself well. I felt a shift developing in my personality. The first year of my Inner Brooklyn Volcano was rising—and the lava inside was getting hotter by the second. The last thing on my mind was studying. Uh oh.

Since I frequently expressed myself to her, Mina had given me some books that were inspiring and helpful. Some of the books weren't translated, so I had no choice but to plow through the Farsi text. The books were about overcoming different obstacles with love and developing your self-confidence while in a transition mode. One was a book written by Deepak Chopra, which had been translated to Farsi, and I couldn't find the English, original version. So I read it with difficulty, but read it thoroughly. Another book addressed hope and understanding fearlessness, and Azin always reminded me that utter lack of fear was dangerous, as the emotion is a survival mechanism.

One of my favorite books about love was by Leo Buscaglia called *Born for Love*. The author was in fact popularly referred to as "Dr. Love," and I wanted very much to meet him—until I found out he'd died in 1998! At least he'd left behind something in his work for a lost girl in the wild Exotic East that helped to express myself:

Dear soul,
Please guide me through the darkness
Through the silence of shouts and dead ends of imagination
We are one but barricades stand in between molecules
Can the bud know its meaning?
Will the bee continue making love to the flower?
Can tenderness be found again in the mouth of a volcano
From where it was born
Softening the dark lines of extremist
If love is the answer
Please release this hostage to the blowing wind?

The books and writing poetry helped me tame the anger inside me and diminished my free-floating anxiety. They also ignited a romantic and passionate feeling toward writing poetry as a form of expression, something I had not felt before, and this too vented my inner turmoil. Things had changed drastically over the last few months and I think I was finally doing pretty good for someone that had been run over by an emotional bulldozer.

I closed my book and notebook, eased back into my pillow, and listened to the wind hiss through the trees outside. Tomorrow was another day of this physical reality...isn't that right? *Shab bekhier, Doctor Love* (good night, Doctor Love).

After the spiritual moment had passed, I started filling out university forms to study Italian language and literature. I was fully aware that attending the Languages section of university wasn't going to be easy, despite not having to study math, biology, or physics for the *Konkoor*. The learning process would be a consuming grind.

Iran hosted a handful of universities, two of three of which qualified as excellent. In truth, I didn't really care where I got accepted. It was just one of those times. The decision was made! I had to imprison myself with books and study materials—that included Arabic. Ugh! But if that would get me out of boredom I would gladly welcome it!

The next months were brutal with having to finish up my final months of public school and also studying for the *Konkoor*. But I was a devoted, if not an enthusiastic, study slave! I graduated high school, and my schedule for the two months in between graduation and the test was:

-Rise at 4 a.m.

-Study until I got ready at for the 7 a.m. bus

-Come home from school at 3 p.m.

-Study until 7 p.m.

-Eat some delicious H$_2$O food

-Study again for the *Konkoor* until 12 a.m.

-Eyes would slowly start to close...

Then my mom and dad would drag my body into bed and the same schedule would repeat the next day. I did insist on taking the occasional mini-break, but as far as going out, or even answering the phone, well, my parents had taken an inordinate interest in covering that! "Thank you, but Shaghayegh is studying today. What? Yes *azizam*, she will be studying for the next couple of months, until the *Konkoor*. No, you may not. What? How dare you take that tone with me! Maybe your parents should teach you some manners!" Then the line would go dead and whoever called got the picture!

My friends didn't have to study as hard as I did because Farsi was their first language. English was three-quarters my first language, and Farsi was the last quarter. So I had to study triple hard. Anyone attempting a face-to-face meeting was met politely at the door, and promptly given their three or four-month notice. No friends, and certainly no mountain hiking until after the *Konkoor*...Emperor's rules!

I nonetheless was driven by the urgency to get into school, so I swallowed hard and kept my nose in the books. What little free time I had was limited to family dinners on Thursdays (which was like Friday night of Iran, since it was the beginning of our weekend). My new life was a dive from making some real human friends to getting a new type of friends—these books!

The entire prep included the various studies of Farsi and its related literature. Plus Arabic, grammar, Islamic studies and, easiest for me, English. I didn't so much study English as give the material a cursory glance, as the tests themselves were ridiculous. For example:

Fill in the blank: "What is _____ name?"

The answer: your.

See what I mean?

I passed the English with flying colors and didn't worry about it and instead put more focus on the Arabic! Rumor had it that some of the *Konkoor* questions weren't really testing your knowledge of how you understood the content, but instead were making sure every detail *in* the book was looked at. It went so far that a past *Konkoor* question was apparently about the birthplace of a long-time dead publisher of one of the test's textbooks! In truth, these questions were absurd, but past test-takers always made remarks that *any* kind of question could be possible on the test. So I was scared into studying with super-duper detail!

Since the competition was rough, if you missed one question, you'd drop behind maybe 5,000 other applicants! I'd memorize all the authors' jean sizes, panty sizes, and how many cups of water they drank a day if that's what it meant to get into university.

•••

The big moment finally was here. It was the night before the *Konkoor*, the test that would shape destinies, including mine. I'd done my best. Now I wanted to burn all my books. Yes! Burn them and leap over the flames while they crumbled into ash…burn, burn! After all, had they not burned through these months of my life? And who knew what this might lead to?

My cousin and I gathered around my mom's table to eat, laugh, and try to relax—I couldn't even remember how to anymore! I couldn't help but think that maybe I do like this; the pressure, the challenge, seeing what I'm really made of. Who knew? I didn't even know which way was up anymore.

I'd come to learn that Iranian education was completely different: from an early age, it's pumped into your blood that there are "right" things to be doing in your life, and you forget the difference between that and living in the unknown void of what you really *want* to study. The passive automation to move you through life by society's and culture's standards...ugh. So far, this society had cut off my dance classes and my freedom to choose my religion. I wished I could talk with Christina and Jennifer, even they would probably say, "Forget it, let's go bike ride and get some ice cream." But then at least my problems would *feel* magically solved!

I just kept telling myself that all was fabulous. In my mind I knew this mental lava was headed toward a rapid-fire explosive exit!

Dinner rocked: chicken kebabs, grilled tomatoes and a hearty salad. My mom always worked wonders, and this time was no exception. In Iran, family was strength, despite trifling disagreements in matters of religion, education, and relationships. My mom, Ghazaleh, and I all sat together, gorged ourselves, giggled like children, and I singled out Ghazaleh to tease and bug her. She would get annoyed but not too annoyed to forget to giggle.

She was also taking the test, and if she got in and I didn't, well, it would be a catastrophe. Both my parents would have a fit and suffer from MSS (Massive Shame Syndrome). Now, if she didn't get in and I did get in, my parents would be flying, especially since everyone would be saying, "You just came here and passed the *Konkoor*? Bah bah, such a smart girl!" The "bah bah" intensifies how much of a smart girl I am—it's basically meant to intensify any subject. It was all about reputation.

Five in the morning shrilled its alarm, and by seven I was seated in a wooden, uncomfortable chair in a rundown high school that had a hanging wooden entrance door that I was afraid to breathe on, thinking it might fall apart at the hinges. The chair creaked annoyingly with each shift of my aching butt. Soon (and exactly on time) the exam documents were distributed by a tall woman with fierce dark eyes and a rigid face.

Well, this was it. My make-or-break moment; entry into the unknown; a ticket to freedom or prison; the elevator to something or nothing; heaven or hell...

I internally yelled at myself to stop it already! No reason to drive myself crazy!

While taking the test, my favorite cake treat, the Persian *Teetop*, was passed around. Yes! It was the best pound cake, stuffed with chocolate cream. With each bite, my memory of any type of Twinkie was quickly evaporating! It was nice to know the test-givers were human after all, realizing how long the test would be and that we might perish from hunger or low blood-sugar while filling out our Scantron sheets.

Savoring the treat was great, and I found—to no small relief—that the test was bearable and even dull; close to my expectations. By noon it was over. Woo!

Walking out of the depressing, worn out building felt beyond good. What do I do now? Love, shout, dance? An aroma of flowers nearly overwhelmed me. As did the mere (but vivid) sight of trees, its leaves magnified by my couple months of sensory deprivation. It was like emerging from a coma and experiencing the world's wonders anew. Wow, how deep had I sunk?

One thing rang true though: I was set once more to figure out how to enjoy life as much as I could. Living here for these past few months, I still hadn't quite found out what to do to enjoy my life! All I had learned was how to be repressed and forget about my deepest desires, how to cope with inserting Islamic absorption serum into my mind and, sadly, how to pretend. I was determined not to go back to that lifestyle.

6

Back to Life!

June 1997

AFTER SHARING AND BASKING IN various congratulations on just taking the test and having survived "study freakism," I wasted no time returning home.

On the way, I was thinking about calling up all my peeps and getting some adventurous stuff on my calendar! Even though the country was oppressed, rumor had it in school that there was so much more going on *underground*—and I definitely wanted to explore that!

I had been through several months of academic incarceration...would my friends even recognize me? Or would I recognize them?! Would they look the same (I thought the last as I was balling)? Maybe they've all departed the country, married, or had kids for all I know!

Honestly, being genuinely happy with this whole mandatory Islam thing was doable, but annoying. I still wished *dancing* was mandatory. Nothing wrong with wishin'! It would be more fun under the burka!

You'd be saddled with babies, the weekly Duas, going to the mosques and always wearing that wretched scarf, wimple or burka. And stay tuned...more exciting activities to follow. That's what it seemed to me: a lifestyle I completely rejected. Everything was about reputation and how everyone else looked and accepted you; Pretending 101. With that in mind, some people would buy the most expensive cars and take expensive holiday trips to keep a high profile and reputation. This even extended to a sixty-million toman ($50,000!) wedding price-tag, 350+ guests, lamb and kebab catering, the best DJ in town, all while putting yourself in deep debt! Believe it or not that was the norm for some people. That would mean you were unable to afford the "big deal," and god forbid if anyone discovered your wallet was really running without fuel!

Back home, I padded past my mom, who stood at the kitchen counter fiddling with fresh flowers bursting from a case like silent explosions. "Well, well. I've been thinking about you, praying for you...how did you do?"

I bent and sniffed the flower display, which included some to the most beautiful scented flowers, like red roses (the national flower of the mothership), sunflowers, orchids, gardenias (my mom's favorite), and the most beautiful purple tulips. Iran was numero uno in flower production and everywhere anybody went or whatever occasion it was, it was "Mr. Florist to the rescue!" The trick here was to pick the colors carefully according to the occasion, and this even included the birth and death of the holy prophets and other religious holidays! For deaths, it was usually white. For everything else it was a rainbow of anything!

I bent and sniffed the display again. "Nice! I did fab, but I'm exhausted." After saying what I said I realized my English accent while speaking Farsi was slowly melting away even though it was surely still there. Thank god there were no signs of the Farsi in my English. That remained untouched.

"I can imagine *azizam*."

"That was the longest running study period I've ever had. Think it was because I had to read everything over and over and over again! I wouldn't wish that on my enemy!"

My mom softly chuckled. "In your world, 'you gotta run for the touchdown!'" she said. "Go have a rest. You'll feel better."

Rest, of course, was the last thing in my whirling mind, but I played along. Eager to activate the plan hatched earlier, I was thinking of calling the girls and maybe Shahriyar—he probably didn't even remember me, even if we were to go through all the hiking details we experienced! Oh...he never even had a chance to give me his number...all our communication was through Leila. Scratch that! I def didn't want to hang with her.

I called Mina and told her to spread the word to Azin and Nooshin and their boyfriends and whoever else wanted to join. I needed to relax and this was my alternative to my soothing Brooklyn bike rides. My new "ride" was going to a coffee shop only to have the religious cops show up at anytime and bash the evening. Party crashers.

Coffee shop time was considered somewhat of an expensive pastime for the North Tehranians; others would sit at home sipping tea with the five o'clock evening news. Times were tough.

I had to keep up the "worn-out" charade in front of my parents, as if I weren't going out to meet with someone I liked. Yes, I'm a broken, post-*Konkoor* student in dire need of a breather.

84

I knew my excuse would fly, but my demeanor had to be its equal!

Later, I emerged from my room with practiced effort. "I'm going out to relax with some friends I haven't seen in months." Nice declarative sentence. Solid delivery.

Peering over a magazine, my mom said, "Oh. Good. Of course. When will you be home?"

"Before nine-thirty, maybe sooner." The correct answer is always "I will be home soon," because committing to a time would be impossible. No big deal. Just a small belated get-together with long-missed friends, Mom.

Incredibly, I turned and stepped out of the house with no further comments from anyone. Now, like some exotic flower, I was ready to bloom and spread my adventure-deprived wings.

I had to exit the house with a vanilla and blah attire to let the folks know it was a regular, no-big-deal friend gathering—all girls! If they smelled any male involvement, my dad's protective side would arise and I would be banned from going. I didn't get this side of him because he wasn't like this in Brooklyn. Or maybe it was because then, I was a bit younger. Now, he was all, "You have grown into a beautiful flower and guys here are all hungry to get a taste of you, smell you like a flower and throw you to a corner." What did that mean? What if *I* wanted to throw a guy in a corner? I was the girl…I should be making the calls…weren't my feelings to be respected?

The minute my toes stepped outside the house I changed the dull, white scarf and transformed into a blue sassy one, painted some glossy red lipstick on my bare lips, and my feet dazzled with heels used only for strutting the runway at the Mercedes-Benz fashion show. Indulging in all this was fun and also a mystery as to how it might work in the face of so much opposition and judgment.

If the religious cops didn't see you or if they saw you but weren't PMS-ing that day, you might be in luck.

Girls could put on makeup outside and could decorate as much as they wanted, but at times if the black religious crows were in a bad mood they could bug you about it. At that point they could either ask you to wipe the makeup off (which would be a tad bit difficult if you didn't have eye makeup remover), or they would ask you to stand still while they took it off for you! The latter would most likely end up in redness on your face—they didn't seem the gentle type!

I usually changed clothes to make it seem it was a super duper normal get together and that I wasn't in the least bit dressing up for anyone, especially dudes. Even within those guidelines you could push the fashion to such an extent that it was still in the Islamic guidelines. The theme was "sexy IS back and always on ON," but on the Islamic highway, which seems crazy, but it worked. Shorten some pieces and tighten some other pieces and *voila*!

Some topics for me to keep in mind when stepping out on the town:

1. Don't get caught by the religious cops, regardless of how much makeup you have on or in your company.

2. Don't get caught by your dad in the company of a guy; and if he catches you with heavy makeup, *that* will definitely lead to suspicion.

3. Don't get caught by gossip-creating family members—keep your mental drama satellite radar up!

4. DON'T GET CAUGHT. Period.

There was too much thinking going into one coffee shop gathering. I felt like Bonnie and Clyde—the domesticated version! I sprinkled some pepper and spice on my outfit, letting my inner self shine, and it gave me a rush of long-suppressed excitement, as

though I was being stalked by the paparazzi. What a change! Now I
could at least breathe without my parents breathing down my back.
I was finally out of the house, without any guilt for the books. In
fact, I wanted to burn those books! Turn them into ashes!

I knew the clock would soon strike twelve. For me, that was
when the moon stepped out of its hiding spot: nine-thirty.
Everything would come to a finish before midnight for me! I had
bypassed my parents, and now had to be wary of the not-so-cute
clad in olive green *Komiteh*, and the female version of them, the black
wearing burkas crows, aka "black crows." They were the ever-
vigilant, annoying "authorities" packing outright otherworldly
questions and searching for a few easy bucks—which I was willing
to pay to them to leave me alone.

Ok, now I needed to chill out! With so much fun ahead, why
think about that?

I would gamble on the 50% chance of running into them. The
coffee shop moments in Tehran were the best. It was all about
experiencing friends and the possibility of making new ones.
Sipping tall cafe lattes, fresh-made pineapple juice or the infamous
black Darjeeling tea (which also led to future tooth-whitening
dentist visits), while nibbling on tiramisu, crème brûlée, or ethereal
Napoleon pastry. And also the five-star Iranian Zagat rated, top-
seller potato chips with melted mozzarella cheese and topped with
ketchup and mayo sauce! This was so good but loaded with
calories…but irresistible at the same time—so who cared!

It beat sitting at a desk studying Arabic, something I would
probably never technically use in my life. Was the point of learning
this thorny language that of acquiring radar to detect others using it
around you? Or filling gaps in my knowledge of the Quran, a book
I might never read ever in my life, or might not *want* to read and
understand? Ugh!

My mind was still racing from the exam! Calm down already…

Not far from the coffee shop I laughed with myself, heels clacking away, recalling the somewhat elaborate scheme my friends and I had devised in case the "cops" questioned anyone. Not many options existed for posing as married people, or cousins, because a few males were present. This way, in the event of any individual being interrogated, he or she would have the "right" answer. Right, in this case, having the same answer as the *other* person. Any demand for I.D. was quickly handled with: "I don't have it." Persistent questioners wanting telephone confirmation of any assumed identity were taken care of by employing a more sophisticated method. Two unknown friends on the other end to answer questions with solid answers, and no blowing anyone's cover!

Was this complex planning really worth the considerable trouble? Yes, it was! Without a doubt, yes! Planning around my dad was one thing; planning around the religious authorities was a whole different ball game.

Around a few pushed-together tables in the cafe we all first shared our stories about how we escaped the mamma and the papas and each strategy that was shared was so different than the other person's, we laughed until someone said she was at my house! That was not funny AT ALL! I would fry if my dad found out. Then she said she switched the last two numbers around so I would lay still. It made me think we were as clever and devious and no-budgeted as independent filmmakers. We *had* to be. Any slip-up would result in a major disaster. The authorities here didn't always play nice! In fact, they never played nice unless they smelled cash nearby—and their sense of smell was faster than the speed of lightning. Zap!

Like all good things, the night was coming to an end and thank god we didn't have to run from anyone. It seemed they were in some other neck of the woods and spared us our night!

I made it home by ten o'clock, and that was okay due to parental understanding of just how hard I had worked over the past six months. Come to push a bit further, eleven o'clock would have been fine too, but midnight would have been *really* pushing it. At any rate, there was nothing to do in the streets at eleven o'clock after having eaten in Tehran. Maybe a stroll in the park.

In my dim room I felt a wave of loneliness, so I plucked a pen from the holder on my desk and wrote in my lined journal about all my suppressed feelings in a country I was trying to find a partnership with.

Fun times for me…but I had made good with it. The female animal was awakened inside of me and I wanted more adventure. This hide-and-seek wasn't doing it for me and I was hungry to break loose. That said, I knew I had the great Emperor to deal with, and I was going to have to work very hard to sneak past the lion king. Grrr.

7

Girl, Accepted

August 1997

ON THE DAY THE TEST results were to be announced, the streets convulsed as if in protest. Every accepted, failed, humiliated, confused, carefree, nerdy, stubborn, religious, and happy-go-lucky student moshed and twitched and flew around waving newspapers in an attempt to locate their names among millions, to see whether they had a chance at higher education, or in my terms, a chance to do anything to escape boredom.

Newspapers rattled and crinkled back and forth between ink-smeared hands, from one grinning face to another pinched with grief, all in anticipation of finding their name in long blocks of tiny-fonted text—the kind similar to fine print, especially in pharmaceutical advertisements.

Some names were so alike they might give false hope to many thinking they were accepted, but given the chaos, even several minutes of that would be good.

I maneuvered and weaved through the crowds, searching for a paper.

Usually they sold out by eight o'clock on such an occasion, but I had on my lipsticked smile and pepper personality in hopes of getting a paper from some hipster (or hipsters) in case of an eventual hook-up. You never know!

Being accepted and not accepted was, at this point, far from my control. Whatever was going to happen would happen—no one on Earth could make changes to the newspaper. Some highly imaginative types might wish to pen their names in, but there was no covering up reality at this point.

Everything about college was a 180-degree flip from the norm I was used to and I didn't think acceptance in school was very well-rounded. In Iran it's eating your brains out, giving a test, dying to get ahold of the results, which weren't computerized and so old-school. The nerdiest, brainiest, and some which had a parent who died in the Iran/ Iraq War, got precedence. So either you were super-duper smart or not anything, but had a dad that died for your country! That latter was really unfair! I could understand the first part...yeah, you're a brain for a living. The second part I couldn't even digest...so someone gets to veg out, watch MTV videos, and also go to an Ivy League-equivalent school in Tehran. The same school that I had to study six months for while I was aging in my little cell, and another douchebag gets to walk right in just because of the war. What if we lost in the war—then he couldn't go to school because his folks couldn't handle weaponry correctly?

That was complete bullshit, but Ghazaleh told me that the ones who did get accepted were to be honored at the Nobel Peace Prize or something, atomic energy kinda material!

Me—not so much. I was just electricity, ready to be used if I was to advance among the first two groups. It was good in a way because there were no interviews, no essays, no need for references, blah blah blah…it was all summed up in one test. Forget calculating an average of all your strengths; just be a good test taker. That, I was a superhero in!

"Ouch! Hey!" I said as some idiot elbowed my back. I wanted out of this mass of people, some of which could use a bath or a Tic Tac.

A spindly guy dressed in over-sized haphazard clothes like a scarecrow looked as if he was going to grope me, so I turned and nearly collided with an attractive young man with abrupt, brown eyes.

"Well hello," he said. "Need a paper?"

"I sure do."

"Please, take mine."

Very respectfully, I ripped the paper out of his hands but had no idea how to make sense of the list—not to mention comprehending the different universities and their corresponding cities and how this was printed and categorized! I only knew of the three main schools located in Tehran.

The nice-looking guy wore an expression indicating he hadn't been accepted and didn't really care one way or the other. He smelled like lime oil. The way he glared gave me an impression of empty good-looks, of shallowness, of talking to an empty telephone booth. And like that, he'd already lost interest in me and was checking out other targets.

People were still fighting over papers, and I stepped in a puddle of what I hoped to god was coffee! Leaning against a wall in a doorway sour with rotten vegetables, I found my name—YES—it was my name!

Like flies to sugar, others pressed in on me to eye the precious paper. After a few moments I found my test results too! OMG! I was in! GOAL! Or GOOOAAAL as they say in Brazil!

Given the struggle to keep the paper, I wondered if cutting out the strip on which my name and results were printed might be a good idea. Something to show off proudly if someone wrenched away the paper. Such accomplishment was how you made a name for yourself or for your family.

I gazed intently at the results. Could it be real?

To no one, and everyone, I shouted: "I've been accepted into Per-si-an Harvard; Tehran University!" People around me chuckled as I expressed my excitement among so many introverts.

Iran had a bunch of "Harvards," brutally difficult to make it in, but I had done it! Yes, I can do it and I DID IT! It was hard, but at the end luxuriously sweet! Here I was, fresh off the boat from NYC, packing a heavy Brooklyn-Farsi accent and roughly one half the vocabulary of a Tehranian local, and I'd easily (with lots of kick-butt studying) taken down my considerable competition!

I grabbed a cab then ran into the house, and without any oxygen left in my lungs, I shouted while entering the house like a diva expressing genuine and tearful joy over their precious daughter's enormous accomplishment, and it seemed as though the mountain climb had been a sort of presentiment of this success. A few bumps here and there, but they knew I'd make it. My feeling was like accepting my first (of many) Oscars from President Clinton himself! Kinda going overboard here but that WAS my feeling!

Thank god I did it! And spared myself from marrying some guy in whom I had no interest, nothing in common with.

A new road opened, heading past signposts reading "University" and "Higher Education." There was uniquely-spiced exploration right here in Tehran. There was a proverbial saying in Iran: due to being locked-up, studying for months and months, you forget what you look like, forget how to shower and socialize. But after you get accepted, the rest is like "ash," or literally in English, heavy, thick, hard to digest soup. Basically, if you could survive this, you could survive anything. I am a commando and an Oscar winner! Ha!

Quite the contrary back home in Brooklyn—or what I used to call home—it wasn't that difficult. I mean, I could take my time with writing an essay and preparing for the interview prep...but in Tehran it was isolation until the test date then deprivement of having the type of fun I wanted to have post-test (which was just going to a party and dancing it up). A lose-lose on both ends, no satisfaction at all! Wonder how the others went through it.

My parents couldn't contain themselves either and both were calling the family about how smart their daughter was and how we had overcome the difficulty of learning the ins and outs of these books and being new to this whole system. My dad invited everyone for dinner at our house, which I thought was overdoing it a tad bit, but whatever worked for the popps!

The family was even more excited than me—they had called their friends and conveyed the breaking news: the one-time Brooklyn girl, not even a year in Iran, had gotten accepted to one of the best schools in Tehran! It was a great public relations firm too!

My present for getting accepted was taking driving classes and if I got accepted, I would get a brand-new car. It was nothing big, just a Renault 5, which is equivalent to an Iranian version of the Ford Focus hatchback...you know, the cars without asses! But hey, it was also a part of my newly attained freedom. No complaints about that! Besides, I knew I would swap cars with the parents soon enough.

•••

Rise and shine! The next day my mom proudly took me to my first driving class. While I walked out the door the Emperor kissed both my cheeks and said, "You are maturing, my princess." Was I? I had no idea! Everything was in good shape until we reached the driving school class and I saw the car and my driving teacher.

The guy was probably in his late forties, bearded, smelly, missing a back tooth, and looked as if he was a sales rep selling condoms. His name was Mr. Abbassi. The place looked professional, but this teacher was the flipside of the coin. He didn't even look licensed or like a comprehensive driver. But that was who they handed me over to. The class was known as the highest quality, most convenient, and most trustworthy driving school in the hood. The guy didn't really look such but I, as with all things I'd seen so far, decided to wing this one too. My mom began filling out the paperwork while I was given away to destiny.

The car was a run-down Iranian manufactured Peykan. After observing it 360 degrees, I found two reasons why they would allow this vehicle on the road: it's cheap, and it runs (for the most part). It was faulty mechanically and from a safety side, it was weak. It looked dodgy to me altogether. I could imagine that if I hit the speed pedal, it wouldn't work at fifty miles per hour.

"This is what we're driving?" I asked him.

"Get in kid," he said and pointed to the driver side of the car.

I liked his demeanor because it looked like he wouldn't take any of my shit. Oh by the way, there was no instruction class beforehand. Maybe that was equivalent to registering for class. Something the folks took care of.

Once we were both in the car I noticed inside it had three-foot pedals: speed, brakes, and something called the clutch, which was connected to the manual gearbox. Within ten minutes he explained the rules of the road to me and when to use each pedal. He had brakes on his side as well just in case I forgot or decided to ignore that pedal.

Before we started the car and rolled out of the parking space he said, "Listen to me and you'll be a pro. The details, you'll learn on the way. If you learn to drive in Tehran, you can drive anywhere in the world kid." He was only half-looking at me with his own stamp of verbal approval. He had a FOBish mafia way about him, and underneath those shabby clothes I got the feeling he was one of the best instructors. The tough-love kind. Even though he didn't look the part.

But the first day was horrible! People in this country drive crazy and the pedestrians could care less if they lived or died. All I had to keep focusing on were pedestrians crossing and the crazy drivers popping out from nowhere. The best part was the cars rewinding back a one-way street after they had accidentally passed their turn point. You had to be aware at all times and definitely know where the brakes were. In Iran you probably needed two brakes and a bag of good swear words and hand gestures. The thumb was equivalent to the middle finger (I was a fast learner there). Luckily we were mostly in residential neighborhoods passing in between houses with a right turn here or there.

Mr. Abbassi's name was Jamshid and we started to develop an unusual friendship. This was the gist of the friendship: him pulling the brakes and me pressing on the accelerator, then we start arguing, and it ending with him telling me, "There are no traffic rules in this country, so it's either my rules or the highway kid!" So I'd back down and let him pound the brakes as much as he wanted.

It turned out that he was a civil engineer but couldn't find a good paying job to support his family and had turned to this driving school. I told him my story and he just said, "Good luck! You have a lot of balls to come back to this country. Stay true to yourself kid." What the last part of his sentence meant I didn't get, but felt he was speaking from a place of truth. Maybe that's why he had so much tough love.

It made me sad to see how smart he was but wasn't able to use it. Finding a good engineering job was tough in Tehran, especially one that could support three kids and a wife. He said the country was filled with unemployed engineers, and look now where one of them was now. I told him he had the honor of teaching me—and he hit the brakes again! Ha!

He dropped me off and told me he would pick me up the rest of the week at 8 a.m. sharp, so I better be ready at 7:45 a.m. He would leave if I were a minute late!

Smack on the second day he took me to the main streets and highways and ended with a nice parallel parking lesson. He was fearless and had a no formula and I loved it. The only part I was afraid of was this steep hill that ended with a traffic light on top. Finding a rhythm between putting the car in first gear and immediately pressing speed without the car sliding backwards into the car behind me was a challenge.

"It's so hard!" I complained.

He ignored me or would make a comment like, "Oh really? Let's try and see how it works out…that's my favorite place to drive!" Then he would take me to the exact hill I was afraid of driving on.

After passing him an irritating look I was formula 1-ing it toward the hill! I couldn't wait. I was a student driver anyways, so I had an excuse if I hit anyone!

The hill was six lanes wide and the end point of a highway leading to Vanak Square. The traffic light took two minutes to turn green, so that was the easy keep-your-foot-on-the-brake part. But it turned green for one minute for the cars to climb their way up, and that was the tricky clutch acrobatic part I was to master.

"The speed and brakes have a love/hate relationship so it's either one or the other! Make sure you let go of one if you decide to go with the other. The clutch is a good friend and follower of the accelerator. You pick the speed and it follows. Once in first gear forget the brakes and pound on the accelerator, but with delicacy; treat it like a girl...soft and gentle!"

"Is that how you treat your wife?" I asked excitedly.

"Maybe," he said and quickly furrowed his brows. That meant OBEY, WOMAN!

The heat was building, and the pressure was def on!

This was the pattern:

1. Brakes

2. Brakes, clutch, first gear

3. FAST AND FURIOUS (I forgot the part where I had to treat it like a woman)!

The car jumped forward and there I was flying like an airplane and if Jamshid's foot wasn't fully awake we would be in the yoga cobra pose.

"I said softly! What the hell was that?" he yelled.

"Jamshid, I *am* the girl who needs to be treated softly," I said with a smile and charm.

He gazed at me for thirty seconds then said, "You want to grab some freshly squeezed fruit juice in Tajrish?"

"For sure!" I said with the remaining adrenaline I had left from my first near-accident experience.

He directed me towards the famous juice stand in Tajrish Square where we met a line two blocks long. "My treat—heads up in the car while I go stand in line!" he said and jumped out of the car.

It was the first time I was in the car alone and was scared at the beginning, but I put on some illegal, FOB-ish music Jamshid had in his car stereo, which was hidden in the glove compartment. To change tapes you would have to do the arm stretch—and this could only be done if the car was parked. Not recommended while driving!

He was a cool guy and I felt a certain closeness with him. After fifteen minutes he returned with two big fruit shakes, a smile and a great sense of humor. Don't know where he picked that up. We talked, laughed and joked around and after another fifteen minutes he said, "Ok kid, start the car up. I have another student waiting. But hanging out with you is a breath of fresh air!"

A third person might have thought this was a mini date and this guy is hitting on me but he was really looking for a friend. Someone that was ok with his hidden stereo that he could complain to and not just hear a different version of the complaint back.

The class continued for one whole week in different parts of town until they were completed and Jamshid told my dad to sign me up for the actual test. Per him: "She can drive anywhere in the world, including England, where the driver sits on the other side."

My driving not only received five gold stars by him, but I could jump hoops and do jumping jacks with my car skills! The day of the test was another *Konkoor* type feeling for me. Both parents knew I would succeed, but I was afraid of one thing.

I realized there was a certain kind of culture that I had yet to fully understand and that included people in high school, my cousins, and even Jamshid. I felt layers and layers of feelings dug deep within them, which they rarely expressed unless they felt you were the same as them. They wanted to know if I was from the same tribe—then suddenly if you made a joke with them, it broke the ice! A joke followed by a smile was a bridge-builder and you immediately could get what you wanted. Totally different from New York…or maybe New York was much different.

The Scantron written version of the test was a piece of cake and now I was in the driver's seat with a lady for the second and final phase. She had thick tattooed brows and lips and her tone was army-like. Something like Delta Force. I think she might have been some kind of bad-ass general back in the day when the Shah was around. It was only after 2003 that females began joining the police force; a change after the Islamic Revolution. By the way, this is totally different from the religious female authorities that walked around with their long black burkas covering the entire body head to toenail and catching you because of your bad *hejab* (wearing your scarf crooked or short and had your hair showing)!

Delta Force was pretty strict and tested me on steep hills, parallel parking, and turning my right indicator on when making a right turn. Obviously.

Steep hill was a breeze thanks to brother Jamshid. Parallel had a slight angle but I was bumper to bumper almost behind the car in front and in back, and the last was the same question on the written portion. Right or wrong all driving rules go out the door in Iran. The only rule is to *stay alive*—and that went for driver and pedestrian.

I still couldn't believe I passed, and before getting out of the car Delta Force said, "You just succeeded in one of the hardest countries to drive in—now stay alive!" I felt honored and scared both at once. I was beginning to feel scared with so many people saying how difficult Iran is and telling me to stay alive...

How hard could it be to stay alive here? Or had I just jinxed it?

•••

The time between me getting accepted and getting my driver's license until the time I started school was interesting. I decided to register in the Italian Language Institute to start slowly getting into the Italian mode and getting used to whipping out my hands with the different Italian melodies. The school was dropped from the heavens itself or maybe the people were from a different world. It was heavily connected to the Italian embassy in Farmanieh in Tehran. This was the first time I encountered "brothers" and "sisters" seated in the same room; a real fusion. At times, I wondered if this institute was paying anything to some religious entity to allow the mix but I never figured it out. They didn't even wear scarves or the manto in class—we did though. My best guess was that maybe the owner was a real religious dude, or he had top-notch connections.

Class seating was as such: the guys sat in the back, or to the left; a subtle conformity to separation. The girls formed their own flock. This loose interaction (at least in the public), so much like high school, was marked by shyness, rebellion, and awkward exchanges: "He *looked* at me," or, "I am going to wear my gray wimple with my new pink gloss, tilt back my head, and ask questions in class to get his attention." To the professor, that meant you were paying attention to others; it meant, let me hear your voice...is it delicate? Sexy? Provoking? Annoying? Keep on asking...there is no such thing as a dumb question!

And so the story continued...and it was real funny, but not a joke.

I used my almond shaped eyes over a cheerful, arresting smile and charm, and using these weapons I knew I could attract anyone my way. Even with the New York, Brooklyn-accented Farsi, my confidence put those other negotiable qualities on mute!

Sitting in on my first class, I slyly glanced at two guys in the back. They were probably in their late-teens. One was wearing a long pink un-Polo-like tee and was (hopefully) unconscious of how it conjured comparisons to the Pink Panther. The other sported a poorly-shaped goatee. I surmised these two must have been from downtown Tehran but must have paid quite an amount to be sitting in this class. Or they were rich peeps with no style. No telling what was what!

Registering for these external classes was pricey in Tehran especially since they were extracurricular activities and connected to the Italian embassy. The savings account must've been full, or they were registered for free, *or* there was some networking connection between the owner and maybe the dudes' uncle…anything that came to my mind was acceptable. I mean, it looks like the country had no rules or regulations in this area either! A newborn baby in the hospital could make rules!

I still couldn't judge Iran. It was too soon, and can't judge a book by its cover. Good thing, too!

Our teacher had a special spice and twist to him. Yes! First of all, it was a him and it was the first time I was seeing a *him* teaching me, since in high school they were all females! They were indelible as ink.

I liked the teacher a lot, but it looked like they pulled him out of a Michelangelo museum in Italy, or from the ancient lanes of Capri. He was definitely old school but had this singing accent and very easy-going manner. An example: if someone's wimple slipped in class, he did nothing in the way of chastisement. He didn't even care; he was a good teacher indeed! An Iranian-Italian dude who spoke graduate-level English and Farsi, but with an Italian accent. The accent was had a Pavarotti-like grandeur. He wouldn't scold you for being naughty or wearing inappropriate attire. In other words, he was not a member the religious green uniform-wearing commandos!

The guy was so cool that I didn't even ditch one of his classes. As soon as I walked through the Institute's doors, everything was put in a European mode, a newly found cultural comfort zone for me. The guys were cool, the girls cooler, and the teacher the coolest!

I started making new friends here again, but they totally understood me! Better than high school or Tatbighi. Either I was changing and everyone was looking good to me, or a new picture of Iran was developing in my mind. We had so much fun, but it was a different kind of fun from Brooklyn. I was beginning to how people really were.

At times, I didn't understand their conversations but felt close with them in other ways. They had boyfriends, skipped classes when they felt like it, smoked and laughed and generally were carefree. Also, they appeared not to care about many of the problems confronting them—things that seemed taboo to me in a country like Iran. At the time I had no idea what these problems were because, compared to my sense of culture shock, they seemed minimal—almost invisible!

Bits and pieces of the culture were being revealed to me with every class or social interaction that I had. It was a coin being flipped, swimming into the deep end of the ocean, traveling to Antarctica, driving cross-country from Los Angeles to New York, going on a blind date to discover the guy is a family friend! I think my point is crystal clear!

"What are you doing today?" asked Elham, a girl I'd recently met who sat behind me. She was a year older than me, petite, and was already a freshman at Azad University in Tehran. She was studying English literature as her major and was coming to this institute to tidy up her Italian. Like everyone else she wanted to get out of Iran, so her plan was to apply for an Italian student visa, head to Rome, and become a director. She was doing all her work through the dial-up Internet at home, which disconnected every two minutes! She was a trooper!

"Going to Franco's class. We have a test coming up," I answered.

"Sounds like a good idea but all the mini tests are rubbish except for the big test at the end of the semester. We can always cheat on these, and cheating is a good idea," she said with a wink.

A funny thing was that Elham was Jewish, but I didn't know anything about her until we gradually became close friends. Another completely accepted secret kept by many Jewish families living in Iran. She told me they were a minority and until she trusted someone, she wouldn't expose a lot about her family. Also people in Iran would quickly label her as "*Johoode*" (Jewish) and would automatically have preconceived thoughts, but I didn't really give a damn and it was at the bottom of my list.

Elham was great, with an awesome sense of humor. I—coming from Brooklyn—was totally accustomed to this and her dry Jewish humor. It was like she and Elaine from *Seinfeld* were sisters!

Was our closeness due to sharing Iranian roots and me being brought up in an Italian neighborhood with a bunch of synagogues in Brooklyn? An odd formula, but who cared? And all along, this difference akin to a sill of opportunity forming in my soul, bracing it to engage—and master—the struggle common among many that age and beyond: the art of acceptance.

•••

Days passed, and my friendship with Elham tightened at greased lightning speed. Another girl joined us frequently at breaks, but she usually spent her time studying. We called ourselves the Trio and spent long hours together in mutual witness of every little event. The ugly truth is, sometimes they were the reason I went to this class! My sole priority was to drop my class with the new car the Emperor got for me, pick up the girls, and circle the infamous reputable street called "Jordan," one of Tehran's liveliest streets. It was abuzz with chic cafes, restaurants exhaling garlicky smears of fried food, art galleries, florists, bakeries, and expensive real estate where many embassies kept their playgrounds. And, in a very Tehranish way, this "night-life" was far from any you might experience in other countries.

Aside from all this chicness, Jordan was loaded with hot guys! Tehranians who could drive their fancy cars up and down the streets, making U-turns as needed so not to be eliminated from the hunting game—if indulging in chitchat—from getting the other (usually male-stocked) car's phone number. In other words, snatching the guy's phone number. Then the guy had to wait and call him, then came *if* the girl accepted the date and if the Lord wanted, a relationship would spring to life!

Outsiders might think these cars were lost, and in dire need of a GPS system. Looking deeper still, they might wonder why ninety percent of the thumping, laughing vehicles were filled with chic, made-up-to-the-max girls redolent of exotic perfumes. Or strikingly handsome, jaw-dropping guys! Maybe there was a reason there were no bars— too many hot peeps!

Yup—this was the game and everyone liked to play it. Some could even be called gamblers!

Depending on which car (and which revelers) might pace us, we would exchange numbers or peel off to dimmer side-streets for quiet conversation, maybe even get invited to some underground party. In short, it was the best situation for those looking to do something on a Thursday night (equivalent to Friday night back home).

The street itself was named after Dr. Samuel Jordan, founder of the American College in Tehran (later becoming Alborz High School), but currently known as Africa Boulevard—a name no one ever used! Kind of like the post-revolution name. Jordan was *Jordan*, not the country, but the happening hotspot. An upbeat place to meet good-looking, upper class, wealthy Iranian boys and, in some cases, girls.

At times when the *Komiteh* demanded you pull over, definite excuses had to have been prefigured, ready for instant use, or else get ready to face the end of a really fun night!

One night I decided to visit my aunt and on the way stop at Elham's for a quick cruise in Jordan since it was on the way. I decided to take my dad's new Peugeot to attract attention, since my Renault 5 was not even comparable to the other cars there (and didn't have any air-conditioning). It was similar to hitting a bar and trying to meet some guys, or just to flirt. I drove fast to Elham's and would blame imaginary traffic on my to be late arrival. Racing along the streets, scarf tied against the wind's greedy fingers, I felt like I was in an old Hollywood black and white movie.

The guy had to make the first move, as Elham and I desired, or he would lose any opportunity for conversation. Elham's beautiful green eyes, black hair pony-tailed inside her scarf, and clear polished skin inspired guys to do the extra circles required. Whether driver or passenger, the girls' situation was win-win. Elham stood before a borderline where she could understand and speak Farsi better than the others and, if necessary, could intercede to fill in any conversational drop-outs or blanks. Amen to Elham, or amen to her tongue!

Now, exiting the freeway, the new Peugeot growled like a glistening black tiger nosing toward the street's thrumming crowd. Windows down, we blasted our favorite music, coast-to-coast smiles bright with the fearless passion connecting the same girl-power that connected us from Day Uno.

"Here, turn here," said Elham.

I braked, spun the steering wheel, and made a U-turn.

This was followed by many more, a seemingly timeless stretch spent watching a showroom's worth of purring imports: BMWs, Mercedes, even the new Toyotas—a big deal indeed! Bursts of flirting had us giggling.

Abruptly a horn blared beside them, and a swarthy guy in a black Patrol shouted, "What's your name?"

I smirked. "Why's it *your* business?"

Struggling with divided attention, the guy grinned. "Well, our cars are right next to each other. I wanted to make sure—in case we collide—that I have some insurance information."

How clever! Just leave it to a Persian guy to bring his savvies to the table.

"Do you drive that badly?" I asked.

This intrigued him more and led to another U-turn as Mr. Good-Looking continued battling against the road and the fierce beauty of our eyes. Yes, they were beautiful indeed. Then cut short as the light turned green, Peugeot already in the lead, its polished form mirroring neon.

They should have just made the street into a big, long, (unending) street. The U-turns and the red lights slowed down our communication and it was hard to pick up where we left off!

"Did you look at him!" shouted Elham. "He looks so in-control and like a man...one of those who know *how* and *what* to do with a woman—and that's not even from a touchy-washy standpoint!"

I shook my head with motherly regret. "He is just like the rest of them: looking for bait. He should put his fishing rod back in the water, 'cause this fish is toughie b-a-b-e." Somehow I doubted we'd seen the last of the Patrol guy.

Another U-turn and we hit a traffic jam. I pursed my painted lips together and slapped the dash. "No!"

Some fool in a tobacco-brown BMW, apparently going for a tight turn, had hit the bumper of the car before his, and now everyone was stuck. Ugh! Just what I needed with so little time. I still had to drop Elham off and also drive to my aunt's home before Dad made the dreaded check-up call; short but ever-so sensitive.

Crap...

Of all things, there was an annoying green Honda, its driver famous in Jordan for picking up chicks and basically having one-night stands with them. He muttered something, and I watched the other struggle to conjure some question weighty enough to demand my reply.

All at once he found words, but his target closed her window, signifying complete dislike.

Peering at Elham, I could see now the Patrol guy's car crawling beside us, and our gazes locked.

No conversation, no trivial exchange, could equal those fierce probing eyes, as if penetrating into my very soul and its secrets. If eyes were the gateway to the soul, I warned myself, his must swarm with desire...and who knows what else? A strange sort of recognition surged through me, quickening my heartbeat. This must be communication; the man feeling, caressing the muscles of my inner being.

And in that solitude, its peaceful buffer against the traffic jam's harsh reality, I knew the Patrol guy had buckled a moment of connection. And he was going to use it.

"Do you want to get out of this knot?" he asked, sundering silence.

I sensed levels of intent in those few words. Nice way to pick up someone and take advantage of the situation...

The look and form behind it were pleasing, but I roiled with tension over the constraints of time and consequence. Until something snapped.

"Hey," Elham said, "get with it."

But do I really care?

I drew a deep breath, exhaled slowly, heart hammering my ribs...and told myself to surrender.

As if anticipating this, Patrol guy grinned and eased the force in those hypnotic eyes. "Follow me through this block," he said, "but be careful. There are many dead-ends within these streets."

He accelerated then and deftly angled his car in front of the Peugeot.

Here I go, I told myself, barely questioning this newfound trust. It felt right.

He'd probably help me if I drove into a nasty ditch...wouldn't he? I was putting too much trust in his good looks.

This turn of events was exciting and a bit scary. I felt certain such trust would encompass any failure, mechanical or otherwise. But I was in.

8

Hero of the Night

August 1997

WHAT DID I JUST SEE? Some powerful energy there, to be sure.

Elham knew butterflies fluttered in my stomach—this could be seen in any girl's eyes, even though I was too arrogant to admit it.

No…I needed to connect mentally before allowing any feelings to brew, let alone to start shakin' in the knees!

I wasn't cold and pathologically indifferent; not that way at all! In fact, beneath my rebellious surface was a kind, humane, smart young woman. In fact, I don't think Elham had met anyone like me, and believe me, I'm not sending myself flowers when I say that! I knew I was young, and bound to evolve, but I was semi-stubborn and that was stamped on my soul. If I did allow someone to enter my life, that person was going to jump through hoops, and knowing me, those hoops would probably be spiked.

But those spikes would also be both *ever* challenging and sweet. I always put my unique and beguiling smile to work, and with some teasing, always got my way.

"Snap out of it!" I said to myself firmly.

Turn after turn, the streets kept getting narrower and steeper, as if we were driving along the edge of a mountain. The freeway could be seen in the hazy distance, cars speeding toward the future.

Abruptly the other car's brake lights flared red. It slowed and pulled off onto the shoulder.

I was forced to stop to avoid a collision. "What's he doing?"

In truth we both knew what he was doing and, butterflies were sneaking out of my stomach's cocoons!

The guy opened his door, breaking a swirling dust devil that spun off in the wind. He climbed out and stepped towards us.

Butterfly status: crashing into one another.

Elham giggled, then immediately snuffed it. "Here he comes…" He leaned down by my open window. I caught a trace of cologne, and he gazed at me as if inspecting lamb shanks. "Do you know your way from here?"

He smiled like a hopeful wolf, as if anticipating a "no" from us.

I inhaled sharply and pressed my lips together as if in reaction to some insult or inappropriate joke. Elham caught this and was quick to respond while I supervised the butterflies.

"Yes. And thank you so much. We are in such a time crunch!"

I split my attention between the steering wheel and this strikingly handsome cad. "Thank you." was all that came out of my mouth. I didn't want to get caught looking at him again. The first time was bad enough!

I thought now only about the Emperor and getting to my aunt's place.

He grinned and grinned. "Well, no problem. Just in case you ever do need directions, this is my number."

He produced a slim gold pen and scribbled on a business card. "My name is Arash." He locked me in his dark gaze, as if in fear of losing the moment; but Elham saw the beginning of trouble.

For a moment I was hypnotized, then took the card and returned another "Thank you." My vocabulary basket was suddenly empty.

He looked so different from Green Honda guy. He (Green Honda guy) had pre-written contact info in quantity similar to the ones they put in supermarkets: Sofa for Sale; for further information call XXXXXX and they cut them with scissors into twenty little pieces so the entire population could rip one off if interested. Some girls in Jordan liked the car or wanted a piece of action so they gladly accepted one.

I realized he was staring at my bronze-tinted hands, which, aside from my face, was my only visible flesh with the scarf on. He just stood there, and I asked myself why oh *why* wouldn't a girl fall for him? He looks like money and underground parties and probably knows all the cool people in Tehran—the ones who really know how to party, rather than hanging out in coffee shops and drinking pineapple juice!

Subconsciously I felt as if in a coma and didn't know why.

Abruptly Elham snatched the card from me and dropped it into my bag, knowing full well that her friend—ME—would mull it over and end up not calling him. He seemed like a nice guy, but there was something off about it. Very attractive, yes, and clean and contemporary—he knew his way around clothes. Hard to tell, but I'd place him in a Giorgio Armani-ish kind of category. Strong, double-A type personality. Good, he'd need it if he hooked up with me, to really see between my layers...and also understand my messed-up use of Finglish.

He stood straight and ran a finely muscled hand through his hair. "Okay then, I'll hopefully see you later."

He turned and stepped back toward his idling car.

Elham gave my arm a light slap. "Hey! Why are you looking away? You *know* you like him. It's okay to be attracted to someone!"

I smiled wistfully, "Look, I do appreciate you trying to make your point, but he's just like the other leeches. They see a hot girl, or in this case two hot girls, and bam! Lasers shoot from their eyes and from the south of the border...you know what I mean!"

We both laughed and I pinched her shoulder, something cute I had learned to do.

"C'mon! You like him and you know it," said Elham. "Maybe you should give this guy Arash a chance, seeing how he kinda saved us from cruising down the nasty *Komiteh* lane. God knows what the Islamic guards might have had in store for us. A beating, perhaps? Demands for bribes we could never afford? Or just dealing with their zombie-like deadness to our welfare and safety? I don't want to think about it."

I smirked, shaking my scarfed head. "I get it, I get it! Point taken. I promise to look into it gleefully!" I said as if swearing before the jury.

I checked all around and eased the car back onto the road. "Okay, now let's land you home. I and this piece of metal should be somewhere on the opposite side of town— like at my aunt's house by the golden phone. The Emperor will be checking my status any minute now. Giddy up!" I said and we both broke into a high-pitched giggle because that only pointed to one show: *Seinfeld*. Ha!

I understood exactly what she was talking about and knew, eventually, I would surrender to the urge to call Arash, the hero of the night.

• • •

After dropping Elham off on the corner of her street, I peeled off in the Peugeot as if fresh from an F1 course with Michael Schumacher himself.

Good thing the car was a Peugeot, and could speed and handle better than just about anything on the road. And definitely better than the classic Peykan or "Iranian chariot" which looked like a newborn Tyrannosaurus Rex. Sure, it could move fast, but god forbid you needed to pull the brake at the end. You'd have a personal Armageddon! Usually taxi drivers had Peykans, and young people (if not classified as vodka-swilling, S-Class-Mercedes-worshipping FOBs) declined to drive them.

I arrived at my aunt Elahe's just in time for the telephone call the Emperor made to check up on me.

"Hi! I'm here!"

Both my cousins, Ghazaleh and Bahareh, were there too, and automatically added up my dad's car and my bright scarf together to equal Jordan cruising! I didn't know them that well yet, but suspected it takes one to know one, so we were in the same boat! That said, I still didn't want to tell them what happened with Elham, that way I'd be safe from any loose lips sharing the info with my aunt. Once it reached my aunt, it was only milliseconds until it reached my folks. Trouble!

We first had dinner consisting of an hour and a half of storytelling, laughter, and enjoying Persian-style lasagna, which my aunt prepared in a pot instead of a Pyrex casserole for oven baking.

Rather odd, but delish! So good, in fact, that I got the recipe. I admired anyone who cooked outside the box and didn't limit their techniques and palates in conformity with what they were told or how they were raised. That was real creativity in my opinion. Fearlessness and courage; apply them to everything, at every moment!

I loved the food, the dessert and mingling with the cousins. It was a happiness flavored by actually sitting at the table with family in Iran, a sense of connectedness, forgiveness, sacrifice and generosity.

After dinner came the Persian tea-hour and, of course, the Emperor chose this time for round two of the check-up call. Was this simply because he didn't trust me? I kept asking myself this question until I finally asked him and got the reply, "I trust you. It's *them* I don't trust!" It was always a win-lose kinda game and all part of him being an ultra-super protective Persian dad. Thank god it remained at ultra and super, because more than that would mean war between me and the popps!

"Hi, *khoshghel khanoom*," said the Emperor. "Are you having fun? Did you park the car somewhere safe?" That was a superb greeting. That meant my secret at Jordan hadn't leaked...yet!

"Dad, your car is safe, along with its diverse cousins parked on the same street! And we are having a fab time, so please don't worry!"

"Great, *azizam*. When will you be coming home?" he asked quickly.

I smelled that question from a mile away, so gave him exactly what he wanted to hear; although since I was at a trusted place, he wouldn't have objected had I said I wanted to stay one more night. After all, this was a trusted family member, they were blood related and she would be reporting *everything* to him without the slightest error message!

"Whenever you need the car, daddy." Persian fathers liked attention and respect, and having you throw the ball in their court.

"Whenever you wake up, sweetheart. Drive safe, and always look to your right and left when making that turn." he repeated for the nth time!

"You got it! And good night." I said, relieved that he hadn't suspected anything or heard about me coming late to my aunt's. Whew!

I don't know why I had become so fearful of my dad finding out. I came from the U.S. and wasn't scared about anyone seeing me there. But then again, I really wasn't into guys either. I think this "being scared" feeling had developed recently in Iran. Hiding this from *that* family member because they *may* think bad stuff about me like…I'm sleeping in that guy's arms and god forbid, lost my virginity with someone other than my husband. The whole traditional feeling and mentality with all its stuffy taboo made me sick to my stomach! For crying out loud I was just having some innocent fun playing "hide and seek in Jordan"! Even if someone did get caught, the parents would probably say, "No it wasn't my daughter it was the neighbors," and leap towards the next useless subject to talk about.

Back at the table, we shared tea, fresh pastries, and watermelon slices, the seeds from which my aunt cracked open while discussing all kinds of things, ending with a Turkish or Rashti joke. There were jokes of all kinds in Iran depending on the county you were from. Whoever was trying to be funny or dumb was labeled a "Turk," but it had nothing to do with the actual Turkish people. So why were they labeled as a Turk in the joke? Maybe some Turk dude was too drunk before Christ, made the joke, and there you have it! He messed the whole culture up by getting too wasted on that summer night!

I really enjoyed getting closer to the cousins, despite some lingering cultural and language barriers, which seemed to drop away in actual conversation. As though they were once connected in another life. Perhaps this was testament to the depth of the familial connection. It seemed they had the same type of difficulty I was facing, with the traditional parental leash buckled on. Similar experiences, though slightly different since I came from Brooklyn and my family had seen that part of the world. It didn't mean much! What part of the world you saw...in the end, all that was important was the residential part. The more you're caged, the hungrier you become! I was being hand-taken to that cage.

During our tea-hour, Arash kept popping in and out of my mind and I wondered why. Wasn't I too young to be talking about this? I was about to start university and wanted to explore. If I were to call him, I had to really fit in James Bond's shoes with all this fear mentally growing within. The country's *Komiteh* added to the fear of my dad finding out added to the fear of a neighbor finding out added to the fear of the neighbor across the street finding out, even though it was nobody's business, needed *this* superhero team: Hercules, Sherlock Holmes, Scooby-Doo, and the Road Runner all cast in the new James Bond sequel! Who cared? It was my life. But all issues were so interconnected in this country that I was wasting my time pushing it.

On another note, strategizing made it fun. For now, just for now, I chose to ignore this and focus on the antics of the two cousins.

Once my aunt left the festive room for bed, the night continued, as they did with many Iranians after dinner. It was prime bonding time. For the first time the cousins began opening up, and I could begin to see the true side of them outside of family and studious times. This was the real deal that was kept secret from the rest of the family for fear of genuinely messed up family gossip!

"Did you see him?" Ghazaleh was asking her older sister Bahareh.

"I did," she faintly replied, "but it was for the duration of the class I ditched, so not for long. He is wealthy and good-looking, but I don't know if he wants to get married."

I casually regarded Bahareh; she was *pretty*!

Her dad came from the western part of Iran called Kermanshah, which I had never seen, but knew was a city of mystics whose people were very happy and upbeat. I marked my mental geography map with an X to discover it some time when I could travel in a car without constantly being checked on!

"But you won't know that," Ghazaleh was saying, "'until you go out with him again. I do like the way he talks on the phone. Especially when I say 'wrong number' and hang up on him because dad is sitting next to me!" She couldn't stop herself from giggling.

"Do your parents know about him?" I asked.

Bahareh shook her head, "Nope. If they knew, there would be no going out alone and we don't want to even go near *that* point. That means the old man doesn't trust you!" She gave me a level gaze. "I know you are new to all of this, but Iran is totally different from Am-ree-ka," I laughed at how she pronounced it! "Our parents don't approve of boyfriends, and going out to dinner with them, or even going to the movies, so we do it behind their backs. Not that we want to lie, but we do want to explore and just have fun with it. Are you seeing anyone now?"

"No," I said firmly. I still didn't trust them. I didn't know them well enough yet.

118

Anyway, I was telling the truth—I wasn't seeing anybody. Getting a phone number from someone didn't mean I was seeing them! Deep down, I knew I was going to contact Arash.

After talking some more about Bahareh's male prospect, I thought: Wow, what a life! How do you know if you want to really date somebody, let alone if you want to have sex with them? If a girl were to have sex and her parents found out, there was a 95% chance she would be crucified or put out to join the homeless.

The conversation, however, didn't' get to that point. Mostly it focused on building a plan for a second-round meeting with this guy my cousin was interested in. After a few more hours of talking (and occasionally using my superhero strategy) the plan was set. The strategy consisted of Bahareh taking her big (huge and giant) bag (holding makeup, a funky scarf and shoes), and changing in the parking lot or grocery store down the block. The plan had obstacles, but not to worry—even this was calculated!

Since all summer schools were soooo proper on attendance, they always contacted parents to inquire about absent students. That time was Bahareh's date-time. In this made-up imaginary production we had roles: Ghazaleh would be secretary that day and sit by the phone to read a book that was more than five long chapters, take a bathroom break during which she would unplug the line as she walked away. The phone couldn't be simply unplugged, in the event someone (like my dad) called and got an hour-long busy signal. That would be a catastrophe in itself, opening a can of lost and frustrated worms! It was a production, with me as assistant off-call producer in case things got really bad!

Bahareh, after the date, would have to downgrade to her original appearance, wearing a wimple instead of a colorful, short, edgy scarf accompanied by her ragged black sneakers. She also had to delete any suspicious perfumery scent and put on her nerdy, lens-less glasses to appear as if she'd just received a Harvard Award for Great Academic Achievement.

Since Bahareh and Ghazaleh were pros at this and always planned ways to get around the parents, their plans always worked. When, rarely, it didn't, there would follow months of silent and caged limitation at home.

•••

I slept that night thinking about Arash, the way he had managed to break the ice and speak with me. When it came to guys I had layers of self-made brick walls built in front of me and was warned by the Tatbighi girls that lots of single men in Iran want a way out of this country. So red light if you had citizenship or a green card!

Since the revolution and the differences between the two countries, Iranian citizens had to get some kind of visa to travel to the U.S. and vice versa. Getting that visa was a pain in the you-know-what, and since living in Iran was also a pain in the you-know-what—especially if you weren't for this regime—then you were dying to leave. Some people adored living in Iran but tolerance levels for others had reached its max and they wanted out of the Land of the Caged and into the Land of the Free. Some felt there was no opportunity to grow and others were fed up with how religion was thrust down their throats and they were made slaves to obey. Even if they threw a party in the privacy of their own homes they would bust the door open and see a mixed party or alcohol (not the medicinal kind), giving the host a one-way ticket to paying up or to the interrogation room. Geez! Too much complication!

So I decided if I were to call Arash, I would mention nothing about my green card and simply note that I learned English from a very young age at the Language Institute. If he asked which language institute then I would say it was called Brooklyn Dodgers, but the owner evaporated toward the states in hopes of better dreams.

The next day I went to summer class just to see Elham and have a girly chitchat with her. We had a kebab sandwich together from the place across the street. The place probably received a negative one Zagat reading as far as physical looks go, but the greasy kebabs could receive a Food Network award if served in New York. Simply the best!

We ate more than we talked until Elham asked, "So, have you been in touch with the patrol guy?"

"Nope," I said, devouring the next bite.

"You know you like him, and you might as well have a little fun!"

"I agree…I think."

"Yeah. He looks like a *man* and he looks fun. Let's at least prank call him!"

I merely nodded, as though considering. Prank calling was the norm in Tehran for some girls who wanted to play around and have some fun. The dude would pick up and the girl would blow air and hang up after causing some confusion, or the dude would pick up and girl would flirt hoping she could knitpick his brain. The last had multiple outcomes but one was definitely hanging up as well!

We strolled to the back of the school, where a beautiful rose garden grew, and no hostile Herasat was watching.

Shielded by many trees between school buildings and the parking lot, the garden was a safe place. Unless cameras were hidden somewhere, no one in the buildings could see or hear us. Elham dug out her cell phone. "What's his number?"

While telling her, a chilly rush of uncertainty and (I have to admit) anticipation sped through my heart.

"We're just going to have a laugh, you dork!" Elham went on, "And you know how to bring that out of a guy with your feisty personality! Just act like typical Shaghayegh, joke around, but step on that tail to let him know there are boundaries he can't cross! The phrase is: gentleman and honor must be preserved!" she said, crying from laughter.

I knew, somewhere in the back of my mind, that I was headed into hot water—but who cared?

Elham handed me the cell. I took it and pressed it against my ear. "Alo?" I said almost in question as if wondering if a person, animal, or alien was on the other end.

"Alo, *befarmaiid*," replied a strong and sexy male voice, using the totally formal Persian expression for: "Who is this, and please say what you've called for."

I steeled myself and was an empty telephone with no words when suddenly my tongue started rotating. "Have you heard the new Arian song, just released?"

Where had the words come from? Barely familiar with the band, I knew only they were one of the few Islamic Republic approved boy-girl groups, with super-sizzling guys in the band. They actually had sold out concerts! A big wowzer, but the girls in the band had to sing with full scarves and at times, wimples. Even wearing those, they were gorgeous and singing united no one could really hear what one voice sounded like. Yup, keeping the mystery alive—another weird factor.

"No, I haven't. What's the name of it?" said the manly voice, whose owner must know this was the lost girl from the other night. But he still didn't know my name. Not much beyond that I wouldn't look in his eyes longer than thirty seconds.

I bet on the other end Arash was telling himself, "It's her, the smart one with the sparkling soul, unfiltered and untouched, but solid."

I swallowed hard. "It's called 'The Hero of Jordan on a Dark Summer's Night.'" I think he was smiling but it barely surfaced in his voice. "Who did he save?" A certain charm and energy could be heard in his voice.

"An excellent driver." Surely this was better than "Two scared girls in need of a GPS or better knowledge of windy Jordan streets."

Returned by a soft chuckle he said, "I see. This great driver, does she have a specific name other than 'excellent driver'?"

"That she does."

"Well, is her name as pretty as her eyes?"

There we go with the flattering sweet talk and impulsive conversation specific to Iranian guys! Just the right amount of sugar coating to add, and knowledge of when to add it.

"It can be. Depends on the eye of the beholder."

Elham loved the back and forth, softly giggling and lip-synching to say this, say that, although I had to brush her aside with a serious glare. Sometimes she needed a double "Shhhh!"

He must be enjoying this. "The beholder's eyes saw many beautiful things, but because he respects excellent drivers he would like to clearly hear what their name is."

I swallowed again and liked the direction he was going. "Shaghayegh...but also know that not all excellent drivers have the same name."

"Did you find your way home all right?"

"Yes, it was fine. Did you?"

"Difficult, but I managed," he said with a chuckle.

"Okay good. Then be sure to check out Arian's new song. I have to run."

There was a pause, then he said, "Can you give it to me so I can listen to it at least?"

I knew the map he was following because he had the same compass, but didn't mind following. "You don't want to purchase it? This can be called piracy, and these hard-working artists could suffer."

Now we both were flirting metaphorically, and I sniffed him wanting to ask me out for a date. At this point, though, I wasn't sure how Iranian couples connected or what the dating protocol was. Hmm...going to his home was completely out of the picture, so *where* could we meet without the *Komiteh* sneaking up on us?

A home, of course, would have closed doors. But a lot could happen behind them, and I wasn't about to take any risk with this guy. I barely knew him.

Then Arash spoke. "Let's go to Vanak Mall. They just recently opened the coffee shop downstairs, and no one really knows about it."

This reassured me I might be in good, but still questionable, hands. "Where? I don't know Tehran very well, and if you could—"

Elham quickly signaled that she knew the location. A famous joint, actually. The fact that I knew nothing about it emphasized my lack of Tehran social travel! But I pushed on, "Actually I will find my way. I can make it around 5 p.m. but can only be out for an hour." I could go during my Italian class and afterwards I'd just go home. It'd work...fingers crossed, toes crossed, arms crossed, legs crossed—there was nothing else to cross.

"Good," Arash said. "I will see you there and...don't forget the tape, Ms. Excellent Driver."

"Oh, I'll definitely bring you the single." I giggled with flirtatious glee and ended the call.

Elham stood close, having quietly laughed off and on and thoroughly enjoyed eavesdropping. "You guys have perfect chemistry and make a good couple. A couple who'll annoy the hell out of each other and laugh at the dullest things with a grain of salt."

I shook my head and stretched to smell a rose because I hadn't brought my pom poms to explode with my excitement. "Such an Iranian man expert. Aren't you supposed to be an Iranian Jewish expert?"

"I am, I am, *ghorboone hameghi beram*—I adore them all!"

We both were going through hoops of giggles but I felt a slight chill when something occurred to me. "It's so *hard* to date in Tehran, and I'm not going to even understand half the stuff he says. And on top of that he'll hear my Farsi accent and know I was raised somewhere else and then will question where, and basically be my slave because he'll want a bite of my green card! These question marks repeatedly pop into my head."

"Everyone dates in Iran and everyone knows that everyone dates. It's no secret. Your parents even dated!" she pouted back.

"That might have been in the Shah's time, but not right now with all the *Komiteh* guys thirsty to make some money off of me, right?"

During the Shah era there were no religious or Islamic restrictions. Ladies went out without a scarf and full on mini dresses, Iran had the best cabarets and bars, and the same kind-of concerts as in the west. Nothing with full scarves on stage! After the revolution, with the whole religious spice in play there were a *lot* of restrictions and for us, the teenage crowd, dating wasn't acceptable. Having sex before marriage would end in catastrophe! Maybe it was taboo, maybe it was religion, but it was frowned upon. That's why fashion shows, parties, alcohol were all hush hush! But for an adrenaline junkie like me, that did bring on some excitement. And so we play the game as well.

Elham rolled her eyes. "Listen, even the *Komiteh* guys have girl-crushes, but it's a process and they flow with it. Just play the game and have your radar up when you go outside."

"Is this the part where I say 'What do I possibly do without you'?"

"You could say that, or instead you could treat me to the blood red beets in Tajrish Square."

We left the garden and I hailed a cab to take us to the square. Hailing a cab here was not a big deal since drivers here were crazier than in New York City. I'd heard a lot about Tajrish Square and the yummy roasted beets they sold on the streets. The smell would make you drool. Tajrish was in the northern part of Tehran and one of the city's busiest transportation hubs.

There were cafes and upper-scale boutiques comparable to those in New York's Union Square or Columbus Circle. The market was similar to the one in downtown Tehran, but due to its upscale status it carried vegetables not found in other supermarkets. One of those, at the time, was broccoli. *The* extraordinary, pricey vegetable available only at the Tajrish market. In Iran it was sometimes pronounced *bro-rook-li* with a *Per-si-an* accent. All foreign words had a Farsi twist, and broccoli with a twist was transformed into a classy-prized vegetable—although it clearly wasn't!

•••

The following days were extremely long, and I was getting ready for my first date in Tehran, with a random guy who spoke a language I could but partially speak. Still, I was excited.

And of course the whole concept of strategizing made it even more exciting.

As I had learned from the pros, I took a big bag and filled it with what I needed. My heart pounded, but I was excited to see Arash. I knew I was headed into a little adventure.

I kissed my father goodbye and left the house organically as if bound for my class.

Although I never required much makeup, in the cab I applied some eyeliner and mascara. Cab rides in Tehran were crazy. The Peykans would be filled to the point where the car might actually tilt if just one more passenger squeezed in. Even the space between driver and front passenger was sometimes filled, bringing the occupancy to six riders! Crazy! I never allowed myself to be jammed into that questionable spot where the driver had to manually shift gears. Worse, another reason to avoid this was that the person to my right might be a pervert. I would have a fit if that happened!

But the taxi ride proceeded fine, and I found the mall which, to my surprise, resembled those in The Big Apple: fancy-schmancy!

Out of the cab, I caught pools of fragrance in the air. Especially freshly-kebabed corn cob and its smoky sweetness. There was the hustle and bustle of people walking, talking, bumping into each other and paying no attention, taxi drivers looking for bait, street vendors hawking goods hoping for a toman (Iran's monetary frequency) or two, and colorful fruit kiosks. All of this animated Vanak.

Walking, I saw stores bearing actual brand names, while others were small, privately owned boutiques carrying exports from Turkey, Sweden, China and more, all at highly inflated prices. Local people's salaries could be lower than that required to purchase certain items in these stores!

This type of injustice was really disappointing, but there were so many elements in need of solutions to just fix this one. It wasn't that easy.

I approached a fine marble stairway, very chic, leading to an area of newly opened shops downstairs: furniture, Internet cafes, manto shops, a pizza place, and the coffee shop Arash had mentioned.

I felt tense and a bit afraid. My senses heightened. Why do girls always have to get antsy? My face flushed hotly with apprehension and suddenly I felt as if I couldn't speak. All because of someone whose last name I didn't even know.

My hair flowed freely from the back of my scarf, and without the hair in the front spotlight my big brown Middle-Eastern eyes were in the spotlight. I pulled the scarf toward the front, afraid it was going to fall any moment when I suddenly heard someone behind me. "So you found it all right, and didn't need a navigation system this time?"

There stood Arash.

The "date" version had dark black hair brushed back and hazel eyes with a smile all their own. We were standing at the bottom of the stairs, looking right at each other.

My mind flushed with thoughts. He was so toned, manly, and athletic.

This being Iran, there could be no handshake, kiss, or knowing smile in public, so I nodded and gave a native hello: "*Salam.*"

"I thought the young were supposed to say hello first."

"That's when the older don't make the initial smart-ish comments."

He nodded slowly, as if digesting the elements of a complicated joke. "*Salam* Shaghayegh Farsijani. Should we go inside and grab something to drink?"

"Is this place safe, or frequently interrupted by the *Komiteh*?"

"It's safe. They still haven't noticed it, so it's not on their radar yet. If they *do* come there is a back entrance to the cafe. The guys are my friends."

"Okay."

I felt as if I might be arrested at any moment for being in public and talking to a member of the opposite sex. But what if I were only asking directions, or where he purchased his shirt? Would that be considered a felony?

Inside, we chatted for a while and slowly I let down one layer of my guard and became somewhat comfortable with Arash. He didn't seem to notice my accent, or if he did, he didn't care. I went into no great detail about my life, but did list briefly my likes, dislikes, and where I went to school.

He spoke fluent Farsi and was degreed in engineering, but had made his way into business joining the family's real estate company. They had escaped to London during the revolution, and his father had become increasingly wealthy in privately owned real estate. His father, Mr. Hossein Sarraf-Zadeh, was also a well-known architect who had returned to Tehran fifteen years after the revolution to serve his country. He had returned with incredible wealth, a fact surely recognized by the government and many in that specific industry in Iran.

I realized he had no Farsi accent, so wondered if he spoke English. "So now you have graduated and are not really pursuing engineering like the millions of guys in Iran who are engineers. How do you spend your time?"

Our order was ready. An alcohol-free pineapple juice cocktail, plus the famous chips and mozzarella treat. A high calorie, high cholesterol dessert impossible to turn down even by high-end fashionista manto girls. I couldn't resist...it was better than Brooklyn pizza!

"Where was I?" Arash said. "Oh, we are building the new hotel on Vali-Asr and it is taking a long time to build. It's not like anything else in Tehran. We have to bribe our way through a lot of avenues with the government, but hopefully it will open in two years." He gazed deep into my eyes. "And what are your plans?"

Caught almost by surprise, I said, "To become a choreographer, but that's a completely closed door in Tehran, so I have no idea what I will be doing."

Right after I said it I realized I should have kept my mouth shut. He intuitively knew, at that moment, I was not from Iran. Girls born and raised here would never give that answer. Typically, the response would be doctor, engineer, or let's-see-what-happens, which usually fell into the marriage category. Never was it a desire to become a choreographer. That was a huge insult to the parents. Persians never in a million years would accept that. He probably had a bunch of question marks already maneuvering around his head.

"Do you dance regularly?" he said.

I didn't know he had figured me out from the start. A typical Iranian guy would think I was out of my mind or living in a dream. That type of art was illegal here in Iran. Probably because it "motivated or aroused" men, but there has never been any dance curriculum in the schools, no *legal* dance classes unless they were taught privately or in some underground studio.

"I did some ballet a couple of years back," I swallowed that the location had been in Brooklyn, "but do it now at home with dance videos."

"You mean the satellite?" He chuckled.

"No," I said wanting to wrap up the conversation while he was becoming a smart-ass, "I mean with this Arian single you should attentively listen to, as you will be questioned about it! I have to leave." This gut feeling told me this tape was the beginning of everything in my world.

I was enjoying the conversation with him so much I had barely noticed the clock. It was an interesting talk and he was smart and clever to say the least.

"Do you want me to drive you home?"

"That is the *last* thing I need—to be caught in a car with you!"

He gave a dejected shrug and picked up the tape, wondering what possibly might be recorded on it.

I stood. "And please listen to it till the end. Don't say I didn't tell you so."

"Yes ma'am!" His velvety voice made him sound like some dashing knight.

I thanked him for treating and was ready to jet off.

His downcast eyes looked sad. "Can I have your number?"

"Why? Are you saying you would like to see me again?"

"Yes. That's what it sounds like." His eyes weren't sad anymore but were shaped like "I beg of you!"

I recognized at that moment Arash was a typical Persian playboy, but he was also very respectful of me even though he was in his mid-twenties—and we all know how horny boys are in their twenties! But there definitely was in Arash a protective and caring instinct.

"Well, I have your number so let's see what happens." I teased and left the coffee shop as if I were Cinderella obeying my fairy godmother's wishes that I make a dash for my pumpkin carriage at midnight.

9

Arash to the Max

MY PUMPKIN CARRIAGE WAS AN elegant Peykan cab I had hailed. It also served as my mini fitting room while I erased all traces of makeup and transformed myself back to an innocent schoolgirl.

The driver observed this transformation, and like the nosey taxi hack he was blurted, "*Dokhtar Khanoom*, does your father know where you were?" Nosy civilians! What's it to you? Just do your job! But obviously I didn't let that get out of hand, so I replied, "*Bale Agha.*" Yes Mr. but with a tone that meant "none of your business, so just drive."

That night I thought about my encounter with Arash, and how I had enjoyed it. I wanted to call him, but not at night, because my dad would focus on me and whom I was speaking with and where the person on the other end of the line lived and how they were brought up and on and on and on—so that was a definite no-go.

Instead, I waited until the next day, planning to venture out and buy a cheap second-hand phone from the telephone fixer, and use it to call Arash at night. Iran has a no-return policy on any merchandise brought from any store so if I was stuck with cheapie where I would only hear the voice from the other end and also dial a number—I was stuck with repair after repair bills. But before I had even left the house to do this, the phone rang.

Dad was out, and mom was gossiping with the neighbors about who was seen leaving the house across the street, who got married on the other block—or divorced—the usual type of chitchat between neighbors.

The jangling phone twisted my nerves and before it could ring again I grabbed it.

"*Befarmaiid*," I said in a controlled but very delicate tone.

"*Salam*, Shaghayegh."

Right away I knew it was Arash. "*Salam*. Hey, how did you get this number?"

He responded with a low chuckle.

Had he called Elham to get my number since I used her cell phone last time?

Then it hit me: the tape! It's on the tape…

I had nearly forgotten my bright and brilliant idea of mimicking a serious breaking news update voice, recording my telephone number at the end of the tape I had given him!

Now I remembered telling him to listen until the very end. He had listened attentively!

I laughed but firmed my voice. "How did you like *the* single?"

"Great. It was great, a Grammy-winner for sure. The production was amazing," he said flirtatiously.

"I know. That's how we roll!"

We both played the clever flirting game pretty well. There were girls in Iran who became doctors, and some that married them. I was none of these. I was a category of my own I guess.

"How are you?" Arash asked.

133

"Good. But I can't talk for long."

There was a pause then he cleared his throat. "There is a party one of my friends is throwing in Shahrak Gharb on Thursday night. Could you come with me?"

Wow! Shahrak Gharb was like Beverly Hills relocated! Was he asking me out? I didn't know much but got the feeling this could be an introduction to Tehran's underground community; all the parties everyone talked about but I had never witnessed firsthand. I wanted to explore and understand what this was all about. And I had heard that lots of stuff happened at these parties. Lots and lots of stuff. Risky? For sure. I thought I might bring Bahareh along. Then again, I still hadn't developed that deep trust with her. If she came she would surely find out about Arash and even worse that I was going out on a date with him, and if she delivered this to my aunt and my aunt to my dad, I was in the gutter! Then the Emperor would closely monitor my every move! But the pro side was that I had someone to go with and whom I trusted.

So I had to take a risk and that was better than not exploring it through.

"Well, I don't know your friends but would love to come. Can I bring a friend?" I hope I didn't give the wrong impression making him think it was a guy.

"Who?"

Was that a tinge of concern there?

"My cousin."

"Of course. Do you want to go over to your cousin's, and I could pick you up from there so we all go together?"

"Sure, or we can come there and meet you," I answered, hoping he would counter.

After a pause he said, "I will pick you up from her house. And don't worry about the *Komiteh*, you know you can always pay them off. They are money hungry!"

Wowzer! Protection from a dude in Tehran! Feeling secure from the *Komiteh* was the best feeling sometimes.

I was super stoked. It was my time to see the underground community in Iran; see how everyone really partied! Was it old-fashioned? How was the music? The drinks, the girls without mantos, the food...the drugs? There were so many unanswered questions in my head.

My cousin was a sure GO, and all they had to say was that we're going to my friend's place for an all-girls party. I pictured it as a shower sauna, reading "Ladies Only" at the entrance. What could be easier?

I heard a clicking on the line. Arash was tapping his finger impatiently. "Okay, let's do it that way. Whatever you want."

That came out rather suspicious. That could mean whatever I wanted until he got what he wanted, which was sex! Ok, I was reading too much into this whole Iranian taboo crap. I needed to undo some labels in my head. I gave him her address and warned him to be punctual. There wasn't much of a buffer to fall back on. We had to get to my aunt's place on time.

After tagging each other goodbye I realized I couldn't wait to see him. I felt very playful talking with him; the goosebumps had spread all over. He brought out the best in me. I felt like he was giving me something but had no idea what it was. Maybe a new perception on life. A new understanding. Whatever it was, it felt warm and I completely hugged it with open arms.

•••

The black two-door Patrol pulled up, and I totally saw Arash eyeing me full force. He probably wanted to see how I look without this manto and scarf and was counting the seconds. It wasn't like I was going to bed with him, but I felt the same way!

Bahareh looked hot, maybe she was a good catch for Arash's buddy. I would gamble all the cash in my father's checking and savings account on her returning with more than five hot guy's phone numbers…and a husband if they had a chance to speak with her!

We climbed in and off we went! Aside from my brief introduction of Bahareh, not much was said. Excitement and some tension were in the air. We arrived fashionably late. That's mainly the reason why all Iranian hosts give a start time two hours earlier than intended. The house, like others in the Shahrak Gharb area, was similar to a villa. Stepping into the foyer, I thought I had entered an alternate warp-zone. The girls there looked fresh from a photo shoot at Fashion Week, one prettier than the other, a painter's palatte of makeup and cutting-edge attire. It was indistinguishable from any American party and reminded me of the parties I'd read about in *The Great Gatsby*. These people were high on life and drinks!

Guided by Arash, we moved deeper into the house and its bumping, thumping beat, through a mélange of perfumes and colognes and oils, and the constant aroma of food.

Despite the seeming chaos, a warm atmosphere of fun and cheerful mingling prevailed. Clusters of people chatted and laughed and danced to get to know each other. Some were speaking Farsi so fast and using slangs, so I just nodded that I understood and was *with it*.

"This is a great turnout!" said Arash. "More than I thought would show up."

We all noticed how a number of male celebrants patted Arash's back, or even gave his shoulders a friendly tap. I learned later they were all his frat buddies, or colleagues turned frat buddies! Arash appeared to be the big, popular cheese, a role he stubbornly played, I bet!

The people at the party were normal people. People you could easily see at a party back in New York on Long Island, so excluding the Mullah and *Komiteh* seasoning at least one night per week. These peeps partied like they meant it.

We moved on, careful to avoid collision with others caught up in conversation or dancing. The place was packed and my eyes kept getting hooked on the extremely handsome and refined etiquette and charm of the guys.

Bahareh was slowly getting into the groove of the party and her little conversations here and there with other people were revealing more of both her social side and her personal life to me. She was flirtatious and fun and had respect for herself. I didn't know if she could keep that respect with the drinking she was doing, but she was on a roll. At the same time, I noticed she also stood beside me in case I needed her lingo help or if she felt I was alone. My wing girl! I felt cute and secure. Security was the first reason I had even invited her!

I felt we were both in the same boat as far as relying on each other in times of bail. The friendship part was slowly coming into view. We both wanted to live our teenage lives in the face of strict Persian fathers and this oppressive society. Geez—did it always have to be this complicated?

Someone approached from my right. "What do you want to drink?"

Arash introduced his bud Ali who was also the party host. I had no idea what sort of drink to ask for, so improvised. "A glass of Pinot Noir, please."

Bahareh giggled.

Arash turned and said, "They aren't really wine connoisseurs here, *azizam*. They go by the drink type: wine or vodka."

Bahareh snickered, "Or *aragh saghi*!"

I was taken back. The literal translation was "doggy sweat," but what the hell did that *mean*? I made sure I kept a neutral expression. Arash noticed this, admiration clear in his eyes, for he too (in his post-return London days) had been subjected to this ruse. It looked like he respected me for trying to figure things out in this land of mystery and intrigue.

This was my first time having a drink, and where was it but in a religious country! The feeling was two-fold, the alcohol on top of the mindset that I was in Tehran drinking it and not in Brooklyn. What the hell. I was exploring life, but in a completely different way than I had imagined. I was numb but happy. Add that to my teenage free spirit. By the way, there was no drinking age in Tehran because there was no drinking! So it was up to one's own self to decide when to drink. I took it and forgot about New York's drinking age of twenty-one and up. I was getting to like Iran bit by bit. I had scored in this category and I wasn't even nineteen yet. Score!

Arash stepped away toward some guy waving. I seized the moment and cornered Bahareh, "What the hell is *aragh saghi*?"

"Relax. It's an alcoholic drink. Cheap but potent. Iran's version of American moonshine, but distilled from raisins."

"Really? Should I be afraid of losing my eyesight or going brain dead?"

"Not if you stick with the wine—whatever it is. You probably don't know this either. Wine and all alcoholic drinks here are sold underground, or on the black market, another reason why not everyone is familiar with all the wines. It's not like we have cellars and vineyards here!"

"No. But doggy sweat? That's flat out gross."

She shot a casual glance around her, not wanting to be overheard. "Oh, that's just a ref to its nastiness. Lots of people distill *aragh saghi* at home, and it can be disgusting! Here you just get used to it, especially when the underground inventory is hard to find."

I wrinkled my nose as if sniffing something rotten. "I'll try my best. And how do you know about wine cellars and the various types of wine? Hmm?"

Abruptly the music blasted and Bahareh shouted, "Leave it to the movie guy, he is the best, although he needs to upgrade his stock from Betamax to VHS."

I was lost. Movie guy? I just gave a goofy grin and jumped over my confusion. Bahareh seemed not to notice. "We will watch one together some time when you are over at the house."

Here was Arash approaching us with drinks.

Hun—a movie guy? What the hell is a *movie guy*? Blockbuster on wheels? The questions were piling up.

Soon it grew too loud for a coherent conversation. In a quick burst as Arash arrived I said, "To be honest, it's from movies that I know about pinot noir because I have never had it before!" I said that to cover up any information I had of wine so he couldn't suspect I was from a foreign country, but I don't think that was very effective. Half my voice was lost in the music anyway. Got an "A" for effort but Arash nodded and grinned sarcastically as we took our glasses.

I broke out of drink virginity and had my very first toast with Arash and Bahareh: the cousin I was developing a friendship with, and the black Patrol guy that had the hots for me. Always a first time for everything, and I was super stoked to break into more. In truth and deep down, I felt how special this moment was.

The wine was good and tasted like the Capri Sun drinks (with added rose water) mom always dumped in my lunchbox for school. It painted my palate with plums and what tasted like liquid flowers. For all I knew, it tasted like rose water...after all, it was in mostly every cabinet or on every table in Iran!

I noticed Arash paying full attention to me as he drank to the toast. He was observing my every move. Oh god! He wanted sex! Or maybe I was dramatizing it. Bahareh, who I noticed was becoming protective of me, took this in with slight discomfort. "So, how do you know all these people?"

Arash grinned. "Oh, school, parties, going out. Some of them are just guys you see as you drive up and down Jordan, Ms. Bahareh," he pointed out sarcastically. I could see the joke in his expression. He loved pushing buttons, and he clearly knew he had just pushed a big one. "And your point?" she said right back.

"No, I was just referring to traffic and shopping centers that everybody comes in and out of. You know, the people you watch while in traffic, but you never pay attention to the cars racing up and down Jordan," he said implicitly. He smiled a sleazy one, but he was so charming that the sleazy part faded out quickly. The smile was full of nitrous oxide.

I felt Arash was getting to know me faster than I was getting to know him. He was very familiar with his surroundings and me, well, I was still a virgin in every way you can imagine. But I could tell he knew I wasn't the type to merely stand there and obey and laugh at every stupid, idiotic, or sarcastic comment he made. I was my own woman—I was a gladiator and a loyal one.

I brushed my hair on my shoulders, glancing away to the party. Some of these girls certainly knew how to dance. Shaking it like that with their hips and shoulders and sexy turns. The guys were all drooling like dogs.

The dancing here was different from Vanilla Ice or MC Hammer. "Hammertime," hammer pants and flashy dance moves had called it quits and now the hips had to be taught to rotate slowly and generously. It was slower than Arabic and the girls basked in the attention, completely aware of the power they held.

Arash stepped closer to me where I could smell his cologne. "Do you want to dance?"

"Sure, but I doubt you can keep up."

He flashed that bright smile again. "I will try my best."

He was a lucky guy because he was about to witness how "Hammertime" hip-hop and Persian belly dancing fused. You tell me to dance and I will teach you your ABCs, I don't care in which language. Let the music pump into the body and your dance skeleton will arise from wherever it was held captive! If exotic and gorgeous could give meaning to the party, I was there to amplify it.

"Hey, you dance erotic woman! Do you do it intentionally?" said Bahareh while doing the hand portion of her dance move.

"I have no idea what you're talking about! Talk to the legs, hips and whisper to the eyes…" I said laughing.

Arash couldn't stay still and moon-walked his way onto the dance floor with his own set of moves.

At one point he turned salsa-ish on me and, for a few moments, I had emigrated to Cuba. Grabbing space, he freely flung me left and right with the rhythm of the Persian *gher* (beat). Whether Persian, Spanish, or South African, I thrived in the moment—at my first Iranian underground party—not caring whether I knew the language, its slangs, or culture. Every turn and each move liberated me more and more.

Abruptly the music shifted to another tempo.

Everyone shouted: "*Baba Karam!*" Literally, "Daddy *Karam*," which was another big question mark for me.

We cleared the dance floor. Everyone took a hat from somewhere, although not all wore one. But my question was: why were they all suddenly dancing like *men*?

"Are they gay?"

Bahareh gaped at me. "Huh?"

"And what is up with the lip thing? Look! That one guy is moving his lower lip back and forth like he's imitating The Joker. It looks like he's about to start bawling or something. And their arms are out like they're going to punch the other dancers in the face. Why?"

Bahareh burst out laughing and I couldn't control myself either. I didn't know if I was laughing with Bahareh at my comment, or at something else.

"No, crazy, this is a type of dancing called *Jaheli*. They are imitating 'jahels,' ignorant people. It's just a dance style where they have fun, and it's sexy. It goes back in history and is taken seriously."

"Must be the last page in a history book, because I don't find anything sexy in a woman moving her lips left and right!"

God, I was learning more about this culture every second.

Arash, hearing my hearty laugh, smiled broadly. He joined us and I changed the subject. I glanced away quickly, but he got the picture.

I was intently focused on the dancers and said, "Why do ninety percent of the girls have bandages across their noses? Is that like being part of a *nose* club?"

Bahareh shook her head, but Arash took over the convo and said. "Nope, this is a status symbol, and a real one; nearly everyone in Iran has had a nose job. Look around. Do you see an eagle nose in the bunch?"

142

I scanned the room. He was right. Oddly, everyone had perfectly-shaped noses matching their facial structure. Frankly, they were beautiful. I was beginning to get the message. This culture was definitely sophisticated and complex with a measure of insecurity. Not all was as it seemed.

Arash nodded, as if keyed in to my thoughts. "Do you want to see the real Tehran?" He noted our proximity to one another as if we feared attack from the Loch Ness Monster.

"What do you have in mind?"

"Follow me."

I stepped after his lead and climbed stairs that opened onto a den-like space on the second floor. Here the architecture was striking: marble floors and luxurious curtains color-coded with a surrounding of French and Italian antique furniture. Another section of this floor had been designed to recall Iranian, or maybe Turkish, history.

Stunning Persian calligraphy was spray painted across the walls; quotes, proverbial sayings, even single words evoked whispers of ancient civilization and its mysteries. This stretched as far as a love seat in one corner bearing a special sort of backrest or pillow. I later discovered these are called *Poshtis*, because Aziz Joon had some and used them for sitting and leaning. Multi-functional.

"Out here," he said softly. He led us outside onto a terrace overlooking the city. The city where I was born, had left behind, and now returned to. The arresting view strengthened my connection to its beauty, culture, and history, all alive with light, scent and sound. The Milad tower in the distance shimmered like some otherworldly jewel. This conjured pure compassion I never could extract from any book or conversation with an Iranian in some foreign country.

Beside me, Bahareh sighed. "Wow, talk about breathtaking. This is beautiful."

Silence cloaked us, and Arash fixed his attention on me. Shyness rained on me from my hair to my toenails. I could feel he wanted to get closer, touch me, feel my skin. Above all, I think he wanted to just look at me because he was gazing into my eyes. It was overwhelming and I felt luminous passion vibrating in my soul.

He was absorbing me and I was being fully absorbed. Maybe he was thinking about why I said such weird stuff, or maybe he thought I was the hottest dancer alive. It was hopefully the second.

Continuing to look at me he asked, "What do you think?"

"This is *the* Tehran that we see in the news?"

"Yes," Bahareh interrupted, "but *this* is also Tehran from Arash's friend's house in Shahrake Gharb." I giggled, to let him know he was funny.

"The city has layers of spirit, and even with all its red flags, it's so emotionally powerful and happy," I commented.

"Wow, that's deep," Bahareh said, "let's go softer next time cowgirl!"

"*Be rooye cheshm,*" I said with a hint of my cinnamon-tasting femininity. It literally translated to "on my eyes," but it really meant "with pleasure" or "my pleasure" or something charming like that.

I could sense Arash wanted to be alone with me because I wanted the same. But there was no getting rid of Bahareh. Talk about a third wheel.

We talked a while longer until I realized it was pumpkin time and reminded Bahareh that we had better get back to the "ladies sauna" where her mom was scheduled to pick us up from. This put an obvious damper on Arash. To his credit, though, the young man drove us back.

While exchanging goodbyes, he asked me with a serious gaze if I could call him tonight.

"Well, if I can I will. I don't know the situation at my aunt's house."

The ever-eavesdropping Bahareh snuck Arash an optimistic look, implying she'd take care of it.

Everything had gone as planned.

Afterwards at the house, we chatted about our first party together, the adventure of it, the sheer fun, and the phone numbers Bahareh got from some dudes, without their knowledge that their friends had hit on the same girl. Leave it to Bahareh to make her selection afterwards!

Bahareh joining me to the party, Bahareh drinking with me, Bahareh looking out for me, Bahareh making it feel okay to talk to a guy, was sinking in my skin. Totally different from the outside world and the outside girlfriends. A girl my age with the same circumstances and *in* the family understood me and gave me a sense of ease. She was helping me build bridges with the unknown of growing up, and the unknown of growing up in a country that I had yet to understand. She was like a lotion or moisturizer or even fertilizer…or a combo of all!

"So what do you think of him girl?" she asked.

"I think he has a good head on his shoulders and is respectful. Much more so than the other guys at the party. You know, the *aragh saghi*-swilling ones acting like frat boy casanovas."

Bahareh definitely had seen *that* part. "Be careful. They all are respectful at the beginning. Play your cards right girl."

"I don't get it. Why is it always a game? Why can't we just go with the flow and watch what happens?"

"No, things are different here. When it comes to guys you can be playful but also have to be super careful. Some have the opportunity to leave the country, but others have to make money. It's not the easiest thing, nor is living with our parents. They alone can drive you up the wall!"

She started to take off her makeup and continued, "So since that is not fun, and Iran doesn't have lots of opportunities for women like us, we try to somehow make it work. One way is to get married!"

"Ouch. To any schmuck?"

"Well, one that could give you some security and is not an A-hole. You know, one who knows your worth."

"Isn't it like that everywhere? Same thing in Brooklyn. That's just common sense."

"Yeah, but here there is no way out *and* this is an easy way out in this country *and* a way to get folks off your back."

"You seem like you have your facts straight, and that's a compliment."

"I hope so. Iran has lots of talented, smart, and hot people, so either they use their brain to get to a better, more opportunistic country or, with difficulty, find a way out through the marriage route," she said pulling her upper lip to the right side.

I was shocked, but fully absorbed this. She was like a Tehranian cultural encyclopedia book for me, the innocent. She knew what she was talking about.

I was fairly certain, when I thought about it, that some girls—if they tried—could get out solely on their brains. Bahareh was smart where it mattered and had earned one of the highest scores on the *Konkoor*. But my acceptance had knocked her out of the celebration arena or slimmed her showtime attention substantially. In my defense I was new to this country. I smiled at the thought.

"What do you want to do with your life?" I asked her.

"I am going to start school studying civil engineering, by my real passion is fashion. Here, let me show you some of my designs. One day I will start my own company. No idea when that day is."

With that, she stood and walked toward her closet. She returned flipping through a fat notebook. For a while we perused professional-quality sketches of coats, dresses, and accessories. Baharch knew her way around pastel pencils and ink. "It's a tad bit difficult," she said, "to start anything now, especially for us girls and especially in fashion. So we're going to have to drive on a couple of highways before getting on the main one! You know what I mean sista!"

"Your talent is a very hot vehicle fo sho! Hey, you could even do designs for mantos and scarves. That would be cool too."

"I know, I know, but I'm not into that as much. But if these don't make the runway, I will tackle it!"

I loved her enthusiasm and perseverance. Some would easily give up the dream, but it looked like Bahareh had the guts to move mountains.

I abruptly sensed how exhausted I'd become so I climbed onto the bed and burrowed in.

"Okay well, sketch away while I go to bed woman!"

"What?" Bahareh dropped the notebook. "No! Arash is waiting for your call!"

"I can't call him from here! Your parents would execute me, and probably you for being a facilitator!" I laughed while tugging the blanket closer, trying to keep it muffled.

"They're asleep. As long as you keep your voice down and don't get overly excited nothing will happen."

"You sure?"

Bahareh rolled her eyes at the ceiling, "Couldn't be *surer*! Now call—and good *night*!"

I dialed the number as she gave me a sharp smile and switched off the light. Arash—no slacker—picked up on the second beep. It sounded like he had tormented himself counting down the minutes to again hear my voice. "Alo."

"It's me," I said softly. "Were you expecting someone else at twelve o'clock at night?"

He chuckled, "No one but you. I'm glad the wind blew my way tonight."

Ok—so he was a charmer.

"Did I wake you?"

"No, no. I'm usually up doing work for my father. Glad you called. I was waiting for you anyway so how can I go to sleep?" He said this so flirtatiously that if I was still at the party he would have been kissed me and glued himself to my lips.

"I didn't think I would be able to, but here I am."

So this time I did most of the talking, opening up to him further and becoming more comfortable after the party. I even started flirting back with him! Not me, but hey it was midnight!

We talked for five hours straight, until the morning light glowed in the windows. It felt like we were developing boundaries, respect, and unconscious intimacy, but I still didn't reveal anything about my life in America. I was still scared and didn't want the relationship to be built on artificial pillars. Intuitively, I felt Arash had sniffed something out and was waiting for me to confess.

Towards the conversation's end, he asked what I was doing tomorrow, and I now completely realized this guy was into me.

"Class, class, and um, well…maybe talking with you?" Shyness surged through me, and I feared how he might respond.

"Well, good luck on the class parts of your answer, and don't forget to call anytime during the day *azizam*."

148

Wow, he was taking this to another level. I swooned. He just called me darling!

Not excessive nor underrated, and I felt like his *azizam* and fancied it. It was cute and cemented our newly established fresh-from-the-sea bond. Five hours had felt like five minutes.

"Good night," I said, and at 4 a.m. I finally hung up.

Sliding back under the covers with the phone under the blanket with me, I could see Bahareh sleeping in peace and thought, *what a strange but enchanting world.* I was glad to be exposed to it, discovering it slice by slice. As though history had sparked back into life with its enigmas and lessons and wanted to sweep me onto Aladdin's rug to fly me through love, struggles, compassion, and romance, and maybe ecstasy. I wanted to taste them all.

10

Movie Guy

September 1997

THE DAYS PASSED AND MY telephone conversations with Arash increased to twice daily. My hours were filled with class and friends I had made everywhere, but more importantly included the fine-tuning of my mind. This part had to be done right!

Arash, on his way back from work, usually picked me up from college and dropped me off at home. Sometimes we would hit a coffee shop, where I sipped Nescafé and Arash gave a bottle of wine labeled as pineapple juice to the shop owner to pour into a kettle, accompanied by some cash on the side. It was happy hour with topped with wine in a kettle. Leave it to Arash to get around the system!

He had gotten comfortable with me and we enjoyed spending time together. There was never a dull moment with me and he was in the same boat. Sometimes when I didn't understand situations or was baffled by others, I would flat out flood him with questions and he would answer. I didn't explain anything and he didn't ask—I bet he knew and was being a smartass about it! Other times we would have the occasional argument, which ended on both ends with excessive teasing and explosive laughter.

He didn't want to get married and neither did I. We were just enjoying our twenties in the best possible fashion.

Even so, I still resisted Arash's numerous invites to his apartment in Farmanieh. The "Big F" neighborhood was fancy-schmancy and in the northern part of Tehran, about fifteen minutes from our house. Sometimes out of the blue or in the middle of laughing we occasionally communicated in bloody English, which added another layer of comfort to the relationship in a very awkward way. Another clue to how I knew he knew!

It wasn't that I didn't trust him, but that I wasn't ready for more. After all, I didn't yet know what to do with my life, didn't know why I selected what I had selected for college and didn't know how things would go in this ivy-league university with Iranian nerds. There was only one thing I knew for certain: this mysterious country fascinated me!

•••

Bahareh's parents were at their villa in Shomal in northern Iran, and she had invited me, Arash, and a guy she was dating to watch a movie together. She loved to socialize and party when her parents were away.

I first thought it must be some censored, Islamic Republic movie, the ones they sold here in bookstores, altering the branding of distribution houses to make it appear simple and educational. Taking out all swear words, sex scenes and scenes where the woman

151

might be wearing tight or exposing clothing. Nothing too westernized or contemporary and definitely nothing steamy and hot was allowed. Legit stuff. The film was drained to vanilla bla-ness. From every standpoint it was censored: politically, culturally, emotionally, sexually, including abuse, profanity, and violence. All mature content was deleted. So just to be clear, these were all foreign movies produced outside of Iran. Supposedly the German ones had lots of skin...just a rumor.

After everyone arrived, we poured some drinks and since I had lost my drink virginity, now I wanted to try every existing alcohol beverage, whether saghi or non-saghi! I was open to all new possibilities.

The doorbell rang. "Expecting more guests?" I said.

Bahareh stood and shot me a mischievous glance on her way to the door. Shaheen, her boyfriend (or what she called a boyfriend), browsed her curves, including her plump breasts, up and down as she walked to the door. Arash glanced at him and said loudly with a chuckle, "Hey, *cheshmato darvish kon.*" Metaphorically speaking: "Keep those eyes to yourself you dirty bastard!"

In shambled a tall, muscled guy wearing phony Ray-Bans and carrying a suitcase roughly the size of a large TV. It must have been crammed with kilos of souvenirs, or enough clothes for a three-month trip. Despite this he handled the case with authority, no doubt benefiting from his own bulk.

Oh no, I thought in a swirl of fright, should I run out of here? He's probably a drug dealer from the looks of it. A million and one thoughts ran through my head until the guy set down his burden with a thump that shook the floor. I could see his fine-carved moustache was the envy of any butcher. His shiny styled hair was portable advertising for the gel company. Who in the world is this guy? And why was he selling drugs with such confidence?

152

Frankly, I felt sick to my stomach and couldn't imagine Bahareh involved in this kind of stuff. Of course many things here were underground, but this stuff is basically underground everywhere!

I stood by Arash as Bahareh approached him and asked, "What do you have new for me today?"

Beneath the black shades he grinned, stretching that mustache. "Lots of stuff, and you will love it!"

Clenching my jaw in suspense, I watched the guy unlock his anchor of a suitcase. He must have loads of drugs, going by the sheer size of that thing. I didn't want to be too judgmental, so waited while he fumbled with the 1970s-era artifact.

"At last!" he shouted in triumph, opening the thing.

I couldn't believe this. What in the world? The case held an amazing quantity of videocassettes, both Betamax and VHS. So *this* was a movie guy—possibly *the* movie guy! D Blockbuster dude, delivering the latest-and-greatest to your doorstep!

"Just received the newest movies yesterday," he said, "so they are fresh. Fresh off the boat—F.O.B.!" He thought that was funny because something like laughter gurgled in his throat. To me, this immediately increased his greasiness rating to five stars (and a square). How did he get access to all these? Who gave them to him? Most of all, why were they still using Betamax?

I glanced at Bahareh, who said, "Shaghayegh, you know the good ones, so just check out the titles and pick some out. I'm horrible at this stuff!"

"Um...okay..."

I scanned the labeled cellophane offerings, a riot of colors and genres. There was comedy, romance, drama, horror, suspense, documentaries, and in varied flavors of Chinese, German, Russian, and the newly released American films. Wow!

They were priced relatively cheap, 500 *tomans* per VHS—equivalent to twenty-five American cents. Uncensored and straight off the shelf from any foreign market. Again, I simply couldn't believe this.

It was cheaper and more convenient than going to the movies, and you had your own personal delivery boy, with no delivery fees or tips included! This greasy guy made living from this stuff, and even had a wait-list taped to the lining in his suitcase!

I admitted to myself that even the case was interesting, probably dating back to when Iran was the Persian Empire. It sure smelled ancient, but its contents were new and uncensored. Being able to watch blood, or romance, tight jeans, tank tops, and push up bras made a difference in a movie normally blacked-out or otherwise edited for the Iranian version.

Arash leaned over the suitcase while the big guy watched. "Hmm, let's have a look…"

He helped me choose some movies as I complained about the Betamax tapes. "Those are real *old stuff*, you know."

Arash gave a slight nod. "Yes, but at least you see the whole movie, rather than a thirty-minute butchered version!"

We both giggled, fingers poking through titles. Finally, this resulted in five selections: four American, one Swedish. Thi was a cosmopolitan journey, and everyone wondered where the Swedish film stood (but didn't really care, because we would probably start with an American one, to be honest).

Arash took the bill and Mr. Greasy slapped shut his case and lugged it and himself through the door. We gathered to watch the first movie together. My first movie with Arash…I like! It was a complete two-hour ride with only silence between us, where the movie would do all the talking. I wanted to move close to him, knowing he had the same intention. I would never make the first move, but Arash should make his and I will allow his move. In the back of my head I knew Bahareh would get protective and fill the space!

"Wait a second," Bahareh said, and brought down the curtains so her nosy neighbors wouldn't invade our privacy. "Okay, all set to go!"

That particular problem soon solved itself as Arash sat down beside me, sliding his arm across my shoulders and for the first time, gazing into my eyes at such close distance. The mingled aromas of perfume and my own flowery scent aroused him, it was all around and through his eyes. I think it was about to drive him crazy. The movie-watching was a great excuse for closeness, even though he had wanted to take me to a local theater. You can't do anything in a local theater except watch an Iranian produced movie, which also meant buying your own box of tissues and getting ready for extreme emotional ups and downs! Pass, and glad I didn't. That sort of risk is crazy, and might have gotten me in trouble with the "green soldiers."

I snuggled against him, and I too was going to enjoy this movie, these intimate moments. I could feel his mind flashing with thoughts and images, our bodies were getting closer, and I could feel his heat growing stronger. Like most men with toned, muscular physiques, Arash was a girl-magnet and he knew it! I sometimes wondered why he had chosen me, when he could have anyone. But then again I knew what a catch I was! How can I not love that sort of confidence, especially with this hot whirlwind speeding towards me?

"Okay lovebirds," Bahareh said not without compassion, "let's watch."

The movie was actually copied from some theater, and had poor resolution and sound that dropped in and out. At times babies could be heard crying in the background, or audience members bumping and shuffling, probably getting up to use the restroom. These people certainly were not dues-paying extras in the Screen Actors Guild. If only the director knew this was the end result of his efforts, surely the Oscar nomination would be trashed! *If* there was to be one!

This turned the movie into a comedy, earning frequent laughter from everyone.

At the end, no one knew even what the story had been about. Had some famous actor like Brad Pitt been featured, no one would have noticed!

But between the gathered friends hummed a good, light energy. Although the movie had not been a hit, the whole concept of the mustache-guy, his tremendous suitcase, and the Betamax cassettes generated plenty of laughter, even a sense of bonding.

I stood and stretched. "Does anyone think the other movies will be better?"

"I will take a wild, educated guess," said Arash as he stood, "and say one-hundred percent not!"

Turning, he again found himself near me, and I felt he wanted to indulge in my lips, and to forget about the unwanted companions in this moment.

"You never know," Bahareh said, heading for the kitchen, "sometimes the guy filming has a better seat, or maybe some babies have already had their bathroom break!"

Ha! Loved it when she was so great with her snappy remarks!

So, the movie was coming to a close and adios time was getting closer. I didn't want Arash to go and, from his expression, he didn't either. I could clearly see he wanted more time with me, and that he liked our little group, which wasn't stubborn or demanding. "Bahareh," Arash said, "if it's okay with you, why don't I invite

156

some friends over, get some kebabs to barbecue and some more drinks? Call it a mini get-together?"

His eyes pleaded for a "yes, of course Arash!" He knew any suggestion of going to his place would be declined by me, because of the Emperor's check-up calls to my aunt.

Back from the kitchen, Bahareh considered the notion. "It's a good idea, but we really should keep it down. The nosy neighbors could tell my parents, so if we make sure no one finds out, you keep to yourselves going up and down the stairs, and park far away enough to avoid suspicion…I say let's party! But don't forget to shhh!" She cracked up. She loved secret parties, being secretive and strategizing. It was the kick to her life!

"I agree!" I shouted with a giggle.

I softly looked at Arash and saw he was staring right at me. The heat was felt again. He was reassuring me that if that's what I wanted, then that would be happening tonight. Let's not go too far with that thought.

"And I second that," said Shaheen, who was trying to come closer to Bahareh for a big Frenchie kiss—and this plan *clearly* allowed him more time to get it.

The guys agreed to make a stealthy run for supplies and were relieved when Bahareh mentioned they needn't buy charcoal, her parents were stocked. There were even chicken parts marinating in the fridge. Leave it to a Persian mama to leave the house with ample food in the fridge for her chickees. After the two set off, Bahareh and I freshened our drinks (now that I was becoming a pro) and began preparing side dishes to accompany the chicken kebabs, and were mostly successful at not laughing too loudly. Mostly.

Within twenty minutes Arash and Shaheen returned with a rustle of bags and clicking bottles, stepping gingerly as if through a minefield. "Hey," Bahareh said, "What took you so long?" And cracked up because she had made a sarcastic comment.

After a few moments the spontaneous mini-party was underway, and anyone invited would surely accept the invitation. There were times (as we all knew) when money must be put aside in case of a *Komiteh* raid. Arash, who was ever resourceful, already had that detail figured out and reassured Bahareh more than once he had it covered.

The natural smorgasbord consisted of: illegal drinks, alcoholic drinks, hardcore drinks, and protein. That was all we needed. The main drinks were vodka and cranberry juice plus yogurt dip and chips, Mortadella, and a main dish of barbecued marinated chicken. The up-to-now quiet Shaheen insisted on tending the coals and grilling the meat, and did so like the chef de cuisine. He was Prince Bobby Flay of Persia! He sliced a few Roma tomatoes, brushed them with olive oil, and threw them on as well—now he was Mr. Ratatouille!

But the best addition to the night was the company. A friend of Arash's dropped in to play some Iranian oldies and new songs. It wasn't long before an informal choir got going (so much for keeping quiet), chanting familiar songs and some we didn't know so well, but there was a sustained sort of harmony flavored with smokey barbecue and laughter. I felt like I fit right in—to say the most. Ha!

Everyone was sophisticated, and discussions ranged from Iran's state of economy to fashion and to the new skiing piste they were inaugurating in Dizin this coming winter. We teased one another, but no one took anything personal or to the heart. This was very close to the Jewish and Italian humor I had experienced with the girls in Brooklyn. Ah! My girls in Brooklyn...I felt so close to them but yet so distant. Bonding when you're young takes on such a different meaning. Stepping into another culture and seeing the black and white made me feel the richness of both worlds and how I enjoyed being in them.

"Check it out," someone said, waving at a girl cradling a guitar.

Standing in a corner, she gestured soulfully while strumming, long pale fingers fretting with passion's precision. Rich, warm chords mesmerized the group, and some rocked gently in their chairs or even from the floor. This was my first time witnessing an Iranian girl playing the guitar. Nothing irregular or bad about it—a girl who liked the guitar and played without her scarf and at times sang with it. It was simple art, food for the soul.

In this country, though, their humanity had to discipline itself and how it was displayed. Such a complicated, two-sided life. But they made the best of it and, tonight, it turned out to be fun.

Throughout the night I sat beside Arash, but had no difficulty connecting and laughing with everyone invited. All the boys knew he and I were dating, so out of respect they kept their distance. I took comfort in knowing I belonged to him.

After dinner and some more guitar, we opened a poetry book and started reading from it. It was beautiful. I had never heard such poems. Some parts I understood, while others eluded me. The reader gave off a vibe of hardcore mysticism and spirituality.

Finally, I could see the book's cover: *Fale Hafez*.

"Why are we reading this book?" I whispered to Bahareh.

"This guy Hafez was a famous poet back in the day. His poems told of connecting to the beloved, or the 'tongue of the invisible.'"

"Oh."

"Usually we make a wish, then say a little prayer and open a book he wrote called *Divane Hafez* to see if the wish comes true."

"Why not other poets? What makes him *the man*?"

"Because," Arash interrupted and gazed into my eyes, "he communicated deep spiritual experiences, and is a genuine mystic, in love with his beloved."

I was taken by surprise. Arash was so fast in answering this question and on top of that I've never heard Mr. Jordan Playboy (or so I thought) speak like this.

"His poetry is like a *dua*, or prayer," Arash went on, "and he wrote poetry expressing love, spirituality, and protest. Today many use a lot of his sayings as proverbs. So, Shaghayegh *khanoom*, when one wants to know answers to their destiny, they consult Hafez."

Arash was so near that I felt he must know everything about me, burrowing through my soul with that penetrating gaze. At once my doubt melted away. I wanted to tell him how much I enjoyed being with him, tell the truth about my life. All of it. "By any chance, are you trying to indirectly communicate something to me?" I asked.

He narrowed his eyes, as if figuring some complex equation. "Why would you think that?"

"Because you are…" I trailed off and glanced away because I knew I wanted him just as badly as he wanted me.

He sustained himself and I wanted to pause the moment to keep it stretching. His body energy was getting intense and I felt he wanted to reach out and grab me, teasingly wrestle with me because he knew I would be difficult. I would surrender to his kiss, but I wasn't ready to even hug him yet. Nope…the time had not matured yet.

The clock rang one in the morning, signaling midnight was gone and it was time to leave. Everyone ignored this, including Bahareh, who carried on chatting with and enjoying her invited guests. This mirth and music went on until somewhere around three, when the party hit one of those quiet pockets. Peeps began checking out, gathering whatever they'd brought—food not included—and saying thank yous and goodbyes.

I pulled Arash to a hushed dim corner and asked if we could speak before he took off. I wanted to tell him the truth: that I trusted him, that I enjoyed getting to know him.

"Arash…" I began, swallowing hard. My Farsi wasn't working too smoothly in the conversation. He realized and jumped in.

"Did you enjoy yourself?"

"Of course! Did you?"

He grinned broadly. "I always do when I am with you."

Oh the charmer is in *da house*.

"Smart guy," I joked with a wink.

"Or so it seems to me. Do you want to continue this dialogue in English or should we switch channels?"

I froze. Oh my god, he did know! And now he knew why I'd been covering it up! I felt like crap! But I stood there, poised and solemn. "You know?"

"From the very start. You know your answers and questions are not those of girls who grew up here. No. It's obvious, at least to me, that you were from a different culture! But you should know that I don't care because I am *not* after your green card." His posture told the firm truth of this statement and his eyes were so innocent. "Look, I know you are scared because lots of guys want to get out of this country somehow, and getting hooked up with a girl with a green card is the easiest way. But you know, or maybe didn't know, that I was raised in London and already have a ticket out…that is, if I *wanted* one."

"So…"

"So I don't need to trick you and act like I'm head over heels for you and your family, or pretend to love every joke you tell!" he ended with a chuckle.

161

I remained quiet, and wasn't sure how to express myself. Words weren't working at the moment, but I enjoyed hearing what Arash had to say and wanted to hear more. But still, I had to ask. "If you're not acting, then what are you doing?"

"I'll tell you. Simply being, and enjoying every moment with you."

"And your intention is to not take advantage of me, right? Because, as I recall from the girls I've spoken to, that's another issue girls have to deal with today."

"Listen, the fact that you are asking is another indicator that you are not from Tehran's world! Girls here play the game and you are asking me if I want to have your sex?"

"Umm, right. So, *do* you?"

For the first time he looked away. "Whenever you are ready..." he trailed off, then continued, "Have I ever touched you or asked you for more?"

He was right. If he was Mr. Jordan Playboy, he may have had an early retirement or on temp vacation. In all the time we had spent together, he had not even kissed me. Was he laying low until he got what he wanted? A strong urge told me to throw away these thoughts heard around the block and school, from cousins and parents, and the dude in the fruit shop, and just be me and relish my time. I smiled knowing Arash could talk with me without being pushed. We had evolved as an amateur couple until this moment of truth. I could finally, completely be myself.

"By the way, I think my jokes are funny," I had to add that.

Stepping closer, he looked into my eyes, and leaned down.

He lifted a hand and tenderly held my chin towards him. This was the guy I could be comfortable with, who had opened my heart without looking at my breasts (for all I knew). He stirred butterflies in me and every moment he infused me with life.

"Okay," I said closing my eyelids, letting him know I was ready for him. But I didn't know to what extent I was ready for him, so I let him roll the dice.

His lips brushed mine, warm and gentle and soft, and I kissed back, abandoning myself to this exquisite man, this delicious moment. Our kiss was small, long and suspended time. It was the first time I was tasting someone who brought new experiences into my life. New emotions were rising to the surface, passing delicate spaces in my soul and filling them with passion.

I opened my eyes and ended the kiss softer than a midnight sigh.

We stood smiling at each other, a mutual recognition of how right it felt.

I looked back into the room. This is my life. My life. I'm going to seize it, and I don't care how anyone else lives theirs, even if in Iran, even if in taboo.

I turned, and Arash gazed at me like I'd just given him the key to glory.

All at once, my worries, thoughts, doubts about coming to Iran, struggling with language and culture, difficulties at school...all seemed distant and inaccessible.

And for now, everything was perfect.

11

Lost in Translation

FOR ME, DISCOVERING IRAN WAS fun. Now I had a flock of friends and every one of them I connected with in a different way. Some understood me and others didn't have the slightest idea of the changes going on inside—but who cared! I was enjoying both worlds. The crunchy and the tasty as opposed to the salty and bitter.

Sometimes after our Italian class, I would venture out with Elham, and at other times I would spend time with family, and getting to know them hadn't turned out so bad at all.

My dates with Arash had become biweekly, and we would either go to dinner or just have a *majoon*, which is every fruit in a blender mixed with dates or honey or a variety of nuts. Things in Tehran didn't have much direction for a recipe because everything was so yummy, if not highly organic.

We talked, exchanged ideas, laughed, made fun of each other, and that was conducted with one foot in the Farsi pool of words and the other foot in the ocean lingo of English. Fin-glish or Farsglish, it came with no instructions other than we both understood what the hell the other was saying.

At times a question was cut in half by any word that filled in the blank. That word might have even been Italian! It just filled the blank and we both knew we were communicating.

My meetings and talks with him had to be kept on the down low and I had to skip out on some Italian classes or leave after forty minutes of class to make it happen. And the calls caused me to lose lots of sleep and turn into an insomniac. But again, who cared—I was young and carefree!

My mom kept asking boyfriend questions to gather data on if I was doing anything under the rugs. She was a good spy. If she knew, then the pops would def know and then I would be under the radar.

There was a time on the phone with Elham I was telling her about our date and the Emperor picked up the phone from the living room to make a call and he overheard a tiny bit of the story. The next day when he asked about it my quick save was that I was telling her about a scene in a movie I had just watched. Since I didn't have a long list of lies on my record he accepted and that bullet was dodged. My list of lies was long but as long as they were kept hidden from the parents and the family, I was in fabulous hands.

Strictness led to lies, led to moving forward in my dating life.

I would tease Arash, "I won't charge you for the Italian lessons."

"Oh, please do," he would joke back, and we moved through the days hand in hand, and sometimes lip to lip when we could squeeze in a kiss in the darkness of the night and car.

One night Arash asked if I could go out with him to the movie theater, and I (developing the courage to step out with my boyfriend without fear of being spotted by family or the *Komiteh*) replied, "Okay, but I have no interest in the sobbing, boring, emotionally intense Iranian dramas. This movie industry needs to inject more action into their work."

My cover-up and white lie was chilling with Bahareh at a coffee shop. Bahareh's cell phone was turned off during my movie time. She on the other hand was spending coffee time with a massive transformation format of me: Shaheen. It fit the bill.

"This is actually an American movie they're screening, but with some changes. I thought it would be fun to check it out."

"I'm in," I teased, "this will be interesting."

The theater was packed, and a line had formed for popcorn at the concession stand. The majority of people stood outside on the sidewalk where a vendor sold fresh walnuts floating in saltwater-filled jars. The vessels didn't look dirty or smudged, and if they were, the public seemed unconcerned and within minutes had depleted the stock.

Arash and I joined in on the fun and bought some walnuts which were dumped into a plastic bag. Six freshly-salted walnuts in a plastic bag for 500 *tomans*. That was nothing in dollars! Seventy-five cents! I could buy the dude and his jar with my allowance. But then again, I had Arash as the dude so I passed on that portion. Smileys.

I devoured some walnuts right there on the highly polluted street and saved a couple for when inside. It was salty heaven! It was proven to me that salt and walnut made a good marriage.

We headed inside, got seated, and I dug into my walnut bag. The crunch wasn't annoying, as everyone gnawed on some snack, including sunflower seeds, impossible to enjoy without being cracked open. Where was the seed? Who knew, people just had to nibble. Nobody minded. This wasn't New York City where any intrusive sound would provoke head turns, sometimes hostile glares and whispered threats here and there from the ultra sensitive.

I crunched away. "It's a good thing no one's giving us the look. We're making quite the noise!"

Arash nosed my ear and whispered, "They are doing the same thing," and gave me gentle kisses with soft breathy chuckles.

The air was close and scented with hot popcorn. The film was American with famous actors, although dubbed in Farsi. "Oh, I've seen this before," I whispered.

The dubbed version, though, was nothing like that movie I had watched. I listened carefully, picked out words and phrasing mistranslated and badly edited into the wrong places. This gave the movie an absurd, unintended twist.

First I thought I heard them wrong, but other than the voices being completely off and the affectionate words cropped, some slang terms were so poorly interpreted they made no sense in Farsi!

"I smell a rat," an actor said.

This was interpreted literally, instead of slang for "I sense something is wrong, or someone's being dishonest." Geez! It threw the whole movie off into another direction! I couldn't help it. "This is translated wrong! It changes the whole meaning of the scene," I said while laughing.

Arash started laughing because I was laughing. "I wanted you to see this, not necessarily the movie!"

I simply couldn't stop giggling through this drama-turned-comedy, especially when the screen suddenly went black. "What is up with the black?" the audience shouted in unity, clapping and blowing enthusiastic wolf-whistles. A few completely lost it to cackling and rolling in their seats.

I had never seen such a thing! "What on earth is happening?"

Arash had to shout over the convulsive laughter. "This is the censored sex scene, and everyone knows it because everyone has a movie guy! They're making fun of it, like when you know but don't know what's happening. When they think you're stupid but have them all figured out."

"Why aren't you joining in on this home run?" I laughed, setting aside the empty walnut bag.

"You go get her! She's a hottie!" screamed some guys from somewhere in the theatre. Someone across the aisle said, "Atta boy! She was beautiful, wasn't she?" The crowd roared on a soprano note, fading when the next pathetic scene unfolded.

I shook my head. This was easily the most ridiculous, hilarious picture—next to the mustached guy's collection at Bahareh's house—I'd ever seen!

Everyone there knew the movie's plot, scenes, and how it ended, but still they chose to gather here in this theatre, re-watch, and eat dirty but super delish salted walnuts! Strangers building memories together.

I doubted the effect held up for screenings of Iranian-produced movies, but as far as these mistranslated, poorly dubbed foreign jobs went, they were like comedies. Perhaps funnier still was that the entire audience knew this, but nonetheless paid for a few inevitable laughs. Wow! This society bonded in very weird ways. So consciously bringing out smiles in one another, yet quiet about it. Admirable...but man...it was sad!

Inching closer to Arash, I scratched the back of his head and murmured, "Thank you for bringing me here, and showing me a movie with *us* as the main actors and actresses!"

"For you, anything," he stole a small kiss, and we lingered in that intimate darkness.

Many in Iran would probably label our kiss or our date as a right or wrong, Islamic or sinful. But for Arash and I, this was a temporary suspension of mandatory discipline in order to enjoy ourselves whenever, and however, we could.

Amen to that. Where was a gospel church when you needed some soul music?

•••

The day after the movie, I woke up to get dressed for class. Elham and I planned to grab lunch at the famous charbroiled burger and pizza place in Vanak, then head to class.

Gastronomy in Iran should be made a science, that's how good the food was! Every restaurant I went too made me want more, even though I opted for less calories, but I had to let this part go. Food irresistibility was a problem I was dealing with.

For me, food in Iran took on a completely different meaning. Much of it was organic, tasty, juicy, and mouth-watering, but with a twist not seen anywhere else. Even the pizza was different—not like Brooklyn's though. Back in the hood, the local pizzeria I patronized and worshipped made the best mushroom pie pizzas and calzones. Pizza here had every topping one could desire…yet was slathered with ketchup. Ketchup? What happened to tomato sauce? Did they forget it or just run out of stock? A pizza can't go without tomato sauce! They didn't even add pesto sauce or truffle oil—nothing, zilch!

Elham drove her mom' s Iranian-made Renault Pars (assembled from the French manufacturer's parts), which had no air conditioning. To compensate for this lack, Elham's bro had installed some sort of engine, or compressor, in the trunk, proving himself a highly skilled technician and problem-solver. He was hired in my book! For both his skills and looks.

This improvised AC system, by way of a long nozzle, pumped cold air from the trunk into the car. It rocked, and he should put "rockstar" on his resume.

When I saw this contraption, my jaw dropped. It was truly unbelievable and out of this (or any) world! "What in the world of science and creation *is* this?"

"Take a wild guess," said Elham with a smirk. "Compliments to my genius brother!"

Elham's brother was the sort of guy who never went to school. In fact, I think he had dropped out of 11th grade, but excelled in figuring things out through trial and error. He had once aspired to be a NASA engineer and probably would have made it had he not dithered and fooled around so much, leading to marriage at eighteen! He still nurtured ambitions of leaving Iran and going to Texas to pursue his dream of one day flying to the moon.

Now, back from the moon and into reality, he was a gifted mechanic and ran his own shop. It was busy all the time, brought in good money, and he had a wife he adored. So career-wise, he was happy, and it didn't do him justice. His brain could be compared to the maze in the vast Garden of Versailles—many-dimensioned and mysterious—but he always quite brilliantly found his way out. Installing a homemade AC unit in a stick-shift car whose small engine barely turned its wheels was genius. This made my day!

"Let's get in and get going!" I said sliding into the matchbox-shaped Renault. "I'm hungry!"

Elham squinted in confusion. "Where are we going again?"

"You now, the famous charbroiled burger joint in Vanak! I've heard so much about it, and it's time to indulge in something different from *Chelo*. I'm tired of crusty rice. So *bezan berim, andiamo, vamos,* GIDDY UP!"

At that, we drove wickedly into the wild, wild, streets of Tehran where driving was an art.

After a good drive with the sound of music competing with the roar of the AC we pulled up to the charbroiled place where the smell made me start doubling my production of saliva.

"No…" said Elham with her mouth wide open

Already a line nearly a kilometer long had formed which, despite moving quickly, seemed only to get longer. This wasn't fair. We were in starving mode!

Okay, I thought, someone had to wait in line. "Why don't you stay in the car," I said, "and I'll get the pick-ups. Maybe we should have called and ordered a week ago!" I said, pissed but still hungry.

"Wait. Let's see if we can find a friendly face, that way we can just cut instead of waiting for who knows how many hours! Gimme a second while I browse."

Even though I was very hungry, I thought that approach would be kinda rude, barging into the middle of the line smiling and signaling to people behind you: Move over—*we* are here now!

No, that was way lacking in etiquette. If I were standing there and someone tried to pull that on me I would surely object, possibly loudly and file a lawsuit! Okay…I was hungry for sure.

Elham hit the brakes. "Wait here! I just saw Ali."

"Ali? Who on earth is Ali?"

"The dude from Jordan. You don't remember, as usual. I think Arash fogged up your brain so much you can't remember anyone else." She jumped out of the car.

Her greeting was very warm and awkward at the same time— well, at least in my eyes. It was simply a *salam*, eliminating a hug or kiss.

I sat watching, dreading what might happen next.

Would Elham offer Ali money to buy their food? It sure was beginning to look that way, and others were noticing with hostile stares. Here we go. The Irani tarof game! She'd say, "Please be my

171

guest this time and take this money. A burger and a pizza don't cost much." Then he'd say, "*En harfha chie!*" meaning "How could you even think about giving me money? Pah-lease! This is my treat." Then the back-and-forth, "No, please take it," and "I insist, you take it." And the inevitable final sentence "Don't even think about it, *khejalat dare be khoda!*" (God! That is so shameful!)

I watched, knowing that at any moment this could continue for a good amount of time. Going on until either the Type-A personality won this tug of war, or an unusual justice prevailed with one party merely agreeing to buy now, and the other vowing to treat next time. The next time would be TBD. I mean we met them randomly here so what are the odds of meeting them in another place, just the four of us? Why couldn't they just take the bill without a "next time"?

Troubling indeed. In Brooklyn if you didn't have cash on you, you would ask your girlfriend for money, but nobody paid for the other person. This was a distinct part of the Iranian culture. So weird! I never figured it out. I just knew I refused to participate in this little power play of "I have more money and could take your bill...no, I could take your bill and my bill combined!"

Elham trotted back to the car grinning. "Ali has invited us to free burgers and pizza! *And* we're spared standing in line and roasting in these wimples, and missing class in the bargain!"

"But we should pay them back girl," I said, kinda confused.

"They are treating, and when a guy treats you accept!" she continued giggling.

I didn't get this concept, but it didn't matter anymore. I just decided to wing it. Since Ali had extended the invitation and Elham had accepted we had to sit and eat with him. The food was heaven. Flame-broiled burgers and pizza baked to crisp perfection in a brick oven. Stuff this delicious, I mused, ought to be advertised in Vogue, and served along the models' runway in Paris! It made the world go 'round! Forget Brooklyn, this is the cheese!

Part way through lunch, Elham leaned toward me and whispered, "Eating this is better than sex!" A comment typical of Elham: likable, hilarious, and created from her vivid imagination. Vivid.

I managed not to blush but did softly giggle. "Mmm-hmm girl, you just may be right on!"

Ali chewed pizza, oblivious to the topic. "So," he said, blotting his mouth with a napkin, "where are you guys headed now?"

"To an elaborate education institution," said Elham with a chuckle.

"Yes," I chimed in, "that is precisely our destination, in our elaborate Oscar-style mantos and wimples." I had to hiss some laughter at my own corny pieces.

Ali looked at us back and forth as if trying to decide something. "I say you skip class and join us."

"Two questions, Ali Joon," I said. "First, join you where? And, who is us?"

I felt somewhat conflicted. There could be danger here, or maybe just another round of good times. So funny how danger and fun times were turning out to be best buds in Iran.

I also thought of Arash, who was supposed to pick me up from class so we could be together. I didn't want to get dragged into something without him knowing.

Ali sat straight and assumed a casual air. "My dad just bought a villa out in Lavasan, and we are all headed there in an hour to escape the pollution that's cutting our lives in half in Tehran. We'll make kebabs, drink, and get some fun times in." Even more upbeat, he said, "C'mon, it'll be fun and you won't regret it!"

"Well, I have a boyfriend," I said, "so if he is down and doesn't have to work then I will ditch class and join in the Lavasan kinda fun."

I didn't want to ditch Arash even though I totally could have. I felt this security with him and I think I respected him and liked him to the extent that I wanted him to know. His friend was hot and Ali wasn't bad either but Arash was my beau. Damn it! I had loyalty!

On the other hand, the parents would think I was in class so I would be covered there as well. Loyalty to the folks as well! Ha!

I was getting to know myself fully: I liked Arash a lot, and I really had to cover up some deets from my parents. Maybe they were afraid of the system too, if I were to get caught by the green dudes. It was such a lawless country anything could be accounted for. Even the days the green guys got their PMS.

"If they join, then I am in too!" popped Elham.

So the fate of this near-future plan was left in Arash's hands.

Ali studied us with apparent composure, as if he had all the time in the world. The pervasive aroma of seared beef and hot pizza haunted his taste buds, and he couldn't believe—after the fairly heavy lunch—his stomach wanted more. "Okay," he said.

Elham leaned toward me and whispered, "we could have gone, you know. Arash doesn't have to know *everything!*"

"But we barely know these guys. Who knows what we'll be stepping into? Anyway, I also want them to get the picture that I have a boyfriend, so hands off is the name of the game!"

It looked like boys and girls did a lot of jumping around with one another in Tehran. Everyone acted flirtatious and it took a while for two to become exclusive. I know I respected Arash, but on a totally different note he was also fun to be around.

"Fine," Elham said, "call him." Her expression said: I must comply or else no fun.

Ali stepped away in search of something to drink.

Arash picked up in a matter of seconds. Elham probably thought: this'll be a quickie. He'll be the typical Iranian man and say NO to everything. A forbidden everything!

She was wrong, and I was completely wrong in my thoughts as well. Mis-preconceptions!

The call went on for nearly twenty minutes, with plenty of nods and smiles and "mmhmm's" from my end. Ali sat sipping some frosty-looking concoction.

Finally, the call ended. Cutting to the chase, I gave Elham the CliffsNotes version.

Stunned, Elham said: "You mean he didn't give you a flat-out no? He didn't shout 'how dare you even talk and have lunch with other dudes'?"

"What are you talking about? Woman, we are not living in the fifth century. He said 'if you know these people go and have fun, but *do* you know them?' I mean, we're ditching. So I would rather ditch and not be afraid. Besides, if you're crazy for this place they call Lavasan, Arash has a villa there too. We could all go there on Friday and I could tell the Emperor that I'm at my aunt's. Of course I would be lying again so it looks like this is the trend! Anyways they are never home on Fridays. They're usually headed to Darakeh, they love the mountains. It'll be tough luck if he tries to call and check up on us."

Ali, finished with his drink, visibly was getting twitchy and was looking straight at me.

"Hmm...you sure we could make it Friday?" said Elham. "Things happen, and the parents twist and turn all the time with their decisions. What if your aunt decides to randomly pay a visit to her brother, and then there we are, stuck in the house?" She

175

laughed, but half of her tone was completely serious. She really wanted to go.

"*Boro ghomshoo*," I said with a chuckle. Get lost! "It'll be a piece of cake, and we *will*—we *shall*—get out," she declared like a superhero. "Sorry Ali Joon. *Merci* for lunch and the cut in line!"

We all stood, and we apologized for not being able to make it today (and be their girl toys I thought in my head). I felt as if we were part of a secret BF and GF society, formed to guard against public (and official) disapproval. These dudes seemed all right, though. They didn't bite.

I knew Lavasan was gorgeous and also knew it was home to the rich Iranian crowd with their servants and new Mercedes Benzes, and similar to Los Angeles's Calabasas, Bel Air, and Beverly Hills combined. I was excited about seeing this. Who knows? Maybe I'd see some Beverly Hills Chihuahuas!

Back in the car, we drove toward our class. It was refreshing to have a little adventure like this. It was unpredictable and totally out of the blue. What if Arash had joined us and we had ended up in Lavasan, or hadn't had joined us and we would have sailed in Lavasan's direction with two complete strangers? "No rules" was the name of the game in this country. No rules except for the Emperor's, which we kept ignoring for the one goal of having fun.

•••

That night in my room, I went under the covers, pulled out the secret telephone and called my (might as well call him secret as well) SECRET boyfriend.

Fortunately, my bedroom was situated far from my parents', because my laughs and naughty flirts would not always be so quiet.

One loud answer and the cops would awake or at least suspicious thoughts would arise.

The conversation wasn't as long as usual, but plans were set. Strategy: on Friday I would head over to my aunt's, with a little white lie (how every other girl would always label it) and would change directions along the way. Arash would pick me up two blocks north of my house. Then we would grab Elham and be on our way. The only additional point we had to take into perspective was the *Komiteh*.

In a sense, Elham was a third wheel. But she didn't care, she couldn't marry a Muslim guy anyway, and it was hard to find someone Jewish in the crowd in Tehran. They usually kept quiet among all the other Muslims. She settled to simply have fun rather than to fish for a Jewish dude and we really got along very well and enjoyed our time together.

So that was that, we were set. Armed with a bag full of smiles, chips, yogurt dip, raw chicken and meat kebabs, vodka, and blasting DJ Bobo-style music, we were driving into the sunset headed toward our mini-vacation.

12

Living Large in Lavasan

I WAS EXCITED TO SPEND time with Arash and my best buddy Elham in Lavasan, wherever that was somewhere on the road. Only the Indiana Jones of Tehran would know that.

The twisty road threaded through a landscape filled with fascinating sights and a symphony of aromas. The car entered a hundred-yard stretch redolent of fresh green grass, then a low spot swirling with stony bits of dust. Bursts of flowers colored crimson, lemon, white and violet adorned the earth, and trees reached fruit-laden limbs over the road luring the travelers with apples, white berries, and apricots.

The intense heat was kept mostly at bay by the cranked-up AC unit. Arash brought watermelon seeds to munch on, and I observed that nearly every soul in Iran seemed to be into sunflower or watermelon seeds. People took them everywhere, whether watching a movie, driving, or having dessert after dinner; the seeds were the dessert! It could be listed under side dishes and dessert at the same time.

Abruptly Arash braked and stopped the car in the middle of the road and gazed straight at me. Oh! How I wanted to have sex with him when he looked at me like that! I looked back thinking he might be crazy, or he was hesitating to say we were out of gas. "Umm...this is the road, *azizam*," I said thinking maybe I was the one missing something.

"I know silly, but look at those sour oranges and berries hanging from those trees!"

"Oh yeah! This is going to be fun!" said Elham.

After a few moments of gazing out the window to connect the dots, I saw what they were pointing at. They were acting like temporary monkeys lusting after a mid-road snack! "I know what you're going to do. Isn't it illegal?"

"Nothing is illegal in this country!" Elham declared. "Get out! They're calling your name!"

I giggled. "Yeah, what *possibly* could they be saying?"

"I want your sex!" And at that, Elham cracked up.

Arash pulled the car onto the shoulder, and we all climbed out.

We, meaning me and my boyfriend, strode through the tall grass toward the white berry tree. Waving away a cloud of buzzing gnats, Arash appeared to dive headfirst into the ground, then his feet thrust into the air. Handstand time!

"Look at you!" I cried.

In a show of amazing balance, Arash twisted his body and faced me. "No, I'd rather look at you!"

Not used to such "free" displays, I felt a rush of fear. Maybe if I were in Brooklyn I wouldn't feel this scared but then again these two monkeys were jumping on these trees as if the rule was to take other people's fruits and be happy you did it! Well, flexibility's arrow hit me through the heart at that point and transformed me into the

179

same monkey. Arash's handstand came to an end. He brought himself back to his feet, panting with effort but grinning.

"Jump, climb and start eating!"

"Just like that? What if the neighbors see us?"

"Then we split!"

I stepped toward a *shatoot* berry tree, heaved myself onto its bulk and climbed faster than I thought possible. Halfway up I stopped and inhaled the intoxicating sweetness of white mulberries, which literally bled sugar. "Hey, these are delish."

Not even thinking about pesticides (I don't even think they were used here), I plucked a sticky bunch and gobbled them with an explosion of heaven in my mouth. They were as good as any piece of fruit I'd had here. I plucked another pungent bunch and savored it, unable to stop!

Arash viewed this spontaneous feast a few seconds longer, then decided to intervene. "Okay, okay. You'll spoil your lunch!"

This went nowhere, and he was forced to pull me down by the leg of my jeans.

Elham had already scaled a *toot* tree as if a veteran of many climbs, and perched on one fat limb munching the purple berries as if she owned the orchard.

"I know you like them," Arash said, "but we have somewhere to get to!" Laughing, he shook his head.

As if in a *toot* trance, I said: "They were so good, where can we get some?" This sounded like a priority.

By the way, *toot* means berry in Farsi and the word after explains the million and one *toots* we have in Iran! White, red, dark red, etc.

Arash waved a hand before my face to induce normal blinking. "They sell some up the road, but let's first grab some sour oranges for the kebabs. They work well together," he said accompanied with a wink. Must really taste good I thought. The comment sounded like

180

a sexual one and if not I definitely took it as one. Now I *really* wanted Arash.

Back on Earth, I said, "Wait, are you sure they won't arrest us?"

"Again with the fear?" joked Elham. "Get a grip, woman. They will join in the fun. Nobody will call the cops for eating a berry or two—or should I say, in your case, two hundred! Besides, they're dangling over the streets. Someone should better maintain their trees."

Meanwhile, Arash had moved like lightning and jogged up to us with at least twenty *naranjas* (sour oranges) bouncing in his bowled-up shirt. Now I was sure they went great with kebabs.

Back at the car he dumped them into a bag and eased himself into the driver's seat. Peering at me again, he grinned broadly as if to tell a funny story. "So how did you like it?"

I clapped once, jarringly loud. "Let's repeat on the way back!"

Elham hooted in triumph. "Yeah girlfriend! At last! Finally the mafia side is lurking out! You're getting out of that right-or-wrong-or-sinful mode. This stuff is not a big deal here. Even if the neighbors found out, they probably would give you a bowl to put your harvest in."

Arash put the car in gear and we drove off. For twenty minutes or so we recharged while basking in the echo of our fruit-picking gig. Finally, Arash slowed. "Here we are."

He nosed the car into a sandy entrance that looked as though it might lead to some deserted shamble of a house, but opened onto a parking area serving a luxurious, Spanish-style villa. A dream home for sure.

It might have appeared deserted from the outside, but it was breathtaking in design and surrounded by a U-shaped garden bright with flowers, tomatoes, and grape vines, and watched over by white, black, and red mulberry trees on the inside. The villa had accents of

Andalusian (or perhaps Italian) porcelain, and an iron stable-style door added a humble rustic charm. The airy house gave off a dreamy magic, as though it had stood here forever. It would have been perfect for some *Lifestyles of the Rich and Famous*-type TV show.

"Look at that," I said, "the outdoor patio should be featured in *Meditation* or *Um* magazine. Just close your eyes and breathe in the freshness."

We opened the doors and got out of the car. Arash stretched his arms over his head. "The only thing I'm breathing is your perfume." He shot me a teasing glance, leaned down and kissed my neck with a wet kiss that refreshed my skin.

I felt he desired to bring everything to me for me…you get the picture! If this was what made me happy that's what he would work toward. The garden itself seemed a reflection of a Swami-yoga person's soul, and the villa a symbol of its depth.

"C'mon," Elham urged, "let's go!"

Officially parked now, we unloaded our goodies and strode through the incense of flowers and fruit to enter the villa.

Once we went through the door, I marveled at the work of great minds and architects. The interior held a scattering of art and objects from Paris, Spain, and Italy. And the garden certainly could rival any in Holland.

Natural light glowed across white marble stars, tiled walls, wood-and-glass combo floor units, a Persian framed carpet, and a grand piano polished to infinity. And this was just the beginning! Balconies opened onto a stream bobbing with watermelons, cantaloupes, and honeydews corralled by a big rock.

"Why are those melons in the water? Won't they float away?" I asked loudly.

Elham rolled her eyes at Arash. "Well Ms. I.Q., that's why there's a big rock keeping them from escaping. Besides, touch the water. It flows down from the mountains and is very cold."

"I see. Thanks for the enlightenment Ms. Know-It-All!" I fired back sarcastically.

Arash had invited eight or nine others and they were wandering the villa and its calm spaces, some gazing at its art, others at the house itself. After about half an hour, everyone was drinking, eating, and enjoying the mini-vacation. I was surprised by everyone's warmth and never expected to visit this villa and mingle with people so hip, fashionable, friendly, and easy to converse with.

Best of all had to be the uncomplicated comfort of sipping wine on a patio with Arash and Elham cracking wise jokes, all favored beneath the boundless blue sky. Ah...this was Iran at its finest.

I took another sip and turned to Arash. "Do you come here a lot? I mean, this is better than all therapies combined—herbal, aroma, or otherwise. I never knew this even existed in Tehran. Although that said, I just became legal to drink!" I said laughing and allowing myself to drink although there was no age limit and I was setting my own rules.

Arash smiled and stole a kiss from my lips. I guess I was being cute in his book. I couldn't be sure what was going to happen with us, or where we'd end up...but he was bit by bit opening my heart.

"Picture time!" shouted Elham, shattering my reverie. Grrrr.

"I need some rouge," cried one of the girls nearby.

"Here you go," said Elham, "use mine."

This piqued the attention of yet another girl. "Oh, can I use it after you? Mine is inside and I don't feel like getting up."

The cycle continued, until those in need wore the same shade of lipstick and the lipstick made a complete 360-degree circle. I wondered why none of them seemed concerned with catching some disease! Sharing lipstick? Ugh, count me out. I'll go with whatever's left on my lips after kissing Arash, drinking, and eating. Basically none, but hey my mascara was still on!

I didn't care, and the picture was taken as a keepsake from this first visit to Lavasan, where I took advantage of sitting beneath the sky and watching the sunset with someone who accepted me for me and enabled me to feel safe. Such a surprising feeling to feel safe without the wimple or scarf and really being with Arash and not be judged or arrested by the *Komiteh* people.

I felt Arash saw me so differently than the other Iranian girls. Couldn't exactly put my finger on it but I saw myself as so real and easy going. I didn't need a ton of makeup and dressing up crazy to come to Lavasan; I was who I was. Maybe that was a trait I brought from Brooklyn where you have to be yourself or you won't survive. Girls in Iran have so much makeup and at times I felt like they were trying too hard to impress guys. You could call it lack of confidence, or maybe I had too much confidence. Sometimes when they heard I was from New York they would look at me like an alien and listen to what I said and how I said it.

I think the whole notion of the U.S. was so foreign to them they wanted to understand it through me...and I was an open book! Nothing to hide except that I may not know Farsi well enough to explain. But my actions were an open book. In my book there was nothing wrong with talking about sex; in fact, we had sex education in school (and some had sex in school!). Nothing wrong with not knowing about something—I mean you weren't Mr. Perfect all the time, nothing wrong with not knowing what I wanted to be in the future and definitely nothing wrong with kissing and having a little twinkly winks with your boyfriend. Who would oppose that?

I think that was what attracted him to me, because there was obviously no sex involved and we communicated in half Farsi half

English. He said it was the way I made him laugh. Guess that's where the Jewish/Italian sense of humor kicked in. He was right, not all girls in Iran had a sense of humor, and Elham was a diamond in the rough for me. Arash accepted me for who I was, and not through some other lens, including the U.S. citizenship, the golden pass for lots of peeps in Iran.

Maybe for the same reason Arash liked me I liked him back. Most guys in Iran, or at least the ones I saw, were sex fanatics or trying to use the chick for something else. Arash was respectful and fun and understood me—which was why I stayed sane. "Feelings" subjects didn't need to be explained, but then again maybe we hadn't come upon those subjects yet. And so we rolled forward without my parents knowing, without any sex. You know the good ol' dating life was in.

It wasn't until Elham received a call and then the time had come to call it a wrap.

We weren't sure what the call was, but I had to get back home. I didn't know if I should go to my aunt's or my house directly. So with a big, fat white lie leaning on my shoulders, we headed towards Tehran.

•••

We got on the road shortly after sunset, the clouds blushing crimson, violet, and gold. The ride was quiet, tinged with both warmth and a little melancholy. This latter I was more particular about. I didn't want to leave freedom, but duty called.

We dropped off Elham with whispered goodbyes and drove on.

After a short while, the car pulled over to the curb at my house. "That's odd," I said.

"What is?"

"Our lights are never off."

"Well, go up and see who's home or what happened. I will hang around here. Shaghayegh, are you scared?"

I narrowed my eyes. "You are so funny...of course I am *not* scared! But wait for my signal before you leave!" I brushed my lips against his, reluctant to climb out.

"I'll miss you," I whispered seductively.

I mounted the stairs with urgency, slipped my key into the lock and opened the door. "Hello? Anybody home?"

The house stood empty.

Hmmm…this never happens. Unheard of on a Friday! Especially unheard of when I hadn't arrived home and the folks didn't know where I was!

I rushed into the kitchen and could see a scribbled note attached to the refrigerator: *Aziz Joon in the hospital, come to hospital, we are all there. Was worried about you. We will talk later. Dad.*

Shoot…did he know I lied? How? Had he spoken with my Aunt? I was screwed, and even though this is disgustingly bad to say, I'm glad my situation was temporarily being ignored because of another situation. I didn't know how my father would react or if he knew, but I was getting nervous! The last thing I need in this caged country is another cage! I brushed the thoughts to a drawer in my brain for the time being and focused on getting my physical self to the hospital.

I think the note had been taped there for a couple of hours. Anxiety surged coldly through my nerves. This was my grandmother, my blood, the only one in the family I potentially could just let loose with and not worry about a thing. She was well-traveled, kind, and protected me from my parents. Maybe she protected me because I was cute, or because I was the far away granddaughter. My dear Aziz Joon….

Tears burned in my eyes, but I knew the doctors here were the best of the best, at least most of the time!

I called my dad's cell. After a few seconds, he assured me all was well, and that I ought to come by for a bit to see Aziz Joon. "But how could this have happened? She's still very young for an elder woman." I knew this was beside the point, that anyone could be hit by misfortune.

Dad explained to me how Aziz Joon was hit by a sudden heart attack and, after calling 911 and waiting an eternity for help to arrive, had been transported to the wrong hospital! How lame can you get! This was a human life they were dealing with but, then again, the ambulance driver—if confronted—would probably softly say, "I'm sorry," or (offended), "Hey, I did my best, and besides no one mentioned *which* hospital she needed to go to!" Which was all bullshit. No one gave a rat's ass in this country.

Yes, that would be your answer. That and a dead body. Typical! No rules in this joint! And that was the story of calling 911 in Iran on *good* days.

I hurried out of the house and jumped into Arash's Patrol. He was still outside and playing a game on his phone, but when I told him, he sped toward the hospital.

"Wow," he said, "what a bungle!" And seemed unsurprised that the driver may have made a mistake.

"This stuff happens here, sometimes often," he said chuckling. "Liability is kinda different in third-world countries, but at least the doctors make up for it."

I felt imaginary horns sprouting from my head, not comprehending how anyone could so carelessly deal with such sensitive stuff. But she's alive, and that's all that matters. I really hoped this type of emergency never happened to any hypothetical family member—or anyone else's for that matter!

As usual, the highways were crowded so we took side streets, only to arrive at the hospital doors where we were blocked by a motorbike dropping off its passengers. Livid, I cried, "I don't believe this!"

Normally the bikes carry one or two riders, but I could see what resembled some stage magician's trick, as a wind gust bellowed the long flesh-concealing chador of the female passenger, revealing four kids underneath! Not even counting the male driver, this was a full-blown family. How could the bike take so much weight? Stranger still, how were those rumpled kids geometrically arranged one atop the other? A real achievement, calculating the setup and hiding it under the chador!

"Tell me you saw that!" I exclaimed. "It was like an optical illusion."

Arash rocked in his seat trying not to burst into laughter. "Oh! Wait! There's room for one more kid."

"What?"

"Believe me, you have not seen the power of these motors and the power of that chador babe!"

Babe? That was the first time he called me babe and with a British accent. This was a culture shock for sure. I suddenly felt closer to him than when he called me *azizam*. I felt awkward and more emotional than usual. Brush it off Shaghayegh. I reminded myself I was in Iran and in the hospital driveway. Get into the groove woman!

"Oh please, this is...well, this is just so damn funny," I said, and totally lost myself in a giggle fit. "And worse," I managed, gasping for breath, "that bike is a regular racer that barely has room for the driver!"

"Ah, it is multi-functional. Everything is multi-functional in Iran!" He watched me and moved closer to my innocence. Every time he joked and took another layer of my fears off my back I felt closer to him. I already wanted him, but this built up the sexual tension even more.

I jumped out of the car and told Arash I would call him "secretly" tonight. Or maybe not, because I might have to linger with my parents at the hospital, or even worse, if my dad knew I had lied the restrictions would begin as soon as I got home.

Time would tell.

I passed through the swishing entrance doors and headed for Aziz Joon's room.

Standing in the doorway, I peered in at the flock of people gathered around the bed. My heart sank to look at this.

Now I fully understood the term cacophony, because here it was. Multiple conversations in progress, plus a barrage of questions posed in various ways, with much repetition at my grandma. She sure pitied the lady in the second bed, although presently she looked anesthetized—or worse.

I stepped into the chaos, waved at Aziz Joon, my mom and dad, if they even noticed. This was more interesting than the motorbike situation. No easy task!

"*Salam*, Aziz Joon—" I began, but was immediately drowned out by the others. I would have to wait my turn and take in the action and the N amount of people that had fit into this hospital room. If only the gathered crowd would give me a break!

"Didn't the doctor have his beeper on?"

"Why?"

"*Mage mishe?*" (How could this happen?)

"So, you have asthma?"

Everyone was asking questions at the same time. How much could an old lady hear? And no one permitted her to answer any of them, and the funniest of all was that she was still in semi-anesthesia mode. That last was the funniest query, a total irrelevancy, since the patient was here because of asthma! Everyone knew that, even the motorbike people in front of the hospital! Well...maybe not them.

The whole thing sounded like a confused interrogation mixed with crazed paparazzi who'd left behind their microphones and had to shout. Nothing was in their minds but trying to support the patient to sleep or death!

I snuck closer, picking up that the husband of the knocked-out lady in the other bed now sat beside my mom. He had slowly gravitated towards the action-packed side of the room maybe to grab a pastry or be part of this chaos.

The room was filled with fresh flowers and pastries, much fingered and crumbled. I remained polite, learning that Aziz Joon was tolerating her guests. Some were family, some friends, some friends of my Aunt, and yet another fugitive from the other bedside! Another phenomenon I wasn't familiar with.

One guy blurted out, "Well, you are lucky! My arm is recently giving me a hard time!" Clearly in need of a good zapping, his wife cast him an evil eye.

Aunt Elahe, Arshia, Ghazaleh, and Bahareh were all there and were tolerating the visitation episode of my grandma's near-death experience. I also realized some of my distant cousins who were vacationing in Turkey and Cyprus (whose names I had forgotten) had hopped on the first plane upon hearing the news. I bet Aunt Elahe spread the news, her tongue was always working at the speed of light. But on a completely different note, that's family, and it was beautiful to have one, all here, dropping their gossip and conflicts to rush to her bedside. I felt the love. My father's family in New York were great too but this was such a different quality of love. Sincere, trusting, and compassionate. At that moment, this love lit my heart, and the pure reality and joy of it was awesome!

Abruptly my zone was violated when some distant family member leaned so close to speak to me that I got assaulted by their rancid breath, and I wanted badly to reach for a potent mint. Worse, I couldn't even understand half of what the woman was saying, and I feared asking her to repeat anything because I would pass out and require hospitalization due to another's reeking breath! All I did was nod politely, as if confirming whatever was being said and quickly turned away to avoid further questions. Geez!

Finally, I made my way over to my mom. "What in the world is this?" I asked so confidently I completely pushed my absence earlier in the day aside.

"Yes, all these flowers, pastries—I haven't had a single one—and family. Although I know they should be leaving soon. Oh god, I'm getting a headache."

"I don't doubt it, but imagine what Aziz Joon is thinking!" I said in a high tone possibly overhead by the others. Who cared? I didn't! That was a tad bit too much for someone that is half-conscious and just had a near-death experience.

The cute nurse who I thought Arshia had a crush on swished into the room with rubber-soled sneakers. Thank god! It wasn't only Arshia eyes she caught but the remaining testosterone in the room quieted down to observe her curves underneath the wimple and long coat.

"Okay," said the nurse with her sensual and half masculine voice, "visiting hours are over."

Another way of saying, "beat it, people!"

Now was the time to say goodbye, which would at minimum add another ten or fifteen minutes. A round of kisses followed by declarations of "hope she gets better" three or four times back and forth between them, then, on the actual way out, repeating that refrain to everyone still in the room and to each other.

At Aziz Joon's side, I lightly kissed her then smiled. I could see the reflection of her love smiling back at me, so pure. Looking in her eyes, I felt a particular beauty, and, even in a room this crowded, knew it thrived in everyone's heart.

Regarding her sweet, slightly troubled expression, I asked, "Do you have a dry mouth from all the explaining you did tonight?" I giggled, but knew it was difficult for her to talk. She was beat.

With a small grin she said, "Next time, I am going to have a board displaying Frequently Asked Questions from all these laymen citizens turned professors tonight!"

Seeing this animated sarcasm tugged a giggle exchange between me and I noticed Ghazaleh had lip-read us and was giggling from a distance too.

"So, what question should I ask that hasn't already been tossed at you, and is among your favorites?"

"How about the questions the nurses ask one another while changing my serum? 'So where did you get your eye tattoo? Or 'I might highlight my hair blonde, what do you think?'"

"Ha! Glad to see you haven't lost your sense of humor." I felt even closer to her. I bent over to give her a kiss goodbye because the Emperor signaled that we should leave.

Obeying Pappa!

Stepping out I glanced over my shoulder, saw her eyes moist with tears but her lips were open and smiling.

I left the room and was hoping my dad wouldn't bring up today and was also planning how I was going to call Arash tonight. He would probably stay up reading his newspaper to make sure I go to bed, or just keep the newspaper covering his face while I thought he was awake. Ha!

"How was today?" he asked while I slammed the car door shut.

"Good," I said, trying to sound neutral. I never lied and didn't know how to. So I customized my tone to a neutral Swiss woman.

He looked at me and I knew he knew that I had lied. The world came crashing down. I hated lying and now I was a liar. Why? Because I had gone on a fun excursion with my friend and boyfriend! Ugh! My father was my best guy friend and I hated to betray his trust. It wasn't like this in Brooklyn. I could go out with my friends and not lie or be worried about something as bullshit as this. It was this stupid environment that forced him to be so protective and also this stupid environment that forced me to lie. Domino effect.

Bet he was worried about how people would view and judge him, and consequently me being the daughter of such an Emperor, judge me. Or was it something I didn't understand. This was one of those times I wish I was in my bedroom in Brooklyn cuddled up with my *Baby-Sitters Club* books feeling freedom of thought, action, and opinion.

"Dad…" I began and looked at him.

Suddenly, he looked at me and cut me off saying, "Let's talk tomorrow, today was too long of a day. I didn't expect this from you."

Silence cut in between us, and once home, to my surprise, he brushed his teeth and marched straight to bed.

I had messed up, but it was my right and my life to go out and have a good time. In my opinion I had done nothing wrong and it was my dad's fault that I was forced to lie. Because he wasn't brave enough to stand up to society and say, "This is my daughter's life and I will support her, but also protect and guide her."

After my mental debate team also marched to bed I felt very tired and gravitated to Arash time.

I called him and we began our normal conversation combined with teasing, flirting, talking about our days, and lots of sensuality. I was getting good at it thanks to Arash! He eased my fear and told me to just be truthful.

"Iranian fathers are very strict because lots of guys are scumbags," he said.

"So does that mean you are one of them too?" I asked quickly.

"Well you do have a point," he laughed. "Don't think I am in the 'A' category though!" he said laughing back.

"I will let you know when you are transforming so you can clean up your act pronto," I said in a sensual tone.

"Deal."

"G'night, plus a wet kiss."

"Wet kiss," he answered, and I closed my eyes, stepping into a dream world.

13

The Interview

IN FARSI WE HAVE A SAYING: "Play, play, with the beard of the father also play." In my opinion, it meant "don't tickle with the tiger's tail," and now I was in the hot seat at breakfast in front of my dad. Going to school in the U.S. and living there for fifteen-plus years had not taken the traditional Iranian out of a man. I was being interrogated!

"Why did you lie to me?"

"Why do you say that?"

"Don't get smart with me. Why weren't you with your Aunt and with Elham?"

"Because you would have opposed if I told you I was with Elham and going to a barbecue."

"Why would I oppose? If I knew this girl and her parents and the rest of the people that were there, I don't want to imprison you," he said softly. "Listen Ms. Know-It-All, Tehran is a dangerous place if you deal with the wrong people, and I just want you to be safe and have fun."

"Dad, I didn't even know half the people at the party, and I know Elham is a good friend. You can't have total control over everything!"

"What if one of the people at the party would have taken advantage of you?" he said.

"Someone would have to invite that possibility. I don't hang out with rapists, dad!" I snapped back.

"I don't want to argue but I am serious and firm—next time you tell me. Not even your mom. I want to know the exact location, people, and I want to speak with Elham's parents to make sure we are both on the same page when our daughters go out!"

He said this and looked at me and made sure he was understood by looking into my eyes. I felt a rebellious feeling coming over me shouting that I would be the one to decide who is good and who is bad, that I would decide if I want to go or not! But I kept my mouth shut, knowing he did have a point. And so did I.

"I will, but I also need you to trust my judgment! I can decide if I should go or no!"

"Yes, you should beautiful, but know I am protecting you," his tone went down so softly that my rebellious feeling shrank and surrendered.

"Guys are guys and there are people of all walks of life in Tehran. I love you," and he kissed my cheek and left the kitchen for a meeting he had to go to.

"Call you mother at the hospital too, she slept in Aziz Joon's room last night."

"Got it," I said while I picked up the phone and called Arash first. This was an ideal time to speak with him in the daytime now that Popps was heading out for a meeting! Smileys!

196

Arash picked up surprised, and I just told him to keep near his phone and that I would call him as soon as the Emperor stepped out...in twenty!

He laughed and had to obey. He had no choice, he longed for my voice! Haha! After those five seconds I called the hospital and made it seem like my first time I had dialed the wrong number.

Aziz Joon was doing awesome and mom would be home later on. Perfect I thought; I could talk to Arash and slip out of the house for a made-up Italian class. I felt as if the conversation with my dad not more than thirty minutes ago was forgotten in the deep holes of my memory. The fear of him finding out my next trip was losing its color too. Yup, I knew that point was the point where I was losing my innocence and fear was loosening its grip on me. It was my life and I had the choice to decide who and where I wanted to go. I made the last call!

When I heard the door slam and heard my father's car engine roar down the street, I knew opportunity knocked. I called the person who I could laugh and have fun with. Arash picked up immediately.

"Just spoke with mom and Aziz Joon is a rockstar!" I said.

"See, I told you the doctors are the best here."

"No, my grandma just got lucky. Your ambulance drivers are idiots!" I said laughing. The joking exchange went back and forth until the story got boring.

Arash, drained now of laughter, confessed that if I ever came to harm due to some derelict ambulance driver, well, he would kill the man. I blushed, smiled, and surged with a range of emotions as if suddenly connected to an electrical outlet. I'm connected, all right, I thought. Connected to Arash. I felt him, wanted him, and missed him....

Word on the street had it that a girl must remain a virgin until marriage. I didn't understand the meaning of that. Why can't a girl explore her sexual side but with her boyfriend and with condom protection? If she isn't slutting around and making porn videos why does she have to save that virginity, which they made into such a delicate and sensitive situation, for the first and last guy she meets? That was really diving deep into it. In our culture, having a boyfriend was frowned upon! The whole sex vs. virginity notion had so many rules and regulations. Why? Because we were a country of taboo or a country of Islamic religion?

My Brooklyn brain was all right with it but now a newly born brain was realizing all this taboo and each question and situation had to have a fair fight with the Brooklyn brain! BTW, Brooklyn beat the crap out of the newly born brain which was a follower. Brooklyn brain was a leader!

Wasn't the whole point of life to live intuitively and organically? This is really bad to say but I felt like religion here laid down the law as opposed to one reaching the inner god within, which is the main point of religion. The manto covered my ass and hip curves, including my boob size, and the scarf or wimple covered my hair—which I should add is very voluminous!

So my questions here are these:

Are my parents limiting me because of this Islamic law? Because I'm sure my dad messed around before getting married BIG TIME!

OR

Are they limiting me because of what my family would say if they knew I had a boyfriend?

OR

Would my parents think it's all right if we had stayed in Brooklyn or just brushed it off? We left a bit too soon for me to figure the last one out! This question will remain a mystery, but my gut tells me it would have been the same story as now. Only now, I see it more clearly because I'm on the other side.

I think if they found out someone wasn't a virgin it was equivalent to betraying the Emancipation of Proclamation. A spotless maiden walking the streets of Tehran that had a hymen and is expected to bleed on their wedding night as proof they are pure. What if the girl was born without a hymen (totally possible)? Rumor also had it that some of the more wealthy women did hymen-repair surgery before marriage. This whole story was over analyzed and confused me. It was blatant ignorance in my point of view! This made me watch the sex scenes and rewind them more often, since it was illegal.

I always thought that could in a way be nice, but a woman must be ready in other ways than sexually. Either way, I had no intention of sleeping with Arash. I wasn't even prepared, but trusted intuition would tap my shoulder when the time was right.

"By the way," Arash said, "I wanted to tell you something."

"Yes?"

"I have some inside scoop from the TV station."

"Um, what does that have to do with me? But please do share."

"Well, there's a guy I know. A sports reporter. He told me the English section is looking for a sports reporter, and you speak fluent English and have the time now so why not give it a shot? It sounds interesting."

I nearly fell over. "What? That is out of the blue. No way!"

"What do you mean, no way?"

"I mean, what will they think of me? What if they do a background check?"

"And so what if they do? This is just a job!"

"Well, for starters I am not religious the way most newscasters are on TV here. And anyway, I would suck! I have never done this stuff before!"

I was glad no one was home. I was excited, shocked and loud. I could hear some fright in my tone too. I felt a wave of energy thinking about it but was scared if they found out we were not religious, meaning we drank, didn't wear a head covering in parties, and well *moi*, had a boyfriend and frequently thought about having sex with him in my head!

"Again, so what? Then you would suck, but give it a try. If you get the job you can say 'Arash said so,'" he joked, but in a serious voice.

"Always the charmer, aren't you?" I said while laughing, knowing that I was convinced.

"Arash, for crying out loud this is the Islamic Republic of Iran broadcasting. I don't like the sound of the first word in that phrase! Aside from the chicks appearing on its program dressed modestly with semi-veiled appearances. My whole way of living is the opposite of religious, cultural and even some national values! Just a disclaimer...that still means I respect it though," I continued *again* frustrated, but was willing to dive in the deep end of this ocean.

TV newscasters in Iran had a specific dress code and that didn't include Victoria Secret Angel bras nor the men wearing the new J.Crew look. I didn't think I would fit in even if I had to pretend and lie again in a different manner. So now in addition to my father I was also pretending. This whole experience was getting better and better! I wanted to try and see what this world was all about and how pretentious or unpretentious everyone was.

I had a good support system if anything went sour: watching *Scooby-Doo* cartoons and listening to MC Hammer to get into the soul of Brooklyn again. Oh, I also had my stubbornness, which was the Queen of Fire. Word.

Although self-confident, I definitely didn't know how to fit into a crowd that wore chadors, burkas almost covering their eyes, and most likely were way older than me. I barely managed in school, and ditched half the time but, since my grades were high, no one really objected. "How am I going to fit this into my Italian class schedule?"

"Stop asking all these questions and just dive into it. If you don't get it that means your class schedule doesn't fit into it."

I was ready to roll the dice, although it seemed irrational at the same time. I always coordinate things and knowingly prepped, while Arash just winged it half the time and things usually turned out right. Was this an Iranian thing or a guy thing? He was a good businessman, and most businessmen are very intuitive so, for the time being, I put him in that category. I wondered if all the girls had the same relationship I had discovered with Arash.

My cousin Bahareh was still in cyberspace going back and forth with five or maybe six guys to see which might in the future provide her with the most comfort. And then there was my favorite Jew, Elham, who could date Muslim guys but couldn't marry one. Tough times man! To see Mrs. Jew and Mr. Muslim married happily ever after would require a miracle. This goes for Iran and the stories I had heard from Los Angeles and New York. I didn't understand where the confusion was. It was just acceptance and irritated me that both sides had such views.

I agreed with Arash's offer to connect with his friend and move forward with the interview, but first I had to tell the fam.

• • •

"I am so proud of you for making this decision!" shouted my mother.

My father had the "this is my daughter and she is going to be famous one day" look on his face.

Geez—it was just a job in the Islamic Republic of Iran and I was just exploring but at this point I didn't even open up that door.

"Yeah, so I thought since I have some time before college classes start I should see if this is a path I want to explore with an actual job."

"Brilliant! I know you will reach high places beautiful!" said my dad. "By the way who gave you this idea?" he continued.

My face went white then black then my lips magically proclaimed together, "Elham."

"A good girl," said my dad. "Helping your friends out and trying to help them find their way. I really like her...so thoughtful."

Elham was scoring points and getting credit on behalf of Arash. I had no problem with that since I got to hang out more this way. More Elham credit meant more Arash time too since I could use her existence to go out on a date with Arash! Ha! My god...one simple lie was making a monster out of me!

A couple of positive things came out of this: my parents thought I had already become a celebrity in my not-yet-determined job status, and Elham received the gold star from an unknown place in a Super Mario Brothers game.

•••

I had no idea what to wear, was a bit nervous, and had no idea how my prospective supervisor would view.

After all, this was the country's national broadcast agency and it was federal. No one could be more likely to be strict about my hair showing, brows being trimmed to perfection, or an inappropriate smile, than their fully-loaded Islamic black burka-long crow sister department, or more simply said, the HR office. Even though I had never actually interned anywhere, I didn't fear any human resource office. But knowing my own level of functionality, I acted in accordance with what looked or felt right in any situation. The rest would work itself out. Things always worked themselves out. Or maybe sometimes they don't, but I probably learned that from Arash.

After getting my attire on, I ventured out. I cabbed it up Vali-Asr Street, the longest street in Tehran. The heat was terribly oppressive, but the driver refused to switch on the AC. This was torment! Who would do this? My wimple, formally arranged and tied, stuck tight to my head. God, how can females work like this? I have an important job interview!

I never wore makeup, so fear of running mascara wasn't among my present worries. Finally, the cab driver said, "I will turn the AC on, but the fare will be doubled." Was this guy out of his mind? The AC was part of the car, right? I could smell the guy sweating, and quite well—thank you very not much! And there was so much traffic...I would pay triple if necessary.

Long story short, I accepted. I had to! I was dripping bullets!

This guy was trying to feed his family, or buy drugs, or fill up his tank, or feed Mr. Sweating Alone, or something...but I had to have that AC running.

My world flipped—from traffic, crazy smelly mania, to a beautiful world of burkas, unshaved cranky taxi drivers, and some who were outside constantly swearing. But even they were beautiful. I needed to feel good. After all, I was headed to somewhere completely out of my comfort zone.

On arrival (grateful to soon be out of the reeking hot cab), I took a quick look in the mirror to make sure even the roots of my hair were covered.

Picking up on my nervous fussing, the driver said, "They are not that bad. Don't worry. They are human, after all."

I managed a flash of a smile and answered softly, "*Merci.*"

The driver wasn't a bad dude after all, and I brushed away my previous negative thoughts about him. But he would probably run the AC until getting another passenger who's burnin' up while he's cooling down!

I paid the double charge and climbed out—without sweat.

• • •

At the main entrance, the security check took forty-five minutes: fifteen to confirm I was registered, and the next thirty minutes were more brutal than the third-degree exercised in top-notch security at airports!

After stepping slowly through the scanner, I was subjected to a body search by, of course, the dreaded black crows. Although no guns, ammo, or swords (anything went here, cold or hot weapons) were found on me, they did find an old mascara and lipstick in my handbag.

"What are these?" demanded one black crow.

Why do you care? was my initial thought, but I quickly swallowed and replied, "A mascara and lipstick."

"Why do you have it in your bag *Khanoom?*"

Khanoom was such an annoying way of saying *Miss.* I hated it!

Because I'm a mature female and might need it, I thought, but dared not say. "No reason, it was left in my bag." I used a low tone, hoping to indeed sound very low key.

"These items will stay with us, as this is not a makeup-driven environment," one said with a fierce dark glare.

"Okay."

I saw traces of innocence in both women, and some measure of neglect. They surely must suffer from being deprived of male attention. Did they ever have fun? Was a kiss ever on the agenda? If so, what kind? When? Where?

They urged me through security and I was on my way. I couldn't help my genuine curiosity about them. Did the crows ever make love? Or feel cool sea water caress their toes? Smile at the sunset, or have a glass of wine under the stars with the man who pleased them? How did they make love? With sheets in between their legs? Obviously they were open with and supported one another, enjoyed each other's company, but I sensed they had also been caged. Or maybe it was due to poor education or simple lack of social awareness, they had not opened up. I felt sorry for them...and then suddenly my mind wondered "did they have sexual fantasies?" But I came back to reality and the grounds I was walking on.

This probably came from patriotism, or because I felt their pain in a way they themselves could not access. Despite that they definitely knew pain—they were still black crows, and would have detained me another forty-five minutes had they found the lip gloss they'd missed in one pocket. Even had I applied it, I doubted my gloss would stimulate any man looking at me or my lips.

With an inner smile I mentally prepared for my interview. How hard could it be? I decided it best to remain calm and centered, listen, and not rebel against the interviewer in the event of disagreement, which was my usual route. Debate to the end! But not in a country with no rules. Heads up.

Striding through the building, I found it surprisingly well designed, even tasteful, unlike some other government or city buildings with their bland colors and anonymous, often dehumanizing interiors.

The place hummed with quiet efficiency; subdued conversations, various clutches of workers drinking tea (the coffee equivalent in Iran), running back and forth with tapes, and a few 4x4 patrols prepping for shoots. All regular stuff you would see in any TV studio, except that some wore burkas and others long black chadors in addition to burkas and mantos. I wondered how they survived, even with constant air-conditioning! Double- chocolate Islamic crows!

A few stood outside smoking cigarettes. Normal stuff. Nothing to be afraid of. So far. A flight of stairs led me to the International English section besides the Sports unit. I knew the people in Sports were considered the coolio sorts, laid-back, and it appeared so. All were guys and all were hot! I approached and they glanced up from work with surprise on their faces. Even my formal attire couldn't hide the "fear of the mystery" in my eyes. But I think these guys were looking at me like I was a chick. Here was a chance for them to flirt with me, step over their regular borders, as if ready to grab a drink and drop some coins in a jukebox.

Either it was my effect, or these men were feeling similar to Alcatraz prisoners! One man stood and beamed a smile and obvious interest. "Can we help you?"

I halted. "Yes. Where is the English sector? I am here for a job interview." I hoped that sounded as delicate as intended. Probably women here should not, or do not, talk to men. Later I could discover they do, but without much eye contact. I'm talking about the ones at the station.

"Please sit here," he indicated a chair, "and let me grab the individual who can help you better. But you are in the right section." He smiled with such a courteous and charming face and his voice was so sensual and noble. I felt they were truly a team. Together everyone formed a kind of logo, self-contained.

From my comfy seat I saw the office equipment appeared new, the furniture modern and high quality. Some of the guys still gazed at me like a chick. They needed more young girls in this joint for sure.

At the sound of footsteps, I turned. There stood my interviewer, smiling as though at a familiar face. He greeted me quietly and let me to a space not too far away.

The dialogue began in Farsi, and transformed slowly into English. I maintained an even, candid line: No, I had not done any journalism or reporting, nor conducted interviews using these methods and on top of that my major in college was Italian literature. The only plus I had going for me was my fluent, without-a-Farsi-accent English. I spoke and knew very good English and that could help the station go up in ranking and help in lots of correspondence and communications. Honestly, in English I thought I was so well versed I could be hired as their top replacement. But that is another topic.

The interview was short and flowed smoothly, yet oddly did not include the usual questions: What are your past experiences? What do you plan on pursuing in the coming years? He didn't even explain the job description. Was this really a job interview or was he taking it easy on me because I had connections? He ended with: "You come from the U.S. and would be a great asset here. The rules here might be different from what you are adapted to, but everyone here is helpful. Just keep up with the team and don't talk a lot, meaning don't give your opinion too much, especially on political matters. The head director is educated and was brought up in the U.S., full Iranian though, and is buddies with the Islamic HR head, so you don't have to worry about much!" He smiled towards the end as if he was telling me "everyone takes their chill pill in this section."

What a mouth full.

I wondered what (other than wearing layers of clothing without smelling) could be so scary about this place. Perfume being out of the question, I made sure (as I was pointed out today) to use deodorant to at least absorb underarm perspiration.

We stood, and the interviewer added that someone would contact me if I should get this job, almost as an afterthought. In fact, this sentence seemed the only part resembling a well-rounded interview.

I thanked the man for the opportunity, but reminded myself to not shake his hand. Just say goodbye.

On my way out, I noticed the room full of applicants wearing heavy-duty wrapped burkas, chadors, with a few girls sporting full-blown moustaches and leafy eyebrows, all in line for the interview.

I had come through the wrong entrance and landed upside down in the Sports section! It was that or I would have found myself crammed against moustaches, eyebrows, and subjected to awkward conversations.

Here sat the Sports guys and like before, they locked laser-like glances onto me. I felt awkward. These guys hadn't seen a cute girl in ages! I thanked them and they bid me goodbye with a please-stay-longer-we-need-estrogen-in-the station vibe. I couldn't help but giggle.

It occurred to me that, had I been stuck into the box of applicants, it would have meant they'd labeled me with a big bold red NO. I felt I was different and it showed in my attitude and demeanor. I wasn't fearful the same way they were fearful. In other words, I didn't give a shit if I didn't get the job, but fearful because this country was so different from New York!

I knew I had rebelliousness, innocence and an honesty that was hard to find. Might as well add confidence to the list since I had stated them so clearly here!

So now, I had to find a phone. I asked the sports dude if I could make a phone call. He showed me the closest phone and whispered very softly while looking in a completely different direction, "the phone lines are all controlled." Then assuming a different tone as if he was saying what he was saying from the beginning, "Dial one, and then your number."

Immediately I sensed that those here could see my layers, and that I was different. This didn't cause me any discomfort, because I felt connected within while on the outside gave nothing away. It was good not to appear awkward. I knew the personal cameras behind everyone's eyes taped my every word and move and stored the kind of evidence that might be shared with HR. Especially the Islamic version of it. The big eagle eye babe!

Plucking the phone from its rest, I dialed Arash's number and, when he answered, said, "Hi, dad. Could you please come and pick me up? Yes. The interview is over." Surprised, Arash didn't immediately grasp this was role-play, but clicked when he heard my voice and his being "Dad."

This was as original as it could get! I must be getting the hang of things in Iran, and role-play was one of them—it came in handy. I was having a little fun to get around the truth in Iran!

He cleared his throat. "Yes, *dokhtaram, hatman.*" Yes, daughter dearest, coming.

He choked back laughter.

"*Merci,*" I said, trying to keep it inside, and hung up. Actually, everyone was trying to keep it inside because they read in between the lines. They were all around my age or a bit older, with the same outlook and frame of mind. They looked charming, naughty and fun. But they all had a difference from me: they were making money and needed their jobs.

You must earn, so metaphorically sell your soul to the company if you have different values and beliefs. Act stupid, eyes locked onto the computer screen. Keep your comments to yourself...exactly like the large corporations spanning the globe.

An alarming thought popped into my mind: Where the hell are we supposed to meet? No! I can't believe neither of us mentioned it! We got caught up in the role-play charade! A rendezvous in front of the TV studio couldn't happen. Cameras all over and yes, this kind of relationship was illegal, as if a drug dealer were meeting with a buyer to buy narcotics.

But lightning struck—I knew where we could meet. And I was off.

• • •

The restaurant where we habitually met was fortunately close by. I decided to just wing it. He was smart enough to guess where I'd be.

And the waiting began.

I ordered my favorite mini-pizza, the *makhloot*. Far from your norm Italian pizza, this Iranian-created mutant smorgasbord came topped with sausage, bologna (*Halal*-type since this was the Islamic Republic), bell peppers, onions, mushrooms, corn, and, if desired, practically any other vegetable, organic or otherwise. The toppings were so densely applied that they overloaded the crust, which seesawed when picked up! The whole thing was probably higher in calories than a traditional pepperoni and mozzarella deep dish pizza. I loved this!

I wanted Arash here, but maybe he could hold off long enough for me to eat and then find me! I didn't want to share my pizza.

14

Job—Check!

AFTER ABOUT FORTY MINUTES OF waiting and munching, I heard a voice behind me. "I knew you would be here!"

Arash grinned and blew a kiss from afar, then savored the warm aromas of meat and cheese. He stepped closer, halted at the table. "How was the interview?"

Trying to handle the loaded pizza, I said, "I have no idea! It was not as frightening as I had imagined. The people were just normal."

Arash observed my obvious enjoyment of the meal and gave a kind of wise-guy smile. "They accepted you."

"What?"

"You heard me. And by the way, *tarof nakoni han*!"

It was just like him to joke around by invoking the Iranian system of sharing-but-not-really-wanting-to-share. I knew he must have talked to his friend (and the main connection), the oil greasing the wheels of business in Iran.

I nearly choked. "Are you serious?"

He nodded. "Your first job is with the Islamic Republic of Iran Broadcasting."

I pushed back into the chair, as if moved by the power of the words themselves. It was so surprising that just because I spoke fluent English they had hired me. I wasn't even in college yet and I just had landed a job as a reporter in the *main news agency in Iran*! The disconnect left my jaw hanging!

I was scared, excited, and wanted to jump up across the table to grab Arash and kiss him and loudly give thanks to the Lord. It was a big job for a first-timer but the fact that they had accepted me as opposed to all the other girls, who were dressed more religiously and "properly," baffled me.

Arash was looking at me with adoration and it really made me blush.

"You made all of this happen. It's such a big shift and a new experience. It's exciting for me and frightening at the same time. I mean, I'm a gal that doesn't even know what she wants. The only thing I knew I wanted was…you know…to become a dance choreographer!" I said giggling. "Then studying Italian literature to get the folks off my back, and now literally working at Channel 6 in Tehran with a paycheck! This life is a roller coaster!" I continued. "But you will be rewarded according to what you have done, Dear Knight!" I said this in English because it sounded weird in Farsi.

"What? I love rewards!" he said with sincere charm.

"Rewards are always better when brought to life, rather than stated with words." Flirtation changed my voice and brought me to more giggles. I didn't know why I giggled so much these days. It was almost nonstop.

Wow! Through Arash's efforts I had secured a high position— and I wasn't even nineteen yet! Inexperienced at practically everything but speaking English, but totally hyped to learn the culture, the world, what I liked...and best of all to have a guy I could really rely on. I still couldn't believe it was real. "What do they pay, you think?"

"Who cares? But for your age it will be a lot of dough for you! This may also open up some career path doors, since you have no idea where you are headed!" he said laughing. To be totally honest I concurred! Was it this country that was derailing me or did it just have a different method of functioning? If I were in Brooklyn I would have at least taken some college classes to see what I liked, or maybe pursued dance. But I wasn't so...delete button!

"Hey, I am an academic of Italian literature and a romantic at heart." The excitement had hijacked my thoughts and emotions. I was flying high. "By the way," I added, "take some pizza—you know I'm not in the *tarof* business."

And Arash joined the fun. Even though he had gotten up in the middle of work, he wanted to be here to share the good news and spend some time with me. He was surprised I had called him from the TV studio, where he knew everything was monitored, and realized something very deep was developing between us. I felt shy. I felt he was helping me know my value and understand love. I made Iran much more *hejab*-friendly for me.

•••

My world changed. I was so job-news-focused, while also going to Italian classes and having a secret love relationship.

Three aspects of life, seeds differently—completely—designed for me in this country where I had to express them so differently. From Brooklyn to Tehran; day to night; black to white. I had zip-lined from the Brooklyn Bridge to the Azadi Tower. Two cultures, two corporations using differing means for oiling the machine...manipulating people and connecting.

I felt like I was cracking. Layers of my soul ripening while diving into an ocean of change and its shock wave. The best part was that I felt like I was in a walking coma, so I wasn't completely knocked out with all this newness.

My agenda was booked: classes some mornings, and this job was from 2 to 6ish in the evenings. Arash picked me up from class, we had our lunch date, and then he dropped me off a block from the IRIB station. A block away prevented anyone on their block from seeing me, and anyone who saw me on the block while I was being dropped off was written off as my bad luck.

The job was fun and awkward at the same time. I was a sports editor and reporter, which was weird for a female in this country. In Iran the sports section was male dominated. The country was mostly male dominated but when it came to sports usually everywhere was male dominated. The exception here was that it was so male dominated that females weren't allowed to go to stadiums either! How was I suppsed to do my job if I couldn't interview male athletes in the stadium? This group included interns, editors, reporters, and any other person with estrogen! That was ridiculous! Watching the game live and up front was only for male eyes and the *Komiteh*, who prevented the "estrogens" from attending matches.

This meant war! Blood boiled to my eyes when I heard this! Rumor had it on the street that some females protested and others snuck into the stadium dressing up as guys and putting on fake moustaches. If the game was going on I preferred the latter because I doubt I would be able to convince them in time to watch the game.

On a completely different note, now we were dealing with issues of identity. After Iran's revolution in 1979, women were forbidden from entering any sports venues, but it was Khatami's time and these policies were loosened a bit, although still in place. The whole dilemma was a clash between the Supreme Leader and the government. The Supreme Leader was calling the shots!

Brushing that aside I got along well with my supervisor and made friendships with the camera guy, microphone guy, and driver, and realized they were simply regular people living an irregular lifestyle. Irregular because their public display differed from what occurs behind closed doors. They weren't what they appeared. They were Muslim, yes, but the kind who converse with women and look them in the eyes and of course, work together. Completely human! The guys were cool and we laughed with each other, but they showed respect and knew their boundaries. The two worlds of sports and English fused for this little editor despite some parts that I hated—but that wasn't related to these peeps.

Portions of my job that I loved and kept me happy:

1. The people were awesome, funny, and humble.

2. The food was not good but the company overlooked this quality—number 2 also points to number 1.

3. My supervisor was very handsome and easygoing—number 3 also points to number 1.

4. It was an eye-opening experience as far as culture! Damn…living as a civilian was one thing, but working alongside "federal employees in a fed atmosphere" was a dive in the deep end.

5. It was super good money.

There was a mix of people; some traditional, some religious, some non-religious. The traditional were cool people too and the heavy-duty burka didn't make them dark. The catch was that the tolerance level for many was different. Some were bad-asses and macho underneath the beard or the burkas! In fact, they had the best jokes in the workplace! But the place had some gaps and the cameras and controlled telephones were sure to catch everything! Everyone was aware not to say anything about the government and the testosterone was very careful of how they interacted with the estrogens. No dating permitted on site! At least that was the rule on the surface of things.

I kept to myself and interacted with my group and the Farsi sports group where I felt more accepted than other places. My responsibilities started out for the most part with lame stuff like logging tapes and taking this tape from this department to the other; I was delivery girl! But I also edited sports updates and was slowly reporting on topics after the political reporter delivered his news. But sometimes I tagged along with the main guy reporter when he wanted to get an interview outside of a stadium with a badminton player, chess wizard or weightlifter (who I thought must hang out with their cousins, the sumo wrestlers, also big as mansions).

Thanks to being an on-air reporter the HR rules were super tight and I had to obey.

I noticed football in Iran was the second religion! One practiced by the entire populace; a religion that unified the nation. Maradona, Ronaldo, and Luis Figo were worshipped here, faces splashed across newspapers and dealing for their rookie cards despite them not being Iranian was an auction! Local footballers had their own following and were treated like rock stars! Girls (but not me) were crazy for them, even though forbidden to express it, and guys would make you their Superman, buy your dinner, and even invite you into their home.

Football was more popular than the Super Bowl, World Series, and NBA playoffs combined. FIFA and the World Cup were followed to the bone, and when word spread that Iran might be entering the Cup if they eliminated Australia, the whole country blocked out their schedule for that time-slot. They actually reserved the entire week for football worship!

Sometimes during the evening, I saw kids playing football in back alleys or on the streets. They improvised goals and nets with round stones and kicked around red and white striped balls purchased for five cents from any grocery store. This was far from commercial standards, so the kids would buy two, tear one open and stuff the other inside. And there you had it: a pregnant football! Harassed by little men scattering in the streets (thank god they didn't have to wear mantos) they kicked that little invention toward stone-marked goals.

The only difference between street, no-rules football, and the professional game was the amazing-*er* passion these kids had. Wearing homemade jerseys in red or blue representing favorite footballers, they mimicked whatever worked to score. In Tehran either you had blue blood or red, colors of the national team, or you weren't part of the club—period. Many even bonded with their team color, perhaps leading to long-lasting relationships! Either you sang your anthem, "Blue is color of the sky," or "Red is the color of blood," and "it's the color of the flag," or you were no fun. Either you were a *Pirouzi* (red) or an *Esteghlal* (blue) fan. Two arch rivals.

Once I saw on TV a Japanese animation series, *Captain Tsubasa* (known nationwide as the Footbalistha cartoon), broadcast daily in the summer. Of course, being a cartoon-lover, I would watch these back to back. Football was in the air and in your veins; a contagious fever that spread through the country.

In fact, when there was a match announcement people left work early and, if necessary, bought black-market tickets. Some traveled from far provinces, pitched tents outside the stadium, or simply slept in their cars to wake into a dream come true. A dream pointing toward a "bloody victory" or a "sky blue victory." During these games the city appeared dead, as though it was the location for some apocalyptic science-fiction film. Considering the density of Tehran's traffic, this was a complete miracle! Some fans seemed more interested in the before and after of the game than the main dish itself. Some wagered, even though betting was forbidden. But who the hell cared? It was fun! These bets usually involved nothing more than food or something equally common, rather than hoopas of mullah.

In other words, I found that football was the body and soul of these players, and the people projected onto them and the game all of their will, love, passion, sadness, loss, and hope...more and more hope, and lots of sweat and blaring horns.

• • •

The day arrived, with Iran two victories away from their first World Cup qualification game and facing Australia. The game would be held in Azadi Stadium in Tehran.

All the men were prepared to go to the stadium or climb its walls if necessary, and all the women would have their homes and meals prepared in advance of the game. Housewives put aside chores, and predictably the men would not even notice. The game was more important than the Royal Wedding, or the inauguration of the first female (assuming one day there would be one) president.

And this lady (*moi*) was ready to tag along with one of the reporters for support and of course, extra help! I really wanted to get into the venue.

Although Azadi Stadium seated 100,000 people and was considered the fourth largest football arena in the world, it had no room for females! Issues in this country were frustrating. I didn't get it. Girls and women were big supporters yet banned from entering. What possibly could be the reason for this harsh treatment and this rule? Excessive hormonal cursing? Or maybe the men lost control after seeing a goal and wanted to French it out. I thought long and hard, and all I could come up with was: wear a hat and speak in a thick voice, and *maybe* you'll pass for man!

A classmate actually had done this and gotten away with it. Obviously she had no boobs, and after cutting her long braids and splashing on men's cologne and looking hairy, she thickened her voice, assumed a hard, tired expression, and dazzled her way in. She claimed that some of the guys were fooled. Whatever.

"Some girls really work their mind and do the craziest stuff," I told my dad, a football fanatic who always tried to make it to the stadium with Arshia. Arshia would get the tickets and off they were in their red Piroozi jerseys.

Arshia gave me this sole piece of advice: "Stop plucking your eyebrows for a month or two, and then you won't even need to thicken your voice!"

It was true even though it was laugh-out-loud. Some girls were hairy, and without the rescuing tweezers, the stadium might have had many male estrogen participants, if you know what I mean!

I really wanted to get in and even though I came to work without any makeup, the reporter refused to take me with him. He said there was no point, that they would find out and he would be screwed. He was right, but I wanted in. Not even my American passport would help me here because the teams playing were both Iranian!

Rejected by all nice professional federal employees to hide me somewhere and take me into the stadium, I decided on an alternative plan: go solo! I called Arash to let him know, and he harshly opposed, "What! You will be walking into a rough, tough, mean, dirty, spitting-machine of a crowd!"

"Can't be that bad, I mean, I always went to Madison Square Garden, and it was all right."

"You wouldn't last an hour. That is how rough it can get."

"I am going." I couldn't be more firm on the matter.

I knew that he knew I wouldn't back down. Arash agreed to at least pick me up and provide a higher view and a clearer perspective before I drifted off into something I thought of as a dream.

"Can I go with you?" He asked.

"Are you trying to unconvince me?" Whatever that meant.

"Yes, but with you I won't win, so let me come and drive you there. Please."

Since we both knew how stubborn we both were, I agreed. Anyway, I was a little bit scared that it could be dangerous.

Soon we were on our way to west Tehran towards Azadi Stadium.

• • •

The streets and entire area surrounding the stadium thrummed with crowds and vehicles. I could not see a woman, not even the black crows, and felt weird and awkward being the only one—but excited to be present at such a historic event!

I glanced at Arash. "How can we get in? Any ideas?"

"You can't. This place is only for testosterones, so you, *azizam*, are a black sheep in this particular family. And by the way you already know that."

"So this is how you were going to take me?" I said, pretending to be upset and curious.

"I said if I can *accompany* you, not take you to the game," he said with a grin. He fixed me with a stern gaze. "You don't understand how heavily it is banned. Meaning not allowed, against the law, illegal!"

What more could he say? Either I was willfully ignorant, or simply could not understand. He had driven me here so I could see the testosterones alongside HIM!

Buses nearing the stadium brimmed with extreme fans, horns blaring at clumsy drivers or simply because they could. Arash shuddered imagining what would happen had I taken a bus to the game. Not only would I have suffered isolation, but a barrage of insults on the order of "I want you!" or "You are mine tonight" or "Hey, how much do you charge?" or "Do you accept coupons?" There would be no limit to the depth of disrespect and awkwardness. So it had been, would be always, for years.

"So we're not allowed inside the stadium," I repeated. I just couldn't digest it. I had always gone to see the Knicks or Rangers at Madison Square Garden and this was absolutely stupid.

"Not allowed," he repeated.

"And again, we are not allowed inside the stadium?"

Arash clenched his jaw. He was probably wondering why I didn't get this.

"Then why do they have sports reporters? What's my purpose?" I said completely annoyed.

"To report on stuff going inside the stadium and reporting on football is def not one of the them. Now you know you can't go inside a stadium!" he said chuckling.

I shook my head as if denying the entire reality. "But if football is the most beloved sport in Iran, and the first on the sports line-up of stories to cover, why am I banned from entering a stadium to watch a game?"

I was a reporter and all the reporters were stacking up in the van to shoot the story, but I soon realized they all were men. So bringing the female reporter was completely out of the question. It was intolerable.

"Because," he whispered with a giggle, "you are special, and can do other duties of the sports section better." That was a spray of cold water on my frustration!

I glared at him. "Am I logically understanding all the backward things you just explained clearly?"

"To a logical backward comprehension, check," he said smiling broadly, and gripped my hand.

I laughed and favored him with that adorable, charming smile. "I need a drink, but that would be banned and backward, no?"

Arash absorbed the words with relish. "How about you come over to my place, we order some wine from the illegal guy, and watch the game at home?" And he might give me a big fat hickey! No!

But I felt a rush of excitement; I wanted to be with him. Not merely because of his patience and understanding, but for helping me moderate this craziness. He was Tylenol to this mental craze! So the Emperor knew I was at work and, with the game starting, was undoubtedly distracted—although it didn't take much for me to be caught on his radar!

This was big. My first time at Arash's house. "Okay," I said, not knowing what to expect. We were going to be alone. All alone for the first time. No Bahareh, no Elham. The football game was the third wheel this time! Ha! No one would even think about looking for a boy and girl, alone, in a black Patrol—the hip car—cruising the streets.

I wondered how it would be, how he would be. I trusted him, of course, and knew he wouldn't hurt me. I was a virgin, a big thing in Iran. Everyone *had* to stay a virgin until wedlock! It sounded so medieval! Otherwise the dude would sniff the flower and the bees would be left without nectar! Given this, how did one discover their sexual desires? In school I always overheard the girls sewing the curtain in cheap clinics, and doctors who were willing to do just that; actually recreating virginity! The curtain doctor!

Being a virgin didn't represent a life choice. It was choosing a life. But this was simply another piece added to the fun jigsaw puzzle of my life. Understanding female entry ban to the stadium was a Sudoku puzzle.

•••

We parked in the garage, climbed out of the Patrol, and headed up as if married or something, talking and teasing all the way up the elevator.

Arash's apartment was well designed and decorated, telling me a lot about his likes and character. "My humble home," he said grinning.

I scanned the place. It had a definite sense of atmosphere and feeling, clearly arranged by an organized mind with an understanding of fine art beyond mere appreciation. Traits usually not found in one man.

Arash noticed my interest. "I collect most of the art on business trips, and must pay a hefty tax just to bring them into the country. A crime, that tax—it should go to the artist."

I agreed completely. There were some fine pieces here, definitely out of the reach of most living in Iran, with its ever-worsening economy.

Arash stepped closer. "Do you want to shower?" What in the world did *that* mean? Was he showing me his perverted side or London side?

But enough...I trusted him.

224

All the stuff the girls said about being careful around these guys, how they first charmed then manipulated you into doing their bidding...well, I wanted to dispose of such notions. "What does that mean?" I asked with attitude.

Quick and calm, he replied, "Relax. It's hot, and I thought you might want to shower after taking off that wimple and manto."

The attitude stayed. "Well, why don't you turn the AC on?"

"It is on, but will take a while to cool this place. Relax, I didn't mean anything by it!" He gave the space a noncommittal wave, as if saying, "look how big it is. It'll take a few to cool!"

"Do you want *sharbat* instead of wine? The illegal guy is probably watching the game too, so we'll save him the trouble of coming over during this football frenzy!"

"Yes, please, that works better. It's so hot! And I am *not* taking a shower my first time in your place!"

A cool, fruity drink was just the ticket, as well as a symbol of Arash's hospitality. My favorite high-calorie, high-sugar drink was also an antidote to dehydration! Arash prepared the drinks, and we crashed on the couch to watch some action-packed football, and bask in the low hum of air-conditioning.

"How are you liking the job?" he asked.

"It has its ups and down but one piece I like is reporting. Maybe reporting will be my future path."

"As a career?"

"Yup! Maybe if we go back to New York I could do sports reporting the legit way."

"It's difficult for a female to have a sports reporter career here. But we do have female reporters. It's definitely there."

"I don't know. Sometimes I wish I could take off to New York again where I didn't have to deal with all this discrimination. It really irritates me—and I don't say that's because I'm a feminist!"

Somewhere in my heart I dreamed of going back and getting rid of all this frustration. The way of life in Iran was so different from Brooklyn and everything was so hard for some odd reason.

"For you it's odd, but people who live here are used to it. They protest here and there but the day I see change is the day I see you put aside your stubbornness!" he said laughing.

"Hey! You need a slap!"

"I'm all cheeks babe!"

I slapped him softly and kissed him with finesse. The Yin and Yang meet.

Iran tied with Australia, and the crowd roared. "Listen," I shouted.

We could hear scattered shouts and jeers and comments through the floor, out of windows, and even from the streets below repeatedly saying, "Iran goal, goal Iran, *ey val Iran, sheere Iran*," all meaning "Iran scored ONE goal" but the *sheere* was funny. That meant lion! Iran roars or something like that!

Arash laughed. "Everyone has magically transformed into a sports announcer and patriotic follower because of this game. But no one can say it better than you," he said ignoring the noise and pulling me into his arms.

Taking advantage of the situation, I wanted to be part of the action so I jumped to my feet and started shouting as well. It was bound to attract attention and as long as it wasn't the Emperor's I was fine. Oh, forgot about the *Komiteh* cops and black crows. But from the window I could see even the *Komiteh* cops and black crows became *cool* and part of the club.

"Maybe there should be many games like this!" I said while downing my sour cherry *sharbat*. "We could head out and make out more often!"

"*If* we could make it this far," said Arash softly.

I felt happy and safe with him. He made no additional attempt for foreplay in the deep end. I leaned and looked into his charming but mischievous eyes. He looked back and said, "I know what's in your head, but it's all good. I enjoy our time together, but I want to be with you when the time is right."

What did he mean? Marriage? I wasn't even thinking about marriage! "You mean sex?" Did I say that cautiously enough?

Arash narrowed his eyes, trying to figure out this tangled web. "Yes. It's taboo in Iran to have sex before you get married, but I think you should have sex when you are ready. All this is bullshit regarding the girl being a virgin until she says yes." He took a long drink. "It's a nice border where love and sex meet. That's where I want to meet you." His direct gaze pierced my defenses.

I felt he really had feelings for me, although at that point I wouldn't call it love...yet. It was the same back, but he was just as mysterious as everything else in this country for me. And I chose for the time being to be in this mystery with him.

"I don't know," I said, voice trembling, "when, or if, I can meet you there."

"Don't worry. Whatever will happen will happen. I just want you to be comfortable and know that, whenever the time comes, *we* will know. It's a bit weird how they think about this in Iran, because everyone tries to be someone they are not, or act one way in front of their families and another with friends. You are lucky your girls are Elham and Bahareh. Be about us; let's just be, and..." he hesitated, "...you don't have to be afraid about this," he pointed at his penis. "It is well-behaved," he joked.

My mind swirled with thoughts. I looked at him with deep regard. "I have so many questions about this, and don't know how to discover it with so many negative things being said in society." My mouth twisted with frustration.

"Let's make it simple. If you are ready and when you are ready you will know, right?"

"I have no idea. I hope so," I said giggling.

"You will, beautiful—just buzz me when you do and I'll take the next jet out!"

I laughed, and that ended the sex conversation. There was so much I didn't understand, as if sex and my natural curiosity and feelings of love were wrong, dirty if expressed openly, and frowned upon.

Why? I remembered my friends in Brooklyn Christina and Jennifer were given their first kisses at sixteen! In Iran, they probably would remark on that as "This girl *pedar madar nadare*," (has no family) or "*Ajab dokhtari*" (what a dirty girl).

Being an observer of all these thoughts, I knew that with Arash by my side I would learn to uncover truth and enjoy it for its own beauty.

• • •

Iran ended up in a draw with Australia, a big thing because Iran was now only one win away from the 1998 FIFA World Cup in France. This also meant smiles, free pastries in the streets, and even free cab rides! The whole country partied like rock stars. They had yet to be *in* the World Cup games, but a party at this stage of the competition was inevitable.

Thousands, in herds and flocks and packs, filled the streets with music and dance. Some younger dancers combined the fluid, twitchy precision of Michael Jackson with old school *Jaheli* moves, resulting in both breathtaking performances and comic mishaps— a nice combo. The girls wore colorful scarves, and even without makeup looked hot!

It was a movie screening for me from the window! "Can we go out?" I asked in a begging tone.

"They get too crazy," Arash said, "and the police eventually will break it up. The black crows might be bussed in to crow them away." He laughed harshly.

We stood together, agreeing some of the dances were good enough to be made into music videos, as if professionally choreographed (not that there were any). A few brave girls dance in their own risqué styles, some as if entranced, waving flags and scarves. Horns blared and beeped from an army of various vehicles, most creeping along to avoid pedestrians and shouting along with them, "Iran! Iran!"

"It's like they all died and went to heaven! It's samba time!"

The yeasty hot aroma of pastries drifted into the window. A cluster of people cried, "Here we come France, watch out Iran is comin! Iran is flying. The *Aladdin* carpet is moving!"

Here was powerful national unity; here was hope, all through the streets and in every home. The naked reality of this, its very sound and smell, had my eyes brimming with tears; the positive kind that had me shaking with life. I had never seen such emotion in *any* stadium, or after any win. These people pulsed and shouted and danced with life itself, and the game gifted them with an outlet for its expression.

I faced Arash, proud to be an Iranian, and he bent down and pressed his warm lips to mine. This one moment in all of time. This moment with my people, my first boyfriend and the passion rooting and bonding us together; it was one I would never forget.

15

Nazri

DAYS PASSED AND I WAS enjoying the job, Elham, Arash, the cousins, and had little get-togethers at my house with Neda and Saloomeh from Tatbighi. I missed Mina, Azin, and Nooshin because they were primarily traveling. Mina was mostly traveling to Canada and her father was in the process of finishing up their immigration work to eventually move there. Azin was in California visiting relatives before her college in Iran started, and Nooshin was in Washington, D.C. visiting her own relatives.

People in Iran traveled frequently but then again they were primarily the upper class. Others traveled too but not too far away but maybe to Syria or other parts of Iran. I think they were day trips to Syria or something, I read it on some travel agency's door. The buses had better be good (I highly doubted it though)!

One day I woke up to loud, religious-type music coming from the street. What in the world was this? Another football scene? Can't be another revolution or else bombs would be coming in from the window! I knew it was a national holiday because I didn't have classes and they told me it wasn't necessary for me to come to my internship.

Climbing out of bed, I padded to the window. What is that? The wide street hosted a sea of black! Men wearing black collared or simple shirts, struggling with some heavy iron object on their shoulders. A water guy, or someone, stood on a corner dispensing water in plastic cups (apparently for free) for the sweating participants getting a cardio workout. Forget sports clothes, these dudes were dressed up and working out!

I could see more water stations spread along the street, and the music grew louder, like a parade but religious. Across the shoulders of the front-line men who voluntarily took part, I could see Arabic script on the cloth covering the metal object's top. Behind this line marched many other men, stretching back at least five or six blocks.

Abruptly the metal's mass would be too much for the front-line's middleman (kinda like the quarterback of the team), requiring a change of place with another. The change itself was funny, I thought, because the metal tilted, shifting its weight unevenly left or right among the sweating few bracing it, until the new man took control.

The front men were the *daste*. Those behind them, but closest to their own front-line, were flogging themselves with something called a *zangir*. It reminded me of Michelangelo's chain in the *Ninja Turtles*, you know, a wooden handle blooming with thin chains. These men wore tortured expressions and looked tranced out, and some had bloody backs! But they liked doing it—no one was forcing them to flog the *zangir* back and forth!

Then I realized something I should have known better than to question! There were no females doing this! It was testosterone world mania again! Well, I don't even think a woman would be able to handle that type of metal dance or whatever they were calling it!

Then I saw some pretty hot girls pacing the men and their struggling shuffle. These were hot mammas! They wore full-blown makeup and what appeared to be new mantos and scarves, as if ready for a nice dinner party or simply lounging somewhere. I had no idea what these pictures added up to, but was curious to find out. They had camels and sheep down there, and more water-guys taking care of them. Nothing made sense!

Hot girls plus men hitting themselves with chains under the hot sun, and others burdened with a length of heavy metal, listening to the squawk and blare of depressing religious music with some peeps chanting in the background. If I heard correctly, this chaos mixed Arabic and Farsi music, with "Hossein" frequently shouted in the background. It was scary but interesting for me.

How should I go out: with regular Shaghayegh clothing, or like the girls with Mac-style make-up?

Easter and Rosh Hashanah weren't this extreme, or maybe I wasn't used to this. The only religious Muslim holiday I knew of was Ramadan, the holy month of fasting; but I doubt they marched in the streets!

The Emperor told me we were going over to my Aunt Elahe's for lunch. We were meeting all the cousins and getting lunch from outside. I quickly got dressed the regular Shaghayegh way, ignoring what was going on outside and headed for the car where the Emperor and H$_2$O were waiting for me.

Again I was in awe as I saw some of the main streets blocked off for the march, similar to how they would cut off NYC for the St. Patrick Day parade. Only this had no beers or leprechauns or any floats!

I wanted to observe and absorb it more before I asked anyone what in the world this was, but I could see my dad looking at me through his front view mirror. He knew I was going to bombard

232

him with questions, and my mom gave me a look or two to make sure I was still alive amid my mental disruption!

If I did start with questions, playing *Jeopardy* with my parents would fall in the category of "I'll take 'What are you watching?' for 1200." All questions included.

Some men were even weeping, but it all had some kind of stylized organization despite the crowd and people talking over one another. The best part was the girls and guys checking each other out. This was a religious gathering, and also a time when the beautiful and handsome Mr. and Ms. Iran fused together, except there was no tiara or swimsuit feature in this particular event!

But it brought certain aspects of the people together, and I couldn't determine whether some really believed in this, even though they were rigorously participating. Perhaps they attended simply to take in the eye candy?

"This event should be respected," said the Emperor, turning the music low. It might as well have been muted or switched off.

Respect, I agreed with. But I struggled against the contradiction inherent with people living in two worlds. I would travel a long road before fully understanding this country I was born into, despite its differences. Didn't these differences give way to a certain passion I witnessed—the same I had felt among my Italian friends in Brooklyn as we cooked, or enjoyed a fun pool day?

Recalling those days brought a smile and tears to my eyes. And Christina and Jennifer—I wondered what they were doing. I missed them, but those memories were what fueled me to fall in love with another part of my soul.

"This whole thing you are witnessing is called *Ashura* and the day after is called *Tasu'a*. The Muslims are mourning a tragedy by holding special ceremonies in different cities and public venues like

233

mosques to offer food to the people," he said looking at me like I'm freaked out.

"What's up with all the chicks all dressed up while the dudes are macho-ing it up for them with these chains?"

"That's trouble! They want to find a hot date. But that is nothing relevant to the mourning!" replied my mom.

"They mourn the martyrdom of Imam Hussein, the third Imam," continued the Emperor.

"Okay, got it. But this is a brutal way of doing it, no?" I asked.

"Everyone has their way. This is Iran's way, which is primarily Muslim Shiites," he replied.

"So this is all to remember him and commemorate him?"

"Yes."

"So they are suffering because he suffered? Reenacting his pain?"

"Yup. You are getting there!" he said chuckling.

Personally, I felt no connection with this whole commemoration. It didn't make me feel good. Christmas made me feel good but that was like comparing apples and oranges and it was a completely different faith. But the cool thing was that they were so passionate about doing this and even the girls with the hot makeup were into it, but in their own way.

Maybe if they had a bar or two in this place the girls would find a place to pick up guys so they wouldn't have to do meet guys this complicated way. Oh the dudes were wearing black but some had gelled their hair and shaved a goatee for the occasion! It was a melting pot of restriction meeting mourning! Geez!

I came back to reality to hear the brakes and find the car parked in front of my aunt's. Inside, I saw the cousins, Bahareh, Ghazaleh and Arshia. The girls were fully dressed in mantos and scarves and ready to walk out the door carrying big pots. Yes, they were kitchen pots. The girls weren't wearing their everyday stuff, but the short, stylish, fancy mantos and scarves. The house held an aroma of mouth-watering food, but only a large bowl of salad was there on the table. Nothing was cooking. Why did we have pots if we were getting lunch from outside?

Makeup-free, I stood outside and pure sunshine beamed through the window illuminating the exotic, natural beauty of my cousins. I realized the "trouble" my mom was talking about included my cousins and myself—only by way of association at this point!

Arshia drove off with one big pot and the rest was given to us. Arshia looked the same as he always did, nothing too hip. My cousins on the other hand were jazzed up! Mind you, at this point I am still not playing *Jeopardy* yet and following the event without the information booklet.

Hastily, Bahareh said, "C'mon Shaghayegh. We are going to get the *Nazris*."

"*Nazris?*"

"Yes, c'mon. We'll explain in the car."

"Girl, is that a Farsi word?"

"Just get in, we'll do the explaining in the car. We want to get rid of the folks so we have lots of time for ourselves!"

She wasn't going to be waited for and so I soon started walking. There was no need even to explain to our parents where we were headed and what time we would be home, so they got a simple, "*Khoda hafez,*" goodbye—and we had vanished.

I jumped into the car where the cousins sat applying makeup before turning on the engine. Still confused, I asked, "Okay, where are we going?"

"We are going to a Hossein party!" said Bahareh.

"Is that where Arshia went?"

"Girl, I have no idea where he went but probably to meet his girlfriend and pick up *Nazri* on the way. We are getting *Nazri* too but into the Hossein party," said Ghazaleh gently applying her eyeshadow.

"So what do *Nazri* and Hossein party mean? I thought this was a mourning for crying out loud!"

Ghazaleh couldn't have been more animated. "Today is *Ashura* and tomorrow is *Tasu'a*. All the hot guys are out and we—the hot girls—are going to check them out, and the rest *khoda midoone!*" Only god knows. "And it doesn't matter that the hotties in the march aren't aware of it, but even they are sizzling."

"That is sick! Sizzling while bleeding. You guys have issues!" I replied.

"Chill out, let me give you the lowdown. One, this is a religious ceremony to remember the third Shia Imam. Two, all the sharbats, chains, and music you hear are part of *Ashura* and how the memory of the Imam is mourned. Three, *Nazri* is free food mosques and some people do give out for free," said Ghazaleh. "You got that part?"

"Yeah but—" I said but was quickly interrupted.

"Holdup! Now for the 'but' part, which is not related to *Ashura* but people do because the country is restricted. One, the girls and guys looking hot is not in any way related to this religious event but since we don't have public clubs or bars we find ways to have fun so we use these events. And we know it might seem irrelevant and rude but whatever. Two, the whole girls and guys gathering makes it a Hossein party. Hossein was the name of the third Imam. Got it? That's the whole scoop!" he said relieved.

"Oh she forgot, *Nazri* is the most delicious food you can eat. It's the same dish your mom might make or the restaurants might serve but it tastes soooo good on this day!"

"All right now you are superstitious! Because it is cooked on this day suddenly it has just the right amount of salt and pepper?"

"No seriously woman, I don't know what it is but it's delish! They are called Hossein *gheymehs*," said Bahareh

"So you stand in line at certain homes giving out these *Nazris* and that is where you can make the best eye contact with testosterone candy!" said Ghazaleh.

"Oh my," I replied, flattered. "So wait a minute, let me get this straight. We give our pots to one of the homes and wait outside until our turn is up and the pot is returned filled?" I asked.

Ghazaleh nodded. "Yup. And it may come flying over some people's head because people here don't know anything about lines! Just know what your pot looks like; there is no number or system! This is not a restaurant. Your pot might even get lost so keep an eye out!"

"But the awesome part is that we usually get different kinds of foods. Kebabs are even given out for free in some joints. The minute we smell the kebab, which is usually in the homes with loads of people lined up, we switch direction!"

"They give out kebabs? Isn't that pricey?" I asked.

"Probably," said Ghazaleh. "A backdrop to the *Nazri* story is that some people, mainly religious peeps, make wishes, and in connection to that wish they will 'donate' or '*nazr*.' Yeah, it's an Arabic word. We got lots of those in Farsi we use! They make *gheyme* stew or do some other charitable giveaway in the form of food or money during *Ashura*. You can look at it as donating to or feeding the hungry."

"Or not so hungry! You consider yourself hungry?" I snapped back.

"No but it's tradition. Don't look into this too deep! Those who eat it pray that the person gets their wish. It's basically holy food," said Bahareh.

"I am really smelling and wanting some Hossein *gheyme* right now!" said Ghazaleh. She was one who simply wanted the food and hoped from a distance whoever made the *nazr* received a fruitful result—but that may have been the last thing on her mind!

"What's up with all the marches on every main street?" I asked.

"Dude, we just told you. This is how they commemorate the event!" said Bahareh. "Listen woman, it'll sink in. We know it's a new chapter in your life and could be overwhelming," she continued.

"To say the least! To what I remember we never had the mix in NYC and the parades were mainly fun! But these people are hurting themselves to show their passion, respect or I don't even know how to feel it...emotional error!" I said while laughing.

"There you go!" shouted Ghazaleh.

"Just accepting and not understanding is the best strategy. Hell, that's how it works best for us too!"

"And to further confuse you the mosques have some poetic recitations in memory of Imam Hossein in the battle where he was martyred. Several parks, which we will check later on today, perform passionate plays dramatizing the Battle of Karbala. It shows the suffering he and his family went through."

"Wow," I said, "that's intense."

The car approached a house with a flock of people in front. Everyone was shouting so loudly for food no one could make out what the other person was saying.

I was taking it all in. This should be interesting. "How do we even get the pot to the front door?"

"We don't. The pot has imaginary wheels!" said Bahareh.

She made me smile. Unloading the car was no treat, but together we accomplished this in record time.

Bahareh carefully pushed her wheeled pot toward the house, halting before a short stocky man with amazingly white teeth. Immediately he passed the pot to another man, and the pot magically moved out of view.

Over the twenty minutes it took to reacquire the pot, Ghazaleh, Bahareh and I checked out the flock, chatted, and watched the passing row of *dastes*.

I noticed a few people exchanging what could only be telephone numbers, and it became clear this event was also unifying different people. Some bore expressions of displeasure, but participated anyway for the greater good, or simply to hang and eat a hearty meal! It was a "let's go with the flow" kind of deal.

I sipped on one of the berry sharbats they were handing out and it was fresh and icy cold. So the story of the sharbat distribution is that since Imam Hossein and his family were starved of water in the Karbala desert before he was martyred, they were now serving cold drinks. That was a celebration especially because I was hot as hell and I was sweating bullets. It hit the spot!

"Ladies, here it comes!" Bahareh said and grabbed her pot from the same man who took it earlier. He favored her with his bright smile.

By the time we returned home we had three pots filled with rice and *gheyme*, rice and kebabs, and *zereshk* (barberry) rice with chicken, *and* Ghazaleh had received three phone numbers from guys. She was contemplating who she wanted to call! The heavy load perfumed the car and required two back and forth tips to get it into the house!

Arshia returned with *gheyme* from another location (I think it was from his girlfriend's house) but he didn't say anything and we got the picture that we shouldn't ask! After lunch, I knew why Bahareh craved *gheyme*: it was absolutely delish! Possibly its ingredients were no different than any other *gheyme* on any other day, but this batch was connected to a special event and charged with the magic present in all holidays.

Although I was touchy about eating too much rice, I devoured the entire dish! Then I thought about Arash and what he might be doing. We hadn't talked that day and I missed him. Using the secret phone in Bahareh's room, I quickly called him and learned that his father had a big *Nazri* event in progress! He had his hands full but wanted to bring me some *Nazri* as an excuse to see me—two offers I just couldn't refuse!

We planned to meet at a park hosting a play for *Ashura*. I wondered whether it might be safe even to be with a guy on such a religious day when all the *Komiteh* people were out watching. Well, I'd seen people exchanging numbers, calling the whole thing a Hossein party, so why shouldn't I see my boyfriend? I hung up the phone and stuck it back in its secret place. I told myself it would all work out, we'll get together...

After a few minutes of planning, Bahareh agreed to drop me off at the play and then head for another round of Hossein partying! "Wish you could join, but Arash would kill us if we took you!" she said.

"I know fully well Arash would never say no. Anyway, why do you always say that? He doesn't own me. I have an opinion of my own. You guys need to know you have a life of your own as a woman too."

It was annoying how she made it seem Arash determined where I went. He was my equal, not my supervisor. Maybe that was a Brooklyn mindset. No one could control me but yet Bahareh even said this at the hamburger joint. I wonder how deep this type of thinking was embedded in this country. It boiled my blood again like the stadium issue! Grrr! Arash had better know that but I think he knew because he was brought up in England and had some white-boy in him.

"We do, but some men just like control, especially Iranian men," added Ghazaleh.

"Yeah, but that's the more traditional version. These days it's half-half," Bahareh chimed in. "Anyway, back to the Hossein party ladies—I want to see guys showing off their muscles holding them *zangirs*," she continued.

"Some don't have six-packs but still are sizzling," joked Ghazaleh. "We support them by following behind these heroic boys!"

I chuckled. "You mean you guys are cheerleaders?"

"Yup, but there is no such thing in Iran! Once we exchange phone numbers, we will know their names and shout them with enthusiasm."

This was better than bar hopping! A meeting of eyes opening a meeting of hearts. So much sensation, desire, and lust in the air! They were searching for love. Inspiring…

In spite of so many closed doors the girls went all out and they were happy. Or it seemed they were happy.

They dropped me off at the park to meet Arash and then drove off to meet their own soul mates!

I stepped across the park and its lush green space and its clusters of animated conversations.

"Your first Hossein party?" Arash said, stepping out of the concealing bulk of a tree.

"A blast to say the least!" I said smiling broadly and happy to see him. "It definitely has a beat to it."

241

We stood in the shade, talking and stealing a kiss or two. I thought about how much I had missed him, even though we had been apart fewer than twelve hours. I wanted him more. I wanted his touch, his cologne on my body.

After devouring the risk and kissing in public on such a religious day he looked into my eyes and god knew what went through his head. I felt safe but then again, I was curious to know what kind of Iranian-British guy he was.

•••

Arash needed to stop at a gas station before taking me back, so he pulled into the least crowded one.

"I won't be long," he said, getting out of the car. I heard him clunk the fuel nozzle into the tank and caught a potent whiff of gasoline. Abruptly a homeless guy approached my window. Now what could this phenomenon be? Brazenly he stuck his smelly head up to me and whispered a speedy string of words. Alarmed, I jerked away. The man backed off, shifted his attention elsewhere, yet repeated his nonsense even faster.

It was something about CDs, but he muttered so heedlessly quick I felt certain he must be selling drugs. The ratty bag he carried wasn't completely closed, and I could see brightly labeled CDs poking out. I glared at him with uncomprehending attention. He repeated his mumbled mantra, and after five or six times I understood. My brain had quality translation software.

"*Navar, disc, pasoor...navar, disc, pasoor...navar, disc,*" and on and on he went repeating these three words. Shut-up already!

Only someone in the loop would comprehend the words: "Do you want any illegal tapes, CDs, or playing cards?"

Aha! He was peddling illegal stuff, trying to make a buck or two. Another one like the movie guy, with the cards falling into the gambling category, so they couldn't be purchased easily or legally; bootleg time for these guys. He was murmuring away so he wouldn't get caught.

At the same time I realized this guy wouldn't approach just anyone, but those he thought might be into this stuff and actually had the money to buy it and be chill about it. Meaning not giving away their identity. But I didn't bother with the response—beyond rolling up my window. The sign language was clear enough: NO.

The scruffy stranger grinned, revealing the blackest, most decayed teeth I had ever seen! No wonder he reeked! He shuffled on with his bag to another victim fueling up. Thank god!

Observing this as he finished gassing up, Arash burst into laughter. He opened the door and eased into the seat. "Babe, you figured that one faster than ever!"

"Lucky for me! You seemed to linger a little longer than necessary out there."

"Haha! He was just trying to sell some entertainment stuff and cards."

"I know! He and his odor were close enough for me to get a look into that dirty, rusty bag of his!"

"Were you able to make out what he was saying? They say it so fast."

"Yes, after six times of repeating it! Does anyone really buy this stuff?"

He turned the key and the engine purred to life. "You would be surprised. This is another way things circle around—these guys are like mobile entertainment stores and, believe it or not, really useful in spreading the latest in the world of the arts!"

"You didn't have him in your face. He was kinda scary, the way he said his sales pitch! You'd think he was dealing opium or heroin."

Arash nodded, "I know, another way of making a living in tough times!"

He shifted the car into gear and drove off to Bahareh's house. We had planned to meet at the same time so we could walk in together.

Arash turned to face me and gave me one of those flirtatious looks that last forever. "Call me tonight?"

It sounded more like a statement than a question. I accepted by just looking back at him and said, "I will think about it." In truth, I couldn't wait to call him.

I didn't feel this had become a habit, but was excited to hear his voice, and talk about anything and everything with him while bugging the hell out of him with my questions! He loved it, and it always ended up with a tease and sexual comments at the end. This had been my first taste of such a religious event in Tehran, which possessed a certain excitement. I found a deep respect for understanding how religion and joy could mix in such a world.

16

Anticipating *Eid*

March 1998

AFTER THE MOURNING IT WAS back to work, summer enjoyment, and prepping for other new surprises coming my way.

I had grown familiar with my regimen. As each day passed, I felt closer to my classmates and people I dealt with. They were kind, real and it invested me with a sense of security and protection.

At the news station we worked hard, then had fun in the late hours when the *Herasat* mostly was asleep, the studio was more relaxed.

The year's end beckoned, the aroma of Spring fresh in the air. Green grass mingled with jasmine, cypress trees, and freshly watered soil. People were having a change of mood, anticipating *Eid*, the New Year.

I recalled watching my mother prepare for *Eid* back home (what was home) in Brooklyn. Now, I observed it as the whole country prepped for the New Year, and found this cleansing, even touching.

It was the same rich feeling but now that I was near the source everything was different! It was like having bread while it was fresh at the bakery, or having a kiss at midnight near the water where you could feel the sensuality. Before, *Eid* would be seeing the whole ritual be done in my hood then celebrating it with one night which was the actual night of *Eid*. Here it was for two weeks total, feeling how the country celebrated the New Year. It wasn't about religion or Islam but a flipping the pages of time to begin a new chapter. Even the taxi drivers were in a better mood and playing happier illegal music in their cabs.

It was exciting; *Eid* in Tehran with Tehranians and their good moods.

Let's roll the dice!

•••

I soon realized even the *Herasat* members in the TV studio were in the spirit too, prepping for the holidays. It was a full two weeks, which meant all the hotshot wealthier Iranians would travel abroad or jaunt off to their fancy villas near the Caspian Sea in Shomal. My uncle kept a big villa there, in *Darya Kenar* (Seaside), and invited the entire family for the holidays. Each gated community bore its own name and employed full-blown doormen and professional security officers, many of them former military police. I heard they were mean and nasty back in their days and beat the shit out of people who opposed them. But now they just had to beat the shit out of cars that were trying to enter through the gate, even if they were villa owners here.

246

Money goes a long way in Iran, and the wealthy surely stood out with their luxury, high-end, homes, cars, even high-end mantos and scarves.

The Emperor had told me to request a two-week vacation for the *Nowruz* holiday and it was granted immediately! Employees were taking vacations left and right and it was like back in NYC where you had to put the request in maybe months before to have it approved! Similar to during the holidays. They didn't have a system like that with vacation days. This is how it went:

"Mr. Director I will be taking Monday through Friday off because I will be headed to Kish (an Island in the South of Iran) with my wife."

"Really, I heard Kish is really nice this time of year."

"Yes, I've heard the same."

"So you are out these days. Let me see if we can have someone in your place," he responds while writing the days on a piece of paper. "Oh, you can go, Javad is here to help," he replies while putting a checkmark next to the days he wrote on his piece of paper, which may float away or land with the other pile of papers he had, labeling it as official! That easy. So, your vacation is granted and the weather chat was just heartwarming! Ha!

At home, my mom was doing the end of year cleaning. Dusting and polishing every hole in the house with the assistance of a hired maid, a tall mid-fortyish man sporting a moustache worthy of Hercule Poirot. Occasionally he brought along his little son because he couldn't afford a sitter, was a widower, and didn't want the kid wandering the streets of the down-est part of downtown Tehran. For a man with an accent and engaging in manual labor, he showed up impeccably dressed. He probably wanted to leave an influence, as everyone here did!

I wondered where he was from? It sure wasn't Tehran. I mused, then figured he must live is some farm city or village outside Tehran where the accent is heavily blended!

My mom warned me not to run around wearing skinny shorts and a tank top when he was working.

"Why?" I objected strongly. "It is our house and we have authority inside our own house! I am going to wear shorts!" I stated loudly.

So again, I was asked to go to my father's office, at the very end of the hall, for another lengthy talk.

"Are you saying that I dress sexy with these gym shorts and I am trying to grab attention?" I asked. "I don't care about this maid-guy and don't care what he thinks!" I continued, now confused more than when stepping into the airport here.

"I get you, but he is a man and from a different place in Tehran. You are too westernized with your thoughts. I just need you to wear jeans when you are around him," the Emperor stated.

"So, if I have too many 'western' thoughts why the hell am I in a country that is too 'traditional' for me?" I blurted back.

"It's a culture clash but you will understand it. Aren't you having fun knowing your cousins more and your culture more?"

"Dad, at this time I am so disgusted with this culture that my answer is NO!" I said and left his office to my room where I could be "westernized" all I wanted! Man, it was ridiculous.

My mom brought me my lunch and the Emperor came to give me some funny jokes, but I told him the jokes were too 'easternized' so he would get off my back. The food was good though and I was eating it while watching *Tango & Cash* by Sly Stallone and Kurt Russell for the Nth time!

Frankly, I wanted to smack the living daylights out of the maid, but afterwards realized the folks were right. On my way back, the way the dude looked at me was as if he had been released from prison and, with no porn magazines available, used whatever he could get. He was a good maid, and the ladies in the neighborhood liked his cleanliness so they had him completely booked. My mom was happy with him and after tomorrow he was heading to my aunt's so I distracted myself the best way I could.

If this guy were in the U.S. he would be making a good load of money because of his résumé! In Tehran it was word of mouth and who knew, this dude was booked until the month's end. He was a highly requested professional!

•••

Prior to the New Year the streets bustled with people from smaller cities outside Tehran, and many Iranians were flying in from Germany, France, and the U.S. to spend the holiday with their families. Others were out in the streets shopping for new clothes. It wasn't about buying a Christmas tree and ornaments or mistletoe (god forbid that one!), but more about shopping to replace the old with the new. That included furniture, clothes, curtains, anything that was smelly, rusting or deteriorating. The arrangement was totally different.

The markets were abuzz selling small goldfish, *Sonbol* (hyacinth), and *Sabzeh* (wheat and barley sprouts) for the table. It was all for setting up the *Haft Sin* table. This involved placing the pieces on the table representing the seven angelic heralds of Life, Health, Happiness, Prosperity, Joy, Patience, and Beauty, each beginning with the Persian letter *Seen*, or S: *Seeb* (apple), *Seer* (garlic—my favorite!), *Senjed* (dried fruit from the lotus tree), *Sonbol* (hyacinth), *Sekkeh* (coins), *Samanoo* (sweet pudding) and *Somagh* (powdered sumac berry). Yup, these were the seven honorable S's!

Among these seven we have the other "happy that I'm here" items on the table too including candles in fine holders, a mirror, painted eggs, goldfish and some Iranians displayed the Quran, the Muslim holy book. I wondered if everyone used the Quran, because this was purely a cultural holiday marking the first day of Spring or Equinox, nothing Islamic based. My aunt didn't use the Quran so it was probably optional.

Maybe it made the Muslims feel good with the start of the New Year. Whatever the reason I digged how chic some tables were arranged. It was like a form of art!

Bahareh came over one night. "It's *Eid* so I gotta buy some new clothes. Do you want to come?"

"Yeah, but I don't like any of the lame designs in these boutiques. They're so old school woman!"

"Duh, you think? I am going to take you to a fashion show! Forget the boutiques. They are overpriced, even though they all have sales going on for *Eid*."

My eyes widened. "A fashion show? You mean a real show where they strut down a catwalk and turn and blow kissed to the crowd with Vanilla Ice in the background?"

"Yeah! Vanilla Ice doesn't have concerts here though. His tour was cut short— food poisoning!" she said laughing.

"Are you playing?"

"Not about the fashion show you geek! This country has got more fuel and imagination than anything you've seen! Let's have some chai and hop into the car. The show starts in an hour and the traffic is brutal, this being the week before *Eid*."

Tea time was anytime in Iran. Everything started and ended, slowed and sped up with tea. You couldn't do anything without tea being in the picture.

"You want some Jack Daniels?"

"Sure, but let's have some tea first!"

The above was always on the agenda!

"So who are the models in the show? Anyone famous?" I joked, though I was really curious.

"*Baleh Baleh, shak nakon!*" Bahareh laughed. Yes, of course, no doubt!

I could hardly contain my excitement. Another facet to this country, one I never dreamed existed!

One thing I was sure of: whoever was throwing this fashion show definitely had some balls of steel! If the authorities found out, they would be busted. No question about it! But how did the organizers screen their guests? Maybe some people were spies and would report them. Another question for *Jeopardy*, for 1500! The questions just kept mounting up...again.

•••

After chai-time, Bahareh, Ghazaleh (who had joined us a bit afterwards) and I put on our scarves and drove off. It didn't take long until we arrived at a regular, nondescript building.

"Impressive, eh?" Ghazaleh said. "Looks like a warehouse built in 1941."

"You've got to go more ancient!" I said, "like maybe the Medieval times."

We got out of the car, walked toward the building, and stopped at the dented basement door. I squinted and leaned toward the entrance. "Listen."

Muffled music could be heard, the type without vocals; techno or European house-style, layered with traditional instruments that sounded like the setar and santoor.

Bahareh poked a red glowing button beside the door, and a bell rang. The door grated open, and they stepped into another world. Right away we could see the place looked much larger than could be presumed from a glance at the exterior. Two big rooms were separated by a long, improvised catwalk. The models displayed themselves in one, while the other displayed racks and racks of clothes for sale from Turkey, Sweden and Italy. Other women milled about, checking out the models, clothes rack, and each other.

"Look at those colors," I said.

Lithe models stepped with fluid grace up and down the catwalk, their designer mantos and scarves mixing contemporary old Persian calligraphy, the nicest I had ever seen! I had entered the land of big creativity, and as far as my eyes could operate without glasses, only women were present. So much for Vanilla Ice! Ha!

So, the brothers and the sisters had separate fashion shows and *only* hung out and met in Jordan, or in private homes to enjoy one another's company. At least they enjoyed it for what it was.

Bahareh tapped my arm. "C'mon, let's go." She took my hand and led me into the mantos room. Brunette women, each with a unique Middle Eastern facial structure and exotic and aloof, dominated the huge space. Any man's paradise, I thought.

A harmony of fragrance haunted the air like invisible music. It was wild, fruity, herbal, and composed by the melange of perfumes anointing the models and guests. I recognized some of the scents as popular brands, but later realized these girls created their own, mixing and matching in awesome alchemy, conjuring a brand new fragrance. Another way to express their artistic side, and to add a truly passionate side.

Bahareh had opened her own little space, shakin' it with mini dance moves, as the models one by one strutted along the catwalk

252

showing off cutting-edge mantos and cutely wrapped scarves. Ghazaleh and I stood transfixed, watching the color-splashed show.

Some models actually smiled. A few narrowed their kohl-lined eyes, lips firm with attitude sharp as their feline cheekbones. All of them were of course sexy, while a few gave off an icy aura of stunning elegance.

Sharbats were being served to all guests, and everyone stood around chatting, making new friends, and sharing ideas.

Bahareh noticed a couple of her friends and the group kept expanding and without really trying we were a group of now strangers-turned-friends within thirty minutes. I felt a kindred spirit between all of us.

These artistic types possessed a rare, bracing camaraderie based on exploration and creativity rather than competition, and I felt at home with them. My previous friends had left a good impression on me, enabling me to see this new crowd in a different light. We drank the *halal* way and some heavily priced mantos were being purchased off the racks and considered "runway"!

Afterwards we all made our way through the noisy crowd and into the clothes-filled room on the other side. Here the chaos was muffled, the women paying rapt attention to the racked merchandise.

"What is the story with this?" I asked Ghazaleh, who busily picked through a pile trying to find items her size and before other chicks could lay their hands on it!

Without glancing up she said, "Well, there are a couple of ladies who travel to Sweden, Turkey, and Italy before the holidays, buy up and bring back the *jens* (products). This stuff is European—fancy-schmancy—and some of it is real nice and sexy, but pricey. There are even designer clothes. Take a look," she said pointing to all the clothes.

"Get otta here!"

"Seriously, look for yourself. These are all American or European brands. Some might be fake, or Asian knock-offs, but whatever. They are as close as it gets and they are nice! Better than your Canal Street!"

"My Canal Street vendors are rockstars!" I said giggling and moving towards the *jens*. I probed the piles before her and found several of my favorite brands. A few were as new as an early-bird spring collection from some designers. This was A-mazing, and heaven for me.

"You know," Ghazaleh continued, "sometimes the new fashion trends get here earlier than in the U.S. Weird, I know, but we are fashion hungry and central and eat this stuff alive!"

I felt she got bull-eyes remembering the bounty hanging and shelved in their closets: all designer, cutting-edge stuff and new fashion brands. I had seriously wondered where their clothes came from, since there was no Rodeo Driver or mall glittering with upscale boutiques here.

If I'd known this show was going to be like this I would have brought my checkbook!

There were piles of denim jeans in a spectrum of colors and styles: shirts, blouses, skirts, dresses, jewelry, makeup and shoes. The mall had been imported to this big room tucked beneath an anonymous building and advertised by word of mouth.

Toward the show's end, I found I had gathered much more stuff than anticipated, and I didn't have enough cash on me.

The lady in charge approached and told me I had made a nice selection, giving me the impression I was looking at a big price tag. This was the time I wished I was in a mall shopping with the Emperor's credit card! There were no credit cards in Iran—cash called the shots!

Bahareh, barely visible behind her own heaped selections, said, "You are doing some major shopping, lady!"

"You noticed?" I said sarcastically.

"Nice—their stuff is good. It lasts, and it suits your style. This lady goes abroad once or twice a year and brings back top-notch stuff."

"I don't think I have enough dough on me," I said with a sad tone. "And I don't wanna miss out since the sizes are limited."

"What? How much do you need?"

"I'm not sure. Haven't looked at the prices yet!"

She laughed. "You spoiled brat! Given that this mountain beats Kilimanjaro's size I would estimate one million *tomans*! Roughly one grand in your language. But don't worry, I can write a check. We are good customers with this lady, she will accept it."

"Really? She would just trust us like that? I mean this is not a credit card company where you would end up in collections or get maxed out of your credit line."

"Yup. She is a cool cat and has been doing this for years," she answered like it was a normal process between them.

I wondered if everyone had this kind of trust here? Relationships even between vendors-turned-friends were trusted. It was like me and Nordstrom having a no-credit relationship and walking in to choose whatever I liked and leaving to pay them back later, no interest applied! Heaven!

Bahareh moved off to talk with the lady, who looked to be in her early forties and whose wardrobe—from head to heels—was certainly European. Later, the elegant proprietress sidled up to greet me, telling me today's bill could be paid after the holidays, or whenever I had time to come by and drop it off.

After a few minutes of conversation, I learned the lady's name was Atoosa. A fascinating woman whose husband was a prominent engineer in Tehran and conceived this business years ago while traveling between various countries. So it started taking off, unconsciously paving the way for other women in the fashion world. In fact, she owned this very basement, and rented it out to women looking to display their products, whether it be for their own designs or designs from other foreign countries. Some girls were even starting to design new lingerie lines, and new manto fashion-wear with funky head-scarves. The scarves were good stuff, I thought, on my head in Tehran and around my neck back in the Big Apple, whenever that time would come. I missed it. Sigh.

Atoosa was a true entrepreneur, and I admired her courage. She inspired many women to pursue their passions, one of those females being my own cousin who wanted to create her own line but didn't have the guts to take a solid step forward. Those who struggled most intelligently and with fierce conviction brought beautiful art into the world. Such a success was a home run in my book and in this country! It was a ticket to someday present their styles on catwalks from New York to San Francisco.

We exchanged numbers and I promised to drop off the money before *Eid*. Amazing—a thirty-minute trust was formed, and all verbally. A thirty-minute Visa deal. It was fab! Bahareh's good reputation extended to cover me and I didn't let her down.

With bulging bags, tattooed smiles, and a few new relationships, we headed home. Along the way I daydreamed about wearing some of my new clothes for Arash, and I knew he would like it.

Once home, the Emperor said we would be driving to *Shomal* (North of Iran) early in the morning.

In other words: giddy up and start packing!

17

Road Trip

"WE WILL BE HEADING OUT the night before *Eid*," said the Emperor, "to bypass traffic and have breakfast in the middle of the road. *Chaloos*, this is," he was referring to the twisty, scenic route towards North Iran, which was also called Shomal. It was a beautiful road filled with nature, kinda of like the highway in New Jersey. But it was twisty because it went up a mountain and had incredible nature on both sides.

"You grandmother, cousins, and Aunt Elahe will be gathering here at six in the morning with some other distant cousins, and off we go. So prep up, *dokhtaram.*" Dear daughter; I loved it when my dad used that term. I felt I belonged to a family that loved me unconditionally, and who better than a Persian dad. A dad that was strict in his very own unique but diplomatic way.

There were so many distant cousins that I didn't even want to ask who they were! These families were so extended and everybody kept in touch enough to go on vacations like this.

This would be my first *Eid*, first experience driving up *Chaloos*, first Shomal visit and spending time with all the family in one house for a week. It was also my first vacation, my first breakfast on the road. But I didn't even get what was so special about eating breakfast with all your folks in the middle of a dusty road? I think the road was so beautiful they hitched a good spot on the road to have bread or cheese or something like that! I just went with the flow on this one. I packed a bag with my new clothes, trendy scarves, new shoes, and was excited to visit this place called Shomal.

Once everyone was asleep, I called Arash from my secret phone to tell him we would be gone for a week. To my absolute surprise he told me he would be there too! "Are you following me?" I asked.

He chuckled warmly. "No! We have a villa there in Izad Shahr. That's the thing to do for *Eid* for lots of Tehran-ians. Everyone drives up to Shomal to chill, hang with family, have barbecues, and to be together for the New Year. It's where all the cool peeps go!"

"Hmm, so it's happening?"

"Let me make it a bit more clear for the New Yorker. It's like when city people go to the Hamptons. Now I bet it's crystal clear?"

"Crystal and glittering and now I am even more hyped!" I said. "Where is…whatever it was you just said?" I continued.

"It's on the other side of where you guys are at, a forty-minute drive. Don't worry. I will ride up to your neck of the woods with my buddies to see you."

"Really?" my heart quickened.

"You will love it! It's really fun."

"Listen, I am going to be with the entire fam in ONE house, so I don't know if I could call you even with a secret phone," I noted.

"Gotcha, but don't worry I will come to the seaside in Darya Kenar, where everyone comes for coffee or french fries most evenings. Hopefully we will see each other there."

258

"French fries?" I knew I'd heard correctly, but this still surprised me.

"Yup. Smothered with ketchup, and even a hookah to accompany that!"

"So, that's the *it* thing to get?"

"Well the menu has lots of stuff you would eat with your fingers, but that's the *it!*"

"Fattening, high-calorie, lots of trans fat—but it's *Eid* and you are supposed to be real happy and free-spirited!" I threw in with a wink like he'd catch it on the other side of the phone.

"By the way, there are a lot of 'Jordan'-type activities there so be careful," he joked, but under that he sounded serious.

Jordan-type activities huh? Another place where they drive around and girls meet the boys, exchanging numbers, hanging out— it was an easternized style Match.com!

"Are you jealous or are you telling me not flirt with other guys?"

There was a pause. "Something like that. But you're on the right track!"

I wished he were sitting right here next to me, close enough to touch me. I longed for the day we would make out hard and strong. No talk of virginity here though; this country was too tabooed for that talk.

"I'll leave our potential Shomal meeting in the hands of fate herself!" I said, having no idea what it was like up there. I had made it this far in this country so Shomal wasn't gonna kill me!

"*Ye boos bedeh zood,*" he joked. Give me a kiss, quickly.

"Nope, I can't. Have to keep my lips a virgin!"

"I've kissed you before though!" he teased

"So, they are still virgins and innocent," I teased back.

"They are not innocent, the way they kissed my virgin lips! Just give it a try," he teased again.

259

"Okay, but it's not working. I can't find a kiss on this end!"

"Try hard!" he said laughing.

I giggled, blew him a muted kiss without getting the phone filled with saliva and dreamed that one day I could be with him without hiding it from my parents and using a secret phone, or kissing him in the darkness of the movie theater. I wanted to express myself without fear of my surroundings.

•••

The next morning, four cars with lots of baggage cruised back to back. Men driving, some with frowns, refusing to wear eyeglasses and others with the oddest morning expression, as if really mourning.

The Emperor appeared most up-to-date in his new Porsche sunglasses and brightly colored polo shirt, as if fresh off the golf course. H_2O, who I considered the most beautiful (inside and outside) woman existing, was happy about returning to the Shomal of her childhood, and reliving memories on the road again.

My mom loved Iran and had sacrificed a lot to detach from the family in order to move to the United States with my dad. She never regretted the move because she adored my dad, but there was no doubt she missed her family when we were in the Big Apple. Aziz Joon and Agha Joon (which simply meant Mr., but *Joon* gave it a sweet touch), my grandfather, who had passed away earlier, were at the top of her list.

Even though I had grown up in an Italian neighborhood in Brooklyn and attended an ethnically-diverse school, I sensed my family unit to be quite different. United, closed, orderly, everybody had to know what everybody (including the extended family) else was doing. There seemed to be a huge emphasis on emotional, financial, and social security. They had to follow one another on the road, talk on cell phones to ensure no one got lost and everyone had an opinion on where to stop along the way.

One might say: "We should drive halfway and stop for breakfast," while another might counter, "*Man mordam* (I would die) waiting that long. Let's stop one-quarter of the way from here." Yet another would counter with, "Traffic will get more intense and we should keep going. Anyway there's a great restaurant about three-quarters of the way from here." Finally, whoever had two votes usually outweighed the others, and the decision was made from there. In some instances, if the most respected elder chimed in all other opinions would be wiped out and the elder given precedence.

My father, who was the eldest of the crew on the road, suggested stopping at a place shortly after halfway, and everyone went mute signaling *chashm* (to obey without question), and then quietly commented, "I can't believe I have to wait that long," but no one really paid him any attention—the decision had been made by the eldest. Complain all you want. It was usually Arshia that complained but he knew when to keep quiet!

Chaloos was by far Iran's most beautiful road. At one point the Kandovan Tunnel connected the dry part of Iran with the green region north of the Alborz Mountains, which lead eventually to the town of Nowshahr in the province of Mazandaran, which is considered Shomal and sits at sea level.

The road was breathtaking, comprised of twists and turns, which depending on the season, opened onto a variety of artist's vistas stretching toward the horizon. Spring was the best time, and I took pictures left and right!

We stopped at a restaurant in the heart of the mountains. Knee high tables covered with Persian rugs functioned as customer seating, with *poshtis* (big pillows) used as backrests. There were similar to the Persian rug on which we sat, but in pillow form, so soft and supporting.

The yeasty hot aroma of freshly baked bread ghosted from the kitchen, turning up the volume of everyone's hunger. Near one corner rushed a miniature waterfall, clearly natural, spilling down into a stream and snaking through the restaurant's center. Chickens could be heard clucking and scratching in the background, and the rest was silence and fresh air.

Fortunately, it took less than five minutes to seat ten people comprising some immediate family, extended cousins, and I noticed Arshia had also brought his friend Hessam along too. Hot dude, but short.

I looked at the menu and I had no idea what to make of it so I just told my mom I wanted *noon o panir,* bread and cheese and fresh walnuts with watermelon. I had no idea what breakfast buffet I was in for!

First out was freshly baked *Barbari* bread, crisp, salty, and latticed. Then they brought out my fav! *Sanghak,* a stone baked oval of sourdough, dimpled and hot. My mom used to buy it from this little Iranian grocery store on Long Island, but this was so tasty it was like comparing food to cars! The bread was the centerpiece of breakfast, fresh and tasty. Then came butter, and a special cream (*sar shir*). Initially I thought the cream was like Philadelphia cream cheese but when I tasted it, it was a sour cream consistency and ricotta flavor. The peeps attacked it once it landed on the table. Then we had the Shomal jams, which was what local, organic jam was to New York's Hudson valley. The names I couldn't grab but one was *Shagagol,* and it was like eating the limbs of a sweet tree!

Eggs followed and then it was wrapping the whole morning up with chai—tea time! So tea pouring had a system all its own: an inch of brewed tea in the glass's bottom, then hot water poured from a pitcher beside a little kettle. I knew the Emperor always drank coffee in the U.S., but maybe that was the "westernized" version of him. I noticed how often in a day tea was brewed—sometimes as many as three times! Then it was poured into fancy tea glasses called *kamar barik* (slim waist). Yes—the teacup had a slim waist, but nothing related to SlimFast or losing weight! Ha!

Tea was priority to Iranians and you had a special place in someone's heart if it was freshly brewed! Caution: do NOT use tea bags! Tea bags were hardly used. Here they were referred to as "Liptons," not the brand, but the actual tea bag. I think they used the brand name because searching for an Iranian tea bag name would end up in a bogus compound word.

I learned an Iranian is evaluated by: their skills at brewing chai, and rice-making. Both are a process, and if you think you can make either within two minutes, think again!

Then came other questions regarding tea: "Would you like it *por rangh* (deep color), *kam rangh* (light color), or *na kam rangh na por rangh* (not too weak or strong)?" The last option was kind of a trick answer...just make tea for crying out loud!

Then came the serving process and I recognized the emphasis the Emperor put on this. If you were a skilled tea-server, somehow (god knows how) you would make a good housewife, and were ready for marriage (the M word) and earned the "*bah bah ajab zan*" reward phrase—what a woman!

Everyone cleaned (or should I say licked) their plates and the whole breakfast was a good two hours long! Talk about Italians spending time at the table! Afterwards they went souvenir shopping. Now, that was weird. Why would you go souvenir shopping when you haven't reached your destination yet?

There was a shop connected to this breakfast joint selling jams, pickled garlic, sour fruit roll-ups, and big round stuffed cookies—

those were the bomb! They were stuffed with walnuts, cinnamon and baked in a special type of roll. The pastries were known as *Kooloochehs* and everyone picked up a box. They were *the* product of Shomal, along with the garlic. My dad took four jars of garlic.

"Dad, we're all in one house for a week, and look at the amount of garlic you're getting. You'll murder my nostrils. Have mercy!"

"Everyone has to have garlic when they are eating their first meal of the New Year with the *sabzi polo mahi with koukou sabzi*! (white fish with herb rice and herb soufflé) And besides they say no matter how much garlic you eat the humidity in Shomal won't let you smell the garlic aroma. Besides, everyone brushes!" he said laughing.

"With what kind of toothpaste?" I said but was just ignored.

This would be interesting. The whole villa had three bathrooms for the entire clan, so waiting in the mornings and nights to use the toilet, shower, or to brush your teeth would be like waiting in a long grocery checkout line. No express lanes here!

After filling the cars with more than the necessary number of jams, garlic and *Kooloocheh,* we hit the road again. A couple of hours more and we were in Shomal!

The entire group shared a strong tea addiction. So strong, each car carried an individual Coleman into which someone would pour tea and pass to the other riders. Out came the *Kooloochehs,* marking my first taste of one, which proved to be somewhat of a beautiful relationship. I swooned with delight. These babes will quiet the most powerful sugar craving and bring happiness to your life! They were heavy, but I could care less.

Watching the views on the road in my *Kooloocheh* and tea solace filled me with peace. The cars were still back to back and communicated so intensively that sometimes we would pull over and people would switch seats to either go in the car with the better music or better conversations. They should make a catalogue for this stuff!

The girl cousins were all in the Emperor's car because he had agreed to put on NSYNC as opposed to his boring *Sonnati* (traditional) music. When I listened to the *Sonnati* stuff it not only depressed me but I also had trouble understanding what in the world Mr. Sonnati Sinatra was singing about! Anything pop soothed my mood, and that was Backstreet Boys included!

The entourage approached the Caspian coast of Shomal, a scenic green blanket stretching to the hazed blue sea. Traffic picked up, cars and other vehicles whisking along like bees swarming to honey—a place to escape the harsh realities of city life.

It was beautiful with rice stalks and locals dressed in vibrant colors with red cheeks in contrast to the black mantos and black crows you might see in Tehran. They appeared to be so carefree and happy. Bright-eyed children waved, selling corn from improvised wooden stands and the warm air carried a whiff of jasmine.

Arriving at the gate, the doorman immediately let us in when my father said the last name of the person's villa we were going to. The doorman bowed and opened the gate. Wow! What a nice welcoming!

We were finally here! The villa was my father's friend's who had opted to go to Los Angeles to visit his family there, so we were using his place. The villa in which we all settled consisted of a couple of bedrooms and three baths. No one family was given a single bedroom, so we were divided: one for the females, and another was for the kids, so if any felt compelled to perform a karate kick in the middle of the night no adult would be injured. The last was reserved for the men, and was where all the men slept together. It was true Iranian family friendliness!

The living and dining rooms and backyard were considered public places, and all the peeps had access to those places. But the bathrooms were another story. These had to be shared in various ways. You really learned to share after this experience. In the women's bathroom, someone might be taking a shower, another applying makeup, while a third washed her feet, all this while engaged in very serious conversation regarding an important subject like Aziz Joon's neighbor's daughter getting a divorce!

In the other bathroom, situated in a remote corner of the house, the men did whatever men do...I didn't really want to go there!

The day of the New Year, *Sal Tahvil* as they called it, the entire family stood together in front of the TV. The moment *Sal Tahvil* was announced was like the ball dropping in Times Square! Everybody started kissing, one from the left, one from the right, and hugging—sometimes double hugging! This was March 21st, the famous worldly equinox, when the sun crosses the celestial equator dividing day and night. It was my first *Nowruz* celebrated in my country and even though I had so many divides in my head, it felt like home.

Once this love and affection died down a bit, it was time to eat! On the long table was *sabzi polo mahi*, steamed rice with chopped parsley, dill, and chives served with fresh white fish. The traditional meal with mountains of garlic on the table! They were a hit!

The entire family stayed indoors that day, basking in the well-earned (or not so well-earned) vacation.

18

Calling "The Man"

THE DAYS THAT FOLLOWED WERE spent mostly in a state of languid quiet—the way a vacation should be spent.

Everyone ate together, shared stories, and almost everyone had the occasional Iranian siesta! The men played poker on the dining room table, having figured out one another's infinite variety of poker faces. In short, they were extremely advanced players—if not professional—though a few thought themselves to be one, and even wore sunglasses at times!

One night Arshia, Bahareh and Ghazaleh decided to throw a party and Arshia had invited some of the peeps he knew in Darya Kenar and the surrounding gated communities. The parents were okay with that just because they were also involved and they drank while on holiday. I didn't know why it was so taboo to drink on holidays and not at parties in Tehran. The Emperor didn't throw a fit and kept saying, "It's *Eid*, let's have fun." Was this a new part of my dad I was witnessing? I felt in Shomal, especially in these gated wealthy communities, the Islamic rules were a bit less overbearing.

I mean the guys were playing poker for one, and now we were ordering drinks and the Emperor was cool with it. Interesting to say the least!

On another note, it felt weird to drink with my parents around so I decided to keep on the down low and let Arshia and his friends do most of the drinking. I wondered if the Emperor was okay with everything while it was the New Year. If so maybe I could get away with introducing Arash. No, bad choice. He would probably turn all conservative and traditional on me.

We didn't have any drinks so we needed to call "the man," the Shomal equivalent of the Ray-Ban wearing movie guy, to bring us a couple of bottles of vodka.

Forgetting that in this country lots of stuff, including the black market, is male dominated, I stepped up to the plate to call "the man." Everyone was fine with it...but that was the thing. I was in a group of family and friends who were the liberal part of this Islamic culture. I felt comfort in that, but it clashed with the outside regime. It was a group within a group within a group. Confusion bomb for a Brooklyn-er! Obviously the guy had a name, but probably not his actual one, considering what he provided! I got his digits from Arshia and dialed away.

"Hello?" I said.

"Yes ma'am," said a gravelly voice, "what would you like?"

Right to the point—all business! "Can we have a couple of bottles of vodka—"

Abruptly another voice cut in: "*Khanoom en karha chie, chi darid sefaresh midid?*" Since that meant "What are you doing ma'am? What do you think you are ordering?" I felt a rush of anger in my gut and felt I was talking to the *Komiteh* or maybe a higher authority!

268

"*Khanoom yani chi*!" I fired back with a New York attitude, curious and frustrated about why the operator had come on the line intruding on my call!

"*Hamin alan ghat konid!*" said the operator with such rage I thought he might fly through the line and strangle me.

I still hadn't connected the dots yet and was still trying to win my debate.

"Who is this?" I demanded.

"*Be shoma hich rabti nadare, hamin alan ghat konid!*" he repeated again.

This was getting annoying!

Arshia, who had grasped what happened, jumped up, hooked the phone away, and hung up.

"What in the world was that all about?" I said. "Oh my lord, was that what and why I think it was?"

"Yup. I totally forgot to remind you, and you quickly switch the channel to the U.S. You can't fight with them here! It's a win for them and always a loss for us in this situation! They have nothing better to do!"

"I totally forgot," I said smiling.

"Don't worry woman," said Bahareh, who had overheard from the kitchen. "I will get some alcohol from the neighbor two villas down, no biggie," she continued.

The operator interrupting the phone line! Wow, that was too much! Even the phone line was tapped! Wowzer! Why hadn't he simply killed the call? You know, snuffed it out leaving nothing but the howling wind? He had to give me his piece of mind and tell me to hang up! Drama...they could avoid this whole power play by pressing a button. But that's probably the point: paranoia. They want you to know they know you're into illegal activity, and prevent you from doing it again. Good luck with that! There was so much division in this country, you would succeed for sure!

Initially I got a bit freaked out, then I saw how nonchalant the others behaved. Good thing for us the neighbors had vodka and also joined the party, which went on until 3 a.m. Celebrating the New Year to the Nth-and-then-some degree was a tradition with a li'l partay over here and a li'l drinking over there! It was really, truly, wholeheartedly festive!

•••

One day, my mom, aunt, and cousins decided to head out to the beach. Excited, I put on my new two-piece fiery bikini and off we went. I wanted to show off with them in front of Arash, but I had no idea where!

Once there, I could see how the beach was set up to keep the women separated from the men. I wall of canvas had been erected, concealing the women and providing a private space where they could swap their mantos or chadors for bikinis. Simple rules: no men, no boys, no cell phones, no cameras. The scene itself was a mix of dull and interesting, nothing I had experienced, at least on a beach.

Some women wore the latest, most contemporary bathing suits, as if models straight from that month's *Sports Illustrated* cover! Their shades and glossy lipstick were irresistible eye candy. They mostly relaxed and worked on their coffee-colored tans. Other women wore bras and underwear, and that was just disgusting! Opposite the cover girls, a few were so religious they didn't even rely on the canvas barrier and chilled wearing their mantos and wimples in the hot sun! My *Jeopardy* question for 2000 was: What was the point of coming to the beach then?

"These are our Olympic swimmers," said Bahareh, giggling. "They are also highly *khosh teep* (stylish)."

The whole view resembled any beach anywhere, without men though. Similar to an outdoor sauna. This def was no longer Coney Island. I turned toward Bahareh. "Where are the guys?"

"Oh, well there is a way to check them out." Her mischievous smile said it all.

"How?"

"Take off your clothes, and swim far out beyond the canvas. The guys usually swim out there too, and then you can check each other out!"

"What's the point of that? Are we skinny dipping by the way?"

"No, you dork. But I love it when we someway, somehow fight the system." she said as she rubbed oil on her legs.

"Can you be arrested if seen that far out? You know, checking out some guy?"

"Yup, we have the 'sea *Komiteh*' on the water too. They are everywhere!" she joked, but her eyes were serious. "Just have a little bit of fun, and don't get too crazy. Or just check out the latest mode in fashion from the girls on the beach—they're wearing it, and they're wearing it before anyone in America."

I looked around and saw my mom and aunt gossiping away in their two-piece bikinis, Ghazaleh reading her book, and as my view expanded I noticed some of the ladies were even topless! Man, who said this was an Islamic country! But no—there were no men on the beach and I assumed no one was a lesbian here. With that assumption everything was cool.

I recalled the latest fashion show in the basement, and its up-to-date designs. This beach was the most secluded I'd ever seen. What happens if a storm comes in and pulls some hot girl in a bikini out to sea? Would one of the sexy guys who is looking over the canvas (hypothetically) jump in and rescue her?

In theory it could happen. But more interesting would be if the guy performed CPR on her! What then? Does he call the girl's father first to get permission? I didn't get it again. *Jeopardy* question for 2200: When do I get enlightened?

I had seen separate sections in the bus and in the TV studio lunch queues, but this was life and death. On the lighter side maybe there was a girl lifeguard that was fast and knew CPR. That was my enlightenment for the day.

I really wanted to spend a day on the beach with Arash, but seeing this one and its set up I knew it had to be at a private pool, or maybe sneaking onto a public beach late at night. I chose not to obsess over this and work on my tan. After applying Bahareh and Ghazaleh's mix of coffee beans and oil, which supposedly gave a real good tan, I laid next to everyone else, chilling. Before I went into hibernation I noticed something that might just be a new wave of fashion.

"Are those the stretch mantos?" I shouted so loud my mom, aunt and cousins jumped to their feet and scanned a cluster of ladies wearing sticky, stretched swim wear—the couture, super-trendy Muslim looks.

A lady overheard me and stepped over to describe this phenomenon. "*Dokhtar khanoom* (missy), these are burkinis, the new revolution of bikinis; a burka plus a bikini." Her smile said, "Muslims can even go swimming with burkas!"

"Really?"

"These new swimsuits," she continued, "are *kheili sheek* (fashionable) and super comfy. Finally someone has come up with a solution!"

I paid polite attention but this was really ridiculous. I guess it was respectable, but if these ladies participated in the Olympics, wouldn't this attire slow them down?

"It comes with a headpiece then a long sleeve top down to the knees, with the skinny pants. The best thing is that some of them have ties to keep the top in place while you are doing the breaststroke. Oh look at that water, they are going to swim, the material is exquisite. *Enshallah* (if God wills) *shoma ham az enha beghirid* (you guys will get the same)."

Umm, this dame must be out of her mind! I just nodded and turned to Ghazaleh, "I think she really wants one. Maybe you should put it on your to-do list and buy it as an *Eidi* gift for her."

I turned to the lady again and asked, "So how would you get a tan?"

"*Madar en harfha chie. Bronze mikham nasham!*" (I'd rather not get a tan!)

The tone in which the woman answered was so funny that I squeezed Ghazaleh's hand and giggled, but I tried not to make it too apparent.

I felt a deeper bond forming with my cousins and loved it. They were understanding and supportive of my lack of knowledge or "*Jeopardy* questions." The only element missing was Arash. Why was I thinking about him so much?

I wasn't in love with him, but he was constantly on my mind…

I wondered whether it was the same for him.

That night, the family decided to grab a bite to eat, so everyone prepped up and we decided to walk to the seaside restaurant. It got packed at night and I really crossed my fingers, because it was Thursday night—equivalent to NYC's Saturday nights—so Arash might come too.

Not only were my fingers crossed, but I had my toes wrapped around one another as well.

19

A Lamb Among Wolves

MY MOM HAD CONVINCED THE Emperor to allow us to go out for dinner alone. He first said we should all go but then my mom reminded him that we wanted girl time and it was a gated community after all…what was the worry? Then Arshia chimed in and said he would meet us afterwards with his friend Hessam so he finally backed up and gave the okay. But we had a curfew and that was 9 p.m. sharp. Car, taxi, or by foot, we had to be at the villa at 9 p.m. sharp. He smiled while saying it but I sensed he was dead serious.

Bahareh and Ghazaleh were dead scared of my dad and since Aunt Elahe was such good friends with them they didn't have any Emperor rules. But when we were together they had to abide by them.

I sat waiting for my cousins to finish up their makeup. It literally took forever. "So, tell me…" I asked, "…how long does it take you guys to get ready? It's not like we have a hot date." I heard a few mumbled curses, but knew the girls didn't care about my comments.

Growing up in Iran they have a solid defense shield, and needed it. I stood and paced the room as if checking out the progress of rebellious runway models.

"All the cuties are out, and even though we lack a car we could still watch them on foot. A car is not absolutely necessary to circle around—if you know what I mean," said Bahareh bronzing every acre of her face. "We'll act like we're out walking, not paying attention even though that's exactly what we're doing!" she continued. Wow, progressive thinking, I thought.

"If someone comes by and you don't like them, don't be afraid to express yourself. Or to say *boro gomsho* (get lost!) with an attitude."

"Why the attitude?"

"Because," answered Ghazaleh, "they like it and it's a turn on! They will have to chase for what's good—they will have to *earn* you!"

"Yeah, yeah...hurry up! We have the earliest curfew!" I insisted.

I kept my cool by thinking about Arash. Bahareh wasn't really seeing anyone and Ghazaleh wasn't into anyone serious either. It seemed they didn't have a boyfriend but then again no girl in Iran "looked like" they had a boyfriend. The weird part was you would suddenly find out that the black crows—the smelly, foul odor moustache girl—in class had a boyfriend. Shocker!

The topping shocker was that they actually *had* a relationship. Good for them! I could see how that would make a good movie: The Black Crow goes out to town with her Beau! Ha!

Chatting and joking, we moved with a purpose, but in our own subtle way. I could see the car play along Darya Kenar's main street was the same as on Jordan in Tehran. No wonder Arash had gotten nervous! Cars cruised up and down the streets, looking for the right person to exchange numbers with.

"Here we go," I said. "Check it out."

A shiny silver Mercedes slowed, obviously interested in us. I had to say, we were hotter than most girls walking the street. The Mercedes pulled up to the curb, and a man leaned out the window. "What's your name, beautiful?"

He was gazing at me, as if I was walking alone.

"*Torobche*," said Bahareh (literally meaning "radish," but slangishly meaning "none of your beeswax") and grabbed me as if to protect me. "*Ba oon ghiyafash tike ham mindaze* (with that face he is teasing too)."

"What's wrong with his face?" I mumbled to her.

Bahareh went on, "*Dokhi joon* (girlfriend!) *en chi bood, to ba behtar az enha mitooni bepari!*" (slangishly meaning "what was that, you could score much better!")

"And by the way might I remind you, you've already got a man!" she said as if protecting me in a way rather than being jealous. I felt the same towards Ghazaleh. Not an ounce of jealousy existed in these girls and they were up there as far as funny, progressive, and accomplished girls. My cousins rocked!

"So you answer with *Torobche?*"

"Yup, and if he is super *poroo* (the type that teases more) he will ask, '*khonat kojast?*' (where is this radish's house?) and you will answer '*to baghche!*' (in the garden)."

"Or," I joked, "you can say *be to che!*" (none of your biz boy!)

Bahareh regarded me with her dark, gentle eyes. And Ghazaleh giggled.

"We pick and choose as we please." And we all put our arms around one another for a big cousin sandwich hug.

"It's a long way to the restaurant, *mikhai auto bezanim?*" (do you want to catch a ride?) Ghazaleh asked.

"I do," I said, "but I don't see any taxis here!"

"No silly, auto means you catch a ride with a hottie dude!"

"You mean just randomly get in some dude's car?"

"Yup, and if you like them a lot you can get their number. You may or may not buzz them up but at least you get a free ride!"

I narrowed my eyes, taking this in. "So, how do you choose which car to jump into?"

"It doesn't matter, as long as the car has wheels and the guy doesn't look like a weirdo, it's all good!"

"Whatever you say," I couldn't believe that was a *thang* girls did here. But in this gated community I felt like they paid off a lot of the black crow people and their *Komiteh* mates!

Before I knew it, Ghazaleh had taken the initiative and was flirting with an upscale car, as opposed to one of the falling-apart Peykans! And we were soon riding in some random stranger's vehicle, heading to the seaside restaurant.

This was so weird. A free ride from some stranger who could suddenly turn away from the agreed-upon route—then what? It's not like we could jump out! What if they captured us and decided to trade us! Ok, the movie *Taken* was becoming too real for me! I was a bundle of nerves. What if Arash saw me? What if the Emperor saw me? It seemed so natural to the girls and even the dudes…it was an epidemic! Lots of girls were doing the same!

I could see Ghazaleh had the hots for the driver and sensed butterflies in her stomach. We eventually arrived at the restaurant and Ghazaleh exchanged numbers but I could feel these guys had girlfriends. Their cells kept ringing every two minutes and they kept declining. Who in Iran didn't have a relationship? Everything was such a show! Everyone was just scared of the other person knowing!

All at once I was shocked. I saw a face so familiar I jumped. That handsome face glared at me, eyes judging and fierce: Arash. Leave it to him to come on a Thursday night! But his face was angry. I had never seen it that way.

Bahareh noticed this immediately and also saw the *Komiteh* in the background.

"Just be chill," she said.

Ghazaleh, who saw us both looking at the same guy, knew that guy must be Arash, Witnessing Arash for the first time she said, "He is such a *tikeh*," (literally meaning "piece" but slangishly meaning hottie!)

"It looks like *gare be khodesh*!" (he has problems with himself!)

I stepped between my cousins and whispered, "Guys I think he just saw us jumping out of that guy's car and is having a cow."

"*Dokhi* (girl), that is what's called *gheyrat*, and all Iranian men have it. It's kinda like jealousy but a bit more extreme. Actually *way* more extreme," said Ghazaleh.

"Yeah, to the point that a fight might break out," added Bahareh.

"Did you look at my girlfriend? And the other replies 'Yes, who are you to tell me who I can and cannot look at?' That's the pride talking. Then the whole thing goes back and forth, until one either lands a punch or one of the girls jumps between them, sparking up the drama!" Ghazaleh said giggling.

I was taking in this movie plot but was also becoming angry about why Arash was so angry! Who is he to tell me what I can or cannot do?

"*Gheyratesh gol karde*, meaning he's a bit too jealous to the point of finding it offensive and wants to protect you. But it seems he is keeping his cool. Some men jump up and punch out the guy on the other end of the flirt!"

"Is this true for all Iranian men?"

"Well, let's just say it runs quite heavily in the blood, especially in Iranian fathers! Like the Emperor! In his blood it doesn't run, it sprints!"

Arash watched us as if lip reading the conversation. It looked like he was calming down as he approached us. He said his *salam* to all of us and introduced his two other buddies he had driven down with. His posture was tense but he got a table and we all sat down. We were all a bit tense! The *Komiteh* was nowhere to be seen yet but Arash had ways of dealing with them if necessary.

Then he stood to go order some food and I followed him to interrogate. I stepped toward the line, then stood beside Arash and said, "Why so upset? I've never seen you like this before." I spoke English so no one around would understand.

"Shaghayegh, this is not the right time to talk," he said softly, not even looking at me. He said my full name and then I knew he was really upset.

"It was the auto, wasn't it?"

Arash glanced at the ground. "What do you think? You got into a complete stranger's car. Forget the fact that you already *have* a boyfriend, do you know these guys can actually *hurt* you? They can rob you, they can beat the shit out of you, rape you!" He was speaking with a flat-out British accent, which I thought was totally hot! But his gaze was serious, and he didn't even know how sexy he appeared to me at that moment.

I wanted to sleep with him right now, but I firmed my voice. "We were just catching a ride. And for your information, I wasn't flirting!"

"Hell, I don't even know how to flirt in full Farsi!"

It was our first back and forth English speaking conversation, and we were attracting more attention than if we were speaking Farsi. The American with a slight Brooklyn accent versus the classy London guy. Everyone from our table knew the noise was from us and let us be.

"And you didn't feel that one might be interested in you?" he snapped.

"What? And if they were, what would happen next?" I sensed this verbal assault had to be the *gheyrat* the girls were talking about; striking with high voltage. Arash knew I had no intention of exchanging numbers and calling the guy, so he was simply venting, and managing it well. This was a completely different side of him...and I loved it! He was fighting for me! He genuinely cared! He wanted me and it was for real. That was when I realized it was the real deal.

Abruptly Arash quit talking, realizing he was overreacting about someone he cared for and who cared for him back. We were just having fun...but he was right. What if those guys were rapists?

Our heated dialogue attracted attention, but the bystanders assumed the man and woman were from *kharej*, or another country, so they looked on as if we were their entertainment, like a soap opera they had switched the channel to! Everyone became special in Iran once speaking another language, and speaking it with a foreign accent! Among them all, English was the black sheep of the lingo family.

We went back to our table once we had emptied some of the negative energy. My cousins were making obvious efforts to avoid eye contact. They changed the subject of the conversation into the weather and asking how *Eid* went for the other guys at the table. I was still upset about how Arash had jumped at me, but there was no use dwelling on it. Arash had been too aggressive. I mean c'mon, cut me some slack! I was just a little lamb in this country; a lamb among the wolves! I'm sure he probably had given autos to girls in the past but also knew that if you were to get in the wrong car, you were screwed!

While in my own bag of thoughts I sensed a hand grabbing mine under the table and clasping my hand. It was Arash, and I knew he felt genuinely sorry. After all, he did have Iranian blood even though he was brought up in London. He didn't look at me as if he didn't want to attract attention but massaged my hand from underneath the table. At the table he started making conversation, and funny ones. He was getting over it, and the massage was definitely helping me get over it too!

It was an interesting night to say the least, and now our early curfew was approaching. Arash got the car ready to drop us off two blocks from our villa, down an alley. Before I got out, Arash signaled me to wait. Bahareh and Ghazaleh caught the drift, and took baby steps down the alley, slowing their pace.

"Sorry I got a little carried away," Arash teasingly said, "but it's for your own good! And so is this." He cupped my face in his hands, leaned, and touched my lips so softly I felt the moist warmness of his. I felt he wanted me right now, right there, to make out...but decided to continue the kiss to substitute for the days we were apart. So unfair! Why did everything have to be behind closed doors? He had to go back to Tehran to take care of his father's business and I was staying here for the rest of *Eid*, without him.

From the distance, my cousins watched our steamy encounter.

After a long minute, I emerged from the car, lipstick worn off my mouth, and bearing a small hickey on my throat.

Bahared suddenly shouted out, "Look at your neck!"

"What about it?" I said with a surprised tone.

"Looks like Arash did the works," she smiled sarcastically and reached for a mirror in her bag so I could see myself.

I checked it out and said, "No worries! This is where wimple and scarf fashion comes in handy. It will cover nicely. You know, this Islamic wardrobe does have alternative saving functions!"

I felt my lamb was turning into a wolf, or maybe the wolf was coming out of its hiding place.

"Be careful," said Ghazaleh. "Especially in front of the Emperor. He is super sharp," she continued.

I knew super-duper cleverness ran in the family and noticed it running through my veins too. It was a total discovery mode for me, and I felt I was surfing the wave of change like a champion. There were times I did feel lost and confused, but whatever! I was living in this country, so why not make the best of it?

We started walking towards the villa when I noticed some familiar faces walking up from the beach behind us. It was my dad, Arshia and Arshia's buddy Hessam. Arash was already gone but I suddenly got freaked out. Had they seen anything? It was too dark right? Now I was worried about covering up this stupid hickey!

My heart started beating and the bad part was that I could hear it clearly. Thank god it was getting darker and my hickey was beginning to hide within the shadows of the night! But I wrapped my scarf a little tighter, just to be safe.

20

Feast Before Sorrow

I FELT A HEAVY SILENCE from my dad but Arshia and Hessam were cracking jokes and telling stories so they managed to lift the mood. The Emperor wasn't speaking much and didn't even look at me. He didn't even look at Bahareh and Ghazaleh that much to be honest.

Oh god, I thought he was going to have a heart attack.

Once home I put some foundation on my neck to color fade the hickey and wanted to call Arash because I was a bit scared, but whenever I neared a phone some family member would pop up out of nowhere—sometimes from the sky itself—so no phone calls were going out of this villa.

During tea time I sensed my mom was a bit shaken up too. I didn't know how to make sense of it all. My mom was a bit on the lighter side, but both the mamma and pappa were going through loops and it was evident even though they were trying to keep their poker faces.

"Keep it cool. I don't think they saw anything," Bahareh whispered in my ear.

"How can I? I feel horrible for lying, but then again it's my life!" I said back.

"We hear you sistah, but I gotta tell you one thing. If the Emperor saw something, he is really respecting you and keeping on the down low in front of these people. Remember the *gheyrat* runs strong here!" she said.

Gheyrat I got, but too much of it I didn't accept. Who was the Emperor to make the calls on my life? First I was born here, then he decides a better life awaits me in New York, then he decides I better get in touch with my Iranian roots before I turned "white" on him, and now this bullshit! I had had enough and was ready to burst.

I missed my freedom in Brooklyn and I missed talking to my girls and not making such a big deal about dates and even kissing guys. Lord, I wasn't even having sex! But if the moment was right with the right person, I didn't even get what was so wrong with that!

All the girls I knew here including Bahareh, Ghazaleh, Neda, Saloomeh, Mina, Azin, and Nooshin were awesome but they all strategized about how to manage their love lives in accordance with their parents. They even made sure their education was aligned with *their* plans.

It wasn't like that in New York. We didn't even talk about this stuff and let life just take its course! This country had no rules because the people made up their own homemade rules in their own minds! Maybe that's why finding a leader in Iran was so hard; everyone was their own leader.

I went out to the backyard to get some fresh air and look at the stars. Bahareh noticed and came to follow me and I told her I needed to be alone before I killed someone. Literally! After about fifteen minutes I heard the back door open and out walked the Emperor. I didn't even have the patience for him.

"What's up?" he asked in his New York accent.

"Nothing, could you please leave me alone?" I asked him politely.

"I just want to ask you a question. Remember, we don't lie in this family to one another," he said, pretending to have a friendly tone.

I didn't answer and wanted to shout at the top of my lungs how fed up I was with this country and all the different ways of thinking here!

"Did you lie to me about who you were with tonight?"

"No. Why would you think that?"

"I went out to buy groceries and saw you at seaside with your cousins and—"

"Are you sure it was us? We left pretty early! Remember our curfew?"

"I will ask you only once," he said firmly. "Were you with some guys? One of them looked like he was very close to you." He continued looking at me.

"What?" I said. My mind was running. He had seen us together and had probably seen Arash holding my hand underneath the table! Out of all the times my Iranian father could catch me, it was this time. Well, at least that was better than him seeing Arash and me making out in his car and ending in a hickey!

There was no way to deny it because he had seen not only me but Bahareh and Ghazaleh too! Dang, I had no way out! But still I decided to deny it. Maybe he was so far away that he had just caught a glimpse and the rest was a bluff. He played poker very well and I knew he was pro at this.

"You heard me Shaghayegh. Did you lie to me? Are you seeing anyone? You better tell me the truth!" he demanded.

The truth! The truth was that you brought me to this bullshit country expecting me to understand everything when I don't even know the culture! That was the real truth...the rest was playing with my head! If I did tell him the truth I would be screwed because then he would know everything. So I opted for the other way, which was telling him that he needed to get glasses!

"No. It wasn't us. You probably saw someone else," I snapped back firmly. I felt like I was being interrogated by the CIA for my life and decisions! Maybe this was how I was brought up "westernized" but I also strongly felt that if he approached me with kindness and as a friend I would have been honest. But this was ridiculous and my way of fighting back was my lying I guess...and making him upset. To be honest, at that point I didn't mind making him upset! I was furious with him! I wished I could take my passport and run away from this wretched place.

"Shaghayegh, I will ask you one more time: who were you with tonight?"

"Why do you care? What does it matter? It's my life! You already ruined it by bringing me to this messed up country!"

He stood back when he saw my defensive side.

"What are you talking about?" he sounded shocked.

"I hate this country! I hate having to pretend! Everyone takes their kids to get a better education in the U.S. and here we are, BACKWARDS in a BACKWARDS country!" I said, letting out all my anger. "Don't sound like you brought me here to get in touch with my roots. I could have done that in Brooklyn by going to an Iranian school or something, but no, nooo, you missed Iran and you guys *love* Iran, and now I'm supposed to love it too!"

I had completely turned the tables from being with Arash to making him the bad guy. But it was the truth, and I couldn't keep it in anymore.

"So because I caught you red-handed, now you are blaming Iran for your lie?" he said, mad.

"You caught me, but not red-handed! I could make my own decisions and go out with who I wanted. The only messed up part is that in this country, people my age are NOT allowed to make their own decisions! Well, dad, I have got news for you. I was raised somewhere else and bringing me here can't change my mentality, even if I do have to wear that stupid scarf and put on that ugly manto!" I answered back in a high tone and was almost about to cry when my mom walked in on us.

"What the hell is going on here?" she demanded. "Kaveh? Is this how you handle stuff? Shaghayegh, what's wrong sweetheart?"

"Ask your controlling Iranian husband!" I said, walking away and afraid that I might burst out crying in front of them both.

My father shouted after me, "You have so much in front of you! Why are you crushing it with these loser guys?"

At that point I knew he had seen us and knew that my mother knew and also knew that I had made my point. If I wanted to see a loser, I would see a loser. Anyways he wasn't a loser and my dad was pissed off because he thought I was lying. I wasn't lying but all this fear and not telling your dad because he has *gheyrat* was really getting to me. He made me lie because he created fear because he was so attached to what others *might* think in our society. This reputation thing in Iran was over the top and no one was themselves!

And so the girl had to be put in a cage until the prince, without any lies, came to pick her up from the castle through the front door. They can't date to get to know one another, oh no, because they might kiss and through that kiss she would lose her virginity! Or if in public, get caught by the *Komiteh*!

Screw that, I said to myself and put my face on my own lap and cried on the stairway in front of the villa. Nobody could see me from here, but I couldn't walk in with red eyes. Crap! So for the longest time I sat on the stairs looking at the stars.

•••

I had fallen asleep when I felt someone trying to fit on the staircase and squash next to me.

"Mom!" I said, almost falling off.

"C'mon, make room for me!" she said laughing.

"There is none!"

"Yes, there is!" and she started tickling me, leading me to sit on the lower step in front of her.

"*Azizam*, are you okay?"

"Depends on how you define okay."

"Don't get smart with me. Your father is just trying to protect you," she said.

"From what? What is this dangerous thing that is happening that I need to be protected from? Why doesn't he hire a bodyguard for me if he's that protective!" I said defensively.

"You know I have never talked to you about sex, but I think it's time, especially since you are growing into such a doll."

"Flattering mom, but I'm all ears. Why is this stuff so taboo here?"

"Well, for one thing this isn't a subject that is discussed. It's the culture primarily and when mixed up with all these Islamic thoughts it's said that a girl should be untouched before marriage. You know, like a virgin," she explained.

"I prefer Madonna's 'Like a Virgin' to the Islamic like a virgin!" I said laughing.

She took in a giggle too and continued, "So it's really shameful if someone has a boyfriend, kisses, and has more intimacy with him. Now, that said I know you are growing and I am not going to mandate anything to you, but I want you to know that you should be private in this area. I am not saying to go and have sex, but respect yourself enough that you have sex with someone that you emotionally connect with. That said, I am still not saying to have sex! But I want you to see the bigger picture," she said, looking away.

"I know it's complicated here and your father is a very Iranian man set in his ways, but you do make your own decisions and both of us are here to share our wisdom with you," she continued.

Wow! Now, that was a touchdown! It was the first time my mom had opened up like this, especially with Aziz Joon wearing a burka, but they were words coming from a person who was here and had seen the other side—which she had. She had grown up here and married the Emperor to go live in the U.S. She had seen both worlds and I could feel her words were golden.

"Let's go back inside. We are leaving for Tehran in a couple of days and you should enjoy Shomal to the max," she urged me. I gave her a mushy kiss and she wiped my tears, just as a good mother does. H_2O proved to be a hero!

21

Feast & Confusion

WE LEFT SHOMAL A COUPLE of days afterwards and I still refused to speak with the Emperor. I preferred all of our communication be made through my mom. I was still furious with him for acting so selfish! He kept trying to make convo but he was out of luck. The issue hadn't resolved with my dad but I think he just missed me and wanted to break the ice. His thoughts were his thoughts and for a guy his age it was impossible to change. Well, for an Iranian guy his age.

I needed a break and wanted to be alone so I was happy we were going to Tehran so I could go back to my room and watch *Tango & Cash* followed by *Home Alone* for the Nth time. It was my only return back to New York! Or should I say the States. Or should I say home. I missed home. I didn't know what to call home anymore really. The city I was born in or the city I was raised in and had an emotional connection with?

We arrived to see an empty Tehran. It looked eerie. I had never seen the city so vacant and traffic-free. A few stores were open, but most supermarkets and *baghalis* (small local grocers) were closed.

I really wanted to the streets to be back to normal, to hear kids playing football in the streets, causing cars to honk horns to avoid being run over. I wanted the sound of melon trucks passing, laden with fresh cantaloupe for sale.

Back home, we quickly unloaded the car. My mom told me that we would be doing *Eid Didani* at my mom's eldest cousin's home. "Aren't they on vacation or something?" I asked.

"No. They usually stay home for the first week because he is the eldest, and the younger have to visit him for respect purposes." So in Iranian tradition the eldest always had the respect factor that the younger had to abide by.

"So he sits there for people to come and visit?"

"Yup. Well, he is a bit older than old, and your cousins will be visiting him too. They might even be there tonight."

"Mom, we just got back from vacay! Do we have to go? Or do I have to come? I barely know him." I threw in the last part to make her feel guilty.

"Oh Shaghayegh, he gives good *Eidis*," she added, knowing my eyes would pop. *Eidis* was the gift an elder gives a younger during *Eid*.

I had no real objection to the visit, but I wanted to rest so I could speak with Arash tonight. I missed speaking with him and joking around with someone who understood me and was from the "other side." I knew going to this *mehmooni* (little visit, or party) would drag on until dinner. All the ladies would start talking, most likely gossip, and the men would start playing backgammon, and next thing you know it's 2 a.m.!

But I knew that arguing would get me nowhere, so I prepped myself up to eat good food and have an extremely boring night.

The arrival at the cousin's house was a barrage of smiling greetings, warm kisses, and repeated voicings of *"Befarmaud"* (welcome) perhaps five or six times. I wanted badly to jump in with: "I got it, lady! And I'm coming in, back off already," but I bit my tongue. I knew the remaining seven days of *Eid* were probably going to be spent this way.

Inside (finally!), the table brimmed with nuts, fresh pastries, a variety of fruit, candies, and of course, fresh tea. The hosts insisted everyone keep eating, so in order to avoid repeated commands to "please eat something," I made sure to keep a piece of pastry or apple near my mouth at all times. Every time the room hit one of those rare pockets of silence, someone broke it with a hearty, *"Befarmaiid-yek chizi bekhorid,"* again repeating the same slogan to have a bite to eat. Mamma mia! Shut up already! It was so annoying, I strategized to keep my hand on my fruit plate so they would look away from me.

As assumed, we stayed for dinner and it was a grand five or six hours *Eid Didani* before they called it quits. I listened to scattered conversations, but all of them were boring and really didn't interest me at all. All I could think about was Arash.

Once home, and everyone went to bed, I called him. He, of course, was expecting my call. I could feel the intensity of our chat as we talked about everything that had happened over the past week, and new stuff that had occurred. Obviously, he got upset over my fight with the Emperor but I felt it was only him that knew where I was coming from. I didn't want to raise my voice at my dad or have a stupid argument but lots of stuff regarding Iran bothered me and he either didn't get it or chose to ignore it. If the latter were true, that would be really hurtful. If the former was true, that would also be devastating because he was supposed to be my support factor and know the consequences of bringing someone to a country with all these heavy rules and cultural angles.

Arash told me to brush it off, that he was my dad after all. I told him I would, but it bothered me and I was just putting it temporarily on standby. That didn't mean that I would speak with him though.

"Stubborn, aren't we?" he joked.

"No, just answering my feelings!" I said. "I have to do what I feel or I will just turn into a slave of this society!"

He also gave me the heads up about the *Eid Didanis* being a vehicle for weight gain since all you did was talk and eat. Similar to Thanksgiving and Christmas, and the time in between when all you do is eat!

We chatted until I passed out on the phone.

• • •

The remaining days were spent in the same format, and I ended up going back to my job, which was ending in a couple of weeks, on the tenth day of *Nowruz*. On the thirteenth day another Iranian tradition kicked in and had everyone running off for picnics and outdoor activities in the park. I wondered if these people ever worked, since they seemed always to be on some kind of cultural or religious holiday!

The last day was called *Sizdeh Bedar*, the last day of the ever-long *Nowruz* holiday. Afterwards, everyone hopefully yet reluctantly returned to regular life.

On this occasion, in addition to the four-car train, some friends joined in for the twenty-kilometer trek to Karaj, where mostly it was green. So again we had the family including Bahareh and Ghazaleh,

Aunt Elahe, Arshia, Aziz Joon and another flock of second cousins. Now I really couldn't keep up with the distant peeps!

Another round of excessive traffic, and this time you could see a strand of green grass (*sabze*), taken from the Nowruz table, displayed in the rear windshield of the car ahead of you driving to the park too.

In the car, Ghazaleh said, "You also have to knot two pieces of grass together. It's tradition."

"Why? Am I maintaining the lawn, too?"

"No, you dork!" exclaimed Bahareh. "They say it's the knot of love! It's actually rooted in our psyche that stuff like goodwill and love exists among everything! Lots of girls do it with hopes of meeting the *one*!"

"But it's nothing like Woodstock in America!" Ghazaleh said giggling.

It was interesting that she even knew about Woodstock! Wow! Satellite TV did wonders! I scowled with sarcasm. "Nice comparison woman!"

"Oh just keep the tradition going. It's fun, and I try to make my knot with trees and Krazy Glue so no one can open it!" Ghazaleh said.

"Stop being so cheesy," said Bahareh.

"Whatever!" Ghazaleh said in return with her upper lip a bit slanted, conveying she was annoyed.

"Oh and this green *sabzeh* has to be thrown in a stream or river towards the end, to erase all negativity from our homes," said Bahareh.

"So in other words, you are polluting the water?"

"*Aroom* (relax), it's grass, so it goes back to nature, Ms. IQ."

I laughed. I looked forward to spending time in nature, especially knowing that Tehran was a city known for smoke and dust.

In the park we made fresh kebabs, had as much tea as you can imagine—while making note of the nearest bathrooms—and played dodgeball with the girls wrapping their mantos around their waist. Classic!

Finally, we tossed the knotted *sabzeh* in the pond, where it basically stood upside-down in the water in front of us. Then we started knotting the grass we were standing on until we were sure we would get married! Ha! Superstitious!

After sunset, we drank another cup of tea (I still didn't know where they put all this tea in their bodies), and we were back on the road again.

I really enjoyed the family time, even the annoying *Eid Didanis*, where we had to pretend to keep eating or the host might come and peel a cucumber for you, salt it, and slice it into fine shapes so you would have no choice but to eat it. And you wouldn't even know if she washed her hands after coming out of the bathroom! Classic moments were adding up.

•••

Initially I had hated coming to this country and now I wasn't so in love with it but it had helped me to understand myself on a deeper level. I mean, it was driving me crazy sometimes but it also helped me understand my culture, a culture I may have never gotten in touch with to such a deep extent if I lived in Brooklyn my whole life. The crappy part was that it had a heavy price tag! I was becoming a more developed female; my thoughts had changed and were becoming rounded, and even though I did give my parents attitude, I respected them. The love was so strong in this country that it made me overlook many cultural restraints.

Then there was Arash. My first boyfriend, my first "guy" friend, who really helped me see everything in Iran, from football stadiums, to explaining every incomprehensible subject, to a romantic love experience.

True, I had not yet slept with him, but I had no problem doing this even with all these taboo thoughts of virginity and marriage. In my opinion, and I am a very opinionated person, there was no problem exploring my sexuality with someone I love so much. I mean, who can predict the future? And who can say whether I'll be forever with Arash?

I had grown to change, love him and enjoyed all the other friendships I had made here. But I wondered about something and that was why Arash stayed with me sex-free. I mean, he was a guy, and at his age, high in testosterone. He was so fun, so sexy, he could easily sleep with anyone he desired. Why was he waiting so much for me? Was I the forbidden fruit?

On top of that he had money. Girls wanted to be with him, claiming he was the whole package. It was awkward but I looked at it as though he really respected and loved me. I hope that was true. I felt that was true.

I walked into this country with useless thoughts creating a dilemma regarding sex, then they slowly mounted and I think it wasn't really until after the talk I had with my mom that it all cleared up. It was unexpected, but the talk helped me see issues through my lens, not a traditional lens. I felt at peace with my sexuality and threw all the virgin BS in the trash!

22

The First Time

April 1998

MY JOB WAS GETTING MORE intense and I felt all eyes were on me now. They had moved me from reporting to an actual anchor position for sports although I still did both! Yes, I was live on air but I don't know why they wouldn't give me the screen. It was just my voice on various news segments even though he (my co-anchor) introduced me with my name and everything! Was it because I was a female reporting on sports? I had no clue. I was also being approached by Channel 4 to do a late-night talk show with another girl and had screen there, but my co-host was a girl. I couldn't make sense of any of it so just rolled with it. It was too much for my brain now. I just donned my attire as I was told and hid my mascara and stuff like that before security check.

I had developed a friendship with everyone and gotten to know how sympathetic they were and how much happiness and love they carried. I knew if one day they fired me or if miracles happened and I went back home to NYC, I would miss the dirty, bearded guard at the door, the black crows, and all my coworkers. They also had work ethic, even though they took every other day off!

But their energy, honesty, and easy-going ways were something I would never forget. Who knew, maybe I would become the main anchor here some day? That would be more complicated than I thought because now I was just a sports reporter, but I knew they had strict Islamic rules and employees also had to pass the *Gozinesh* test, where their ideological views were scrutinized. I didn't think it would be a good fit for this non-Islamic, westernized soul who never prayed or fasted but on the contrary drank, had a boyfriend, and wore open clothing where her skin was actually exposed! Oooh, such a sin!

For now, I was happy. Of course, with Arash.

My birthday was approaching and Arash was arranging a party for me. It was a combo of my college acceptance and my birthday; two in one. I told him he had to do separate parties, but he would tell me to relax! It was a good reason to be next to him. This journey so far had been a disaster with lots of good parts, but those good parts weren't strong enough to change the word "disaster!"

I told my parents I was headed to Elham's for the night. She had gained seniority since getting me in for the internship! I stocked my party clothes in my duffel bag and threw it down the stairs so I could walk out of the house with some books and an apple.

I arrived early to Arash's to help him get ready for additional errands. As always, his place looked spotless and clean, and he had hired catering and ordered good wine and drinks. I was both excited and worried. I had invited all my friends and Arash had invited some of his and you can't go wrong with good drinks and no chaperone!

The worried part came from my parents calling Elham's number, but she had told me she had diverted the line to her cell.

I felt all the people at this party had helped me understand and cope with the newfound, alien craziness of this strange country. Arash was at the head of the line. From the moment we had met, I had discovered a hidden passion and love within me that he drew out, and I managed to experience it with him. All the dinners, the Lavasan mini-trip, meeting secretly in Shomal, and the underground parties he had exposed me to. Our souls had joined, and I knew for sure I was in love.

I changed shortly after because it was now showtime! Guests started arriving one by one and each of them made me super happy. And they all were carrying gifts! I wondered how on earth I was going to sneak these gifts into the house...

Bahareh told me she had bought me the *Firoozeh* gemstone (turquoise stone), the original found in Iran's Khorasan Province, so they had specially designed a pair of matching earrings, a bracelet, and a pendant for me. It was awesome and the minute she told me I had to open it!

I loved silver and some really unique designs I had only seen in Iran and never seen such elegance and beauty on any website or in any NYC store. It was the stuff Elahelty wore. Of course we weren't Elahelty but we were close to it! Wink!

We ate, drank, sang, talked and took lots of pictures to remember my first birthday in Iran thrown by my first boyfriend with my first friends in Tehran. Arash had a balcony and was grilling some meat (at my request, even though there was full catering service—it was my favorite), so we moved outside to look at the Tehran sky. In this sky you could see every single star...or maybe it was because of Arash that I could see every single star!

The air was crisp and the steak kebabs right on! I don't know if it was the weather or company but the food in Iran was impeccable! Even better than NYC where everyone raves about the food!

Neda and Saloome from Tatbighi had come too and they were hitting on some of Arash's friends. The norm. After her hip movements Neda joined me in my third piece of steak and said, "Happy birthday woman! This party is awesome," and bit into some meat. "Oh by the way, I have news for you!"

"Please do share!" I exclaimed.

"We are moving back to Los Angeles in a month or so," she said casually.

For some reason it hurt me when she said that. I liked Iran but also wanted to go back so badly. Why was she returning and I wasn't? Why had her father decided she had to go to college in LA and mine wanted me to stay here?

"That's awesome!" I said. Even though I was bummed about my status I was happy for her. She had a long future ahead of her and I knew she was in love with UCLA and the whole beach vibe there.

"What do you plan on doing when you get there?" I asked.

"First things first, I'll throw away this stupid scarf and jump in the ocean!" she said laughing.

"Jump in for me too! I remember Bar Beach in New York, where we always went...good times. So what is the second thing you are going to do?" I asked curiously. I asked this as if it was a foreign thing to me, or something I missed. I mean it was no big deal, she was headed to California. I guess I felt so overwhelmed I wanted to hear her say things to me like, "I could go here and do that and just be." I wanted to hear her say, "I don't know what I am going to study in college but hey I have two years to decide, no rush." I wanted to hear her say, "I am going to play beach volleyball with my friends." I wanted to hear her say, "We're going to order Chinese food when we get home from the mall and have Oreo cookies." Oh my god! Now that I was hearing myself say all this stuff, I knew how much I missed my life there. Life in Iran was good if only I could have the freedoms I had there. Iran had given me my family, Arash, and it was my homeland. The homeland I was developing a very complicated relationship with! It was all good I told myself, some things that I couldn't find in New York, I found here. But the U.S. was my home too.

Arash came by to join the conversation and added, "If we would have known, it would have been a goodbye party too!"

"It's never too late to announce the number three!" Neda said laughing.

"You mean you are pregnant?" said Arash teasingly.

"I think she might be," I added some spice.

"Shut up guys!" said Neda jokingly. "I think Saloomeh is also headed back but I don't know when. Her dad is fed up with Iran," she added.

Saloomeh was busy flirting and getting drunk, so we didn't spoil her fun. I didn't want to hear about Saloomeh, because I would have turned sad. In my heart I really did want to go back and all this talk was taking away from the birthday fun. Arash noticed and kissed me lightly on the cheek without saying a word.

We brought out the cake, which Arash had ordered. It was in the shape of my lips! While blowing out the candles I had one wish: it was to head back home to New York. It might have seemed like a long-foreseen dream, but it was the only dream my heart desired. Of course, with Arash!

We did another toast before everyone started to wrap up and leave. The cousins, friends, and caterers all went home and all that was left was an awesome memory and Arash and me standing in front of each other. I walked towards him and hugged him so tightly I could feel how much I had grown attached to him.

I tilted my head up toward his ear and whispered, "Thank you for the party."

"I would do anything for you," he replied softly.

We gazed into each other's eyes before Arash took me in his arms and eased me with a kiss. I felt his heat, his tongue, his body against mine, and knew with him everything would be all right.

He tickled my ear with his lips and whispered, "You are the best thing that's ever happened to me."

I knew my feelings were just as true, and hearing him say this made it all the more real.

I turned to his ear, gently kissing it, and said, "Right back atcha."

And we stood there, listening to each other breathe, listening to our souls surrendering to one another. I felt like dew from a secret flower for him and looking at him brought on an intoxicating dizziness. It was like floating on some magical cloud, a potent drug allowing me to step into my femininity. With him there were no taboo thoughts, and everything was lost in the timeless moment of being with him.

"Can you sleep over tonight? I just want you to sleep next to me," he asked. Without thinking of the consequences of where in the world I would tell my parents I was, I answered yes.

"What are you going to tell the Emperor?" he asked.

"I don't want to think about that. I'll let Elham be the mastermind." I answered.

I lay nuzzling and cuddling with Arash, whose languid grin appeared permanent, and gave no thought to the outcome of this either. I think he was fed up with trying to think of this and that too.

The next morning I woke up and found the sunrise brushing the wall with gold. I wanted to stay in next to him but Cinderella had to rush home! The pumpkin ride was long overdue. I called Elham before leaving and she said my dad was worried sick and my mom was in critical condition.

"Just go home. Your dad is so mad it would take the Persian and Roman Empire to keep him in place! He kept asking me where you were, and I acted like I couldn't hear him so I hung up the phone!" she said nervously.

"I'm glad he didn't have our address. I swear he would have come to my door to ask for you woman!" she was so upset that she had lied. Her parents were chill, nothing compared to the Emperor. Maybe it was because she was Jewish. No this was a cultural, traditional, personal thing.

"I am all right woman, but worried for you. Just go home and roll the dice. I hope you had a good time last night!" she added.

"I did, but nothing happened! But it was good to not worry and be cuddling and kissing and cuddling and kissing," I said giggling. "Ok, talk to you later, if I live!" I said just as nervously. I had no idea what awaited me but I knew it wasn't pleasant!

I hugged the beau and rushed out to grab a cab. Oh god, I thought…how can these passionate feelings work in a country you live in, but not be on your side? My blood boiled again but I had to calm myself down. I had to deal with other elements of my life.

23

A Niche to Freedom

THE CAB PULLED UP TO the house and as I was walking and going up in the elevator I could already feel the negative energy through the doors. Or was that my imagination?

I walked in the house and walked straight to my room without looking around. I didn't even want to make eye contact, but from the corner of my eye I could see both parents watching TV on the couch.

After I settled in my room, I put on the *Three Stooges* to get a laugh and shrug it off. I mean what was going to happen? Was I getting punished, grounded, or thrown out of the house? The worst was already done by bringing me to this country, in my opinion. Anyway, in my conscious I knew I had done nothing wrong and hadn't disrespected anybody.

After about thirty minutes my mother came in my room and asked me to come out because they wanted to have a talk with me.

"What is this about?" I asked, still looking at the TV screen.

"You know what it is about Shaghayegh," she answered.

"Actually I don't because as far as I know I am living my life and not bothering anyone else," I said casually, but annoyed.

I paused the video and walked into the living room. The Emperor was there and waited for me to sit. At that point I really thought the title fit him well!

The first question out of his mouth was, "Why did you lie about where you were?" His tone was so intimidating that I felt like he was asking, "Why did you murder the Senator? What were your intentions?"

I couldn't deny anything and I was at the point where I didn't even *want to* deny anything. I didn't just consider my decision making the tail end of my rebellious teenage years but I considered it a clash with such a hide-and-seek culture. This is who I was and this is how I operated; label me easternized, westernized, traditional, stubborn or whatever. I wasn't disrespecting or hurting anyone but on the contrary I felt I was being tortured with customs and beliefs I was forced into.

"Because *you* forced me to lie. If I had told you I was at a party with my boyfriend would you have allowed it?"

"What? Boyfriend?" his voice escalated.

"Yes! Boyfriend! I have a boyfriend and he threw me a birthday party!" I said loudly.

"Lower your voice Shaghayegh. I don't want Aziz Joon, the neighbors and the whole world to know we are having a fight and where you were last night," my mother said.

In my heart I knew my mother felt what I was going through, but was also under the umbrella of these beliefs. Why did she have to conform? I felt she was on the very same page as me but had to keep it on the down low and just obey. What I didn't understand was that was she obeying my dad, obeying to keep face in front of her relatives in Iran, or to keep me from figuring out the truth.

"Mom, I am not speaking loudly. I am frustrated by how all you guys care about in this stupid country is how Mr. X and his lousy gossipy wife Mrs. X view me. Frankly I could care less, and to add to that I could care less about all this traditional nonsense of how a girl should be and not be! Oh, and leave all the Islamic beliefs aside, but I don't find myself in that direction at all!" I added.

"Don't shout Shaghayegh. I can hear you! I won't accept you partying with just any guy and I definitely won't accept you having a boyfriend!" the Emperor said firmly, as if we were negotiating the treaty between Palestine and Israel.

I didn't want to be disrespectful to them and say it's none of your business. "You know, we wouldn't be having these fights if I were still living my beautiful, happy life in Brooklyn. Maybe I wouldn't have wanted a boyfriend and maybe I would have known what I wanted to study. Maybe the pressure to be 'someone' here is not what I am accustomed to! I mean, who brings a sixteen-year-old back to Iran? Who does that? I had already formed my identity and right smack in the middle of my development years you brought me here! All my friends are moving back and you rewind back to a country stuck in the 1970s!" I said angrily, now almost shouting.

He knew I had a point and he knew he had made a big boo-boo. But no one, not even my mom, had the courage to tell him. I mean he was an Iranian man! Whatever! I had no role model and felt so lost at times. My role model was—and this may sound funny—Kevin's mom in *Home Alone*! Yes! And don't even let me go back to *Tango & Cash*!

I felt my mom challenged and she wanted me to get through the end of these crisis years as a healthy, well-adjusted adult, but not only did I want privacy for myself, but it had become an obsession to keep everything secret. I needed a neutral party, and before coming here I found that in my parents. I had lost it now. Oh, and let's not forget about my wildly late puberty stage, which was a no-show-no-tell! Shhh!

"We are trying to be supportive of you, but you have to accept some rules here. What part of telling the truth do you have a problem with?" my dad asked.

"I don't have a problem telling the truth, but I do have a problem with you pushing your rules and beliefs on me. So if you want the truth, you also have to accept that I have my own beliefs and they are definitely nothing like what you, mom, these black crows, or the neighbors believe!"

"Lower your voice! We won't have that in this house!" said my mother in a warning tone again.

"I don't want to be here! Living here has brought all this confusion upon me, and you both were the cause of this!" I said, this time shouting at the top of my lungs.

Both my parents were shocked, surprised and taken aback. They had never seen me like this. I had kept it in the whole time.

"This is your country," said my dad, regaining his tone. "Why don't you want to get in touch with your culture, heritage, and live here for a while and accept the differences?"

"Because I don't accept shoving mandatory beliefs down my throat and I won't accept just being someone else to be accepted!"

"Okay Shaghayegh, this is going too far and you are clearly not opening yourself up. I am not even going to ask you where you spent last night, but you are grounded until further notice. No more Elham, no more Bahareh and no more of this person you call your boyfriend! You will just go to work and come home!" he said angrily.

"There will be no lies in this house and all the calls will be screened. So don't think I will walk out of the house and you can call whoever it is you are calling. You are smart and have so much ahead of you, and at this age you are dating!" he added frustrated.

"People get married at my age!" I cried.

"That's the right way, not by dating!"

"And I assume the *right* way is by some lame intro and by he and someone coming to see you for permission. Is that *right?*" I said sarcastically. Now I had stepped on the lion's tail big time.

"Go to your room and don't come out until you make the decision to accept and respect rules and traditions in this country," he said looking straight at me and pointing to my room. "We can't go back to the U.S. because I have invested in our lives here, so don't even think that will be a solution either."

"Don't worry, and remember if you have another kid, don't torture him or her like you are doing to me! You didn't think of me when coming here. You only thought of yourself and how you missed your beloved country. And for the record, I am not a liar but I am true to myself and stand up for my own beliefs and way of life. I have done nothing wrong!" I said rather loudly and went towards my room, ready to burst into tears and find consolation through Kevin's mom and the warm feeling of Christmas time in *Home Alone*.

God, what does a girl have to do to just *be* these days? I curled up with my pillow and blanket and turned on the TV. My tears were in a coma and wouldn't roll down my cheeks. I was scared of my future and wanted to be with Arash. I had to eventually contact him, but I felt as if all my energy had been drained. It was the sorrow following the feast. I felt so alone.

• • •

Obviously, the show had to go on, so feeling the way I did, I got dressed and went to work the day after. I was in my own shell and didn't want to talk or socialize a lot at work. I just wanted to get my news stories, edit them, practice them and get the hell out of the station. The minute I got into work my director approached me and said they wanted to see me upstairs. Oh god, what now? What was wrong with these people? I had picked up that line from Julia Robert in *Pretty Woman*. I was so frustrated with my living conditions and my family that I was not in the mood to get in a religious pretentious mode.

I walked upstairs to the main headquarter's corporate office area and all the guards were looking at me like, "Oh, this hot chick!" Or maybe it was, "This frickin' American!" Or "How you doin'?" Either of those equivalent thoughts were in their heads when a black crow came out to meet me in the reception area and guided me to the main office of another black crow. It was the Senior HR office, the religious HR office.

"*Salam*," I said respectfully.

"*Salam Khanoom*," she replied back in a strong accusational type of tone.

I waited until she started on whatever she wanted to tell me. When the words started popping out of her mouth, a wave of up and downs came crashing over me. In addition to everything that went down with the Emperor last night, this was incomprehensible to me. I felt my hands fisting unconsciously and it felt like I was having a slight coma. I couldn't react because I felt judged and knew if I did, especially within the walls of a federal news agency where there must be cameras and stuff, I would just be condemned. I felt like saying, "I want my lawyer. Or better yet I want a human rights representative here!" But I knew it would make no difference. The point of complete surrender had been reached and I was in complete shock.

I could hear words like, "Not following Islamic rules; we have been following you; you have an illegal, sinful relationship; you should be ashamed of yourself; you put perfume on at work; you wear open-toed shoes; who do you think you are; you should solidify your beliefs; we want someone with solid beliefs as a reporter and anchor here, not someone who doesn't know what Islam is and who drinks alcohol!" And her last words were, "You are terminated from this point on. I encourage you to go more towards god and maybe take a trip to Mecca to learn more about Islam and make yourself a better Muslim."

Better Muslim? Who said I was a Muslim? I had stepped into a Muslim country and I respected it, but why did I have to be a Muslim and why did I have to follow all this religious stuff to hold a broadcasting position and pretend I was Muslim? What happened to respecting who you are and what you believed in? What happened to being a good person and realizing your full potential and growing that potential?

Then she threw a bunch of pictures on the desk from a private investigator or someone they had hired to follow me around. It was me with Arash, wearing a thin scarf with my hair revealed, partying in Lavasan, and every little bit of my private life. They had followed me around and butted into my personal life to see if I fit in and qualified to be an anchor! The good part was that at least I was smiling in some photos.

I was annoyed, sad, and completely outraged. What kind of better life did my parents want me to have here in Iran? From the moment of this conversation, I felt crushed and confused, with a complete loss of identity! Was I Iranian or American? Oh god...I was so confused I couldn't get up and leave her damn office! These people were from a different world. Words weren't of use to me at that point, and all I told her was, "Whenever you decide to go to Mecca call me and we'll go together!"

"Looks like you are *zaboon deraz* as well!" she said angrily. *Zaboon deraz* literally means "you have a long tongue" but metaphorically means "you are quite the rude one."

"I learn from my elders," I said. I glued a fake smile on my face while looking at her, opened the door and walked out the room as the other black crows were looking at me. I sensed looks that said, "That poor girl," or "she got what she deserved, you have to be a good Muslim to keep your job here like all of us." Other girls I sensed knew what was going on and how I was simply fighting for who I was, which included my background and growing up in Brooklyn.

I went downstairs but felt my legs were walking without me leading the way. I looked at some of my coworkers and they knew what had gone down. It was all around the office.

I was trying to fight back tears because it was enough that I was being questioned and fired for who I was; I didn't need these people feeling sorry for me. I quite frankly didn't care about the job, but was broken because they questioned who I was as a person. Which, after this, I didn't know the answer to.

My colleagues were the best. We had shared so many moments together and I truly loved them. I looked in their eyes but due to Islamic law I couldn't hug or handshake them goodbye. One of them slid me a piece of paper with his email and phone number, looked in the other direction and whispered, "Breathe, this place is like this and you are so real and so different. You are going to make a great reporter, but here, they will kill your fire and soul." Then aloud, so everyone could hear, he said, *"Movafagh bashi!"* (you will succeed!)

312

God, I thought corporate America was bad, but this took everything to another level! I wanted to take a pillow and scream into it! I told myself to breathe now and scream later. Good plan Shaghayegh.

Everyone knew the reason behind my departure: the religious HR had caught up to me and my director couldn't protect me anymore. I didn't know, but for months they had been following me and interrogating everyone about my personal life and how I operated beneath this wimple. I was shocked. What did my personal life and beliefs have to do with me being a professional at work?

I didn't feel defeated but had felt in some way I had let myself down by choosing to work in this place. Because I had. What choice does someone like me have to work anywhere in this country while being opinionated, non-religious, and wanting to be her full female self?

The question blaring in my head was, "How did this happen?"

The answer: my parents wanted me to get in touch with my roots because I was becoming "too white" or "too American."

As I said a dry goodbye to all my coworkers and the guy that always served tea nonstop to the employees, I looked into their eyes and I knew they knew this wasn't fair. This wasn't fair at all! Who had I hurt? What rule had I broken? Why was I the victim of their extremities? As this hurricane was going through my head I saw a security guard in front of me to escort me out of the building.

Security guard? This was obscene! Why did I need someone to escort me out of the building? Was I not being cooperative? Was I the American female interrupter? Angry, confused, mad, and heart broken, I followed the security guard. As I was giving him my building badge he looked at me and said, "*Shoma yeki az mahboubtarin ghoyandeghan Sede Sima boodid, delam baratoon tangh mishe.*" You were one of the most liked reporters here and I will miss you. This made me feel so much more heartbroken because I felt everyone was under a stupid spell here. This guy was escorting me out and taking my badge but also sharing with me his real feelings. Feelings he could have never shared if we were inside the building, or else someone would think we were having an illegal relationship.

I got a cab, put my head on my lap and cried all the way home. The cab driver probably thought I had lost a loved one because he kept looking at me and saying, "*Zengeghie dige*," meaning "it's life." The truth was I *had* lost someone, and that was me. Who the hell was I? One lost chick. I had American roots and Iranian roots but which one was *me*? I didn't feel at home in the country I was born in. I felt like I had lost my identity, or that it was broken into pieces. It didn't upset me that I had lost a job, but that I was questioned for being plain old me. I felt like my character, especially the American portion of it, was under attack and in ruins.

I got home, opened the door, and had to pass the living room on my way to my room. Both the Emperor and H_2O saw me with two big red, puffy and wet eyeballs. I just ran to my room, shut it, locked it, took off the stupid wretched wimple and manto and started crying into my pillow. I cried and cried and cried until there were no more tears left to cry. My heart ached to just be free of all this nonsense. I didn't want to see my parents, my friends, Arash, or any other living being. I made a nest of a room and stayed there, not wanting to go out into this country anymore. My room with my *Home Alone* movie, posters of my time in Brooklyn, and listening to pop music were my home. *Home Alone* was on repeat, literally. It was my medicine. It made me feel safe.

My parents kept asking me what had happened but I would shout from the top of my lungs, "Just leave me alone!" It was all their fault! Bringing me to this damn country I didn't understand and saying things like, "You are a champ and could change!" But it

314

wasn't like changing a coat, it was about changing who I was! I was slowly going into an emotional coma, and I did. My emotions were overloaded and I shut down. I was in my room 24/7 and didn't want to come out. I didn't want to eat, speak, listen or talk on the phone with anyone. I couldn't cope with it anymore. A darkness and resentment settled over me. I missed my real home.

After a week of knocking and begging to please open the door, I let my mom in. I didn't even trust my dad anymore. I think he was out of his mind in every way possible, and super cocky and arrogant for bringing me here without even asking if I also wanted this life change!

I had lost a lot of weight and had dark circles underneath my eyes. Honestly, I had no hope and wanted to die. I didn't care about anything anymore. I wanted to run away. My mom was super careful about what to say because at any moment she knew I would ask her to leave my room and she def didn't want to be locked out again. I felt she was scared I was going to do something to myself. I felt both of them were. They had heard another girl from the U.S. in my situation had committed suicide and were scared to the bone I would do the same.

"So you know my friend, the therapist, Dr. Veeda, who is on TV?"

I nodded.

"She wants to see you. She is the best therapist in Iran. Do you want me to take you?"

Home Alone was on in the background but on mute. I kept looking at the screen while she was talking. I had so much anger I couldn't even look at her face. I hated my parents for bringing me here and I was suffering for their desire to live in this country, the country they call home.

"No," I replied, looking at Kevin going to church on Christmas. Thank god for this movie, it warmed my heart.

"*Azizeh delam*, you are my only daughter and I feel like I am losing you. Can you please come? I can't see you like this. *Azizam* you haven't had anything to eat. Look at you, you have lost so much weight," and then she broke down crying.

I felt bad. Maybe she didn't want this either and it was all coming from my dad. He was the strict Iranian father. She was simply a follower. At times, I felt she obeyed him and didn't have any opinion of her own because it was simply not accepted by him.

I looked at her and saw a broken woman who maybe didn't want to come back either and was forced to do as she was told. Was my dad a dictator? He was so kind and wanted the best for his family, but was our best the same as his best? Then I thought of all the other women I had met in Iran and it all fell into place. They all had golden hearts but had no say in anything and simply had to obey. They were emotionally abused from their traditional parents and from the person they were sometimes forced to call their partner in life. Why weren't they given a choice to pick who they wanted to marry? Not someone whose resume looked good to them or their folks.

I looked at her, trying to understand, and although I really had no desire to see this therapist lady, I did it for her.

"I really have no desire to go out in this country anymore, but will go for you," I said and kissed her wet cheeks.

I went back to watching my movie, indicating it was time for her to leave.

•••

The therapist was a nice lady and I recognized her immediately because she was regularly interviewed on TV, like a Dr. Phil or something. I frankly didn't care if she was a good or cookie-cutter therapist because I was only doing this for my mom. After she broke down crying in front of me I suddenly felt she was a victim in all this too. I knew that if she had the power we would head back to New York and live our Brooklyn life again the way it was. The therapist had known my mom since childhood and when my mom had contacted her she accepted to see me immediately.

She looked at me with an observant eye and knew that I was not here to really get treatment or talk to someone. I was here because of a request. Suddenly Arash came into my thoughts and I realized how much I missed him. I hadn't contacted him since my birthday night and he was probably going nuts. I had no idea what was happening in the outside world, and frankly had no care.

I'm sure this was the first time she was encountering a case like mine. It was the first time I had stepped into a therapist's office and aside from the things you see on TV like on *M*A*S*H* or *Frasier*, I had no idea what to expect. She knew I was in culture shock mode and really just wanted to go home to my VHS tapes, the closest I could get to Brooklyn. I was not interested in advice or telling her about my days or frustrations. I really felt my road had come to an end. I had no thoughts of suicide or anything, but I knew that some of my friends had attempted it. Scary stuff.

The session ended with me thinking "thank god this is over!" I told her how much I hated this country, how I wanted to go back home, that there was no road for me to progress, and about the shit that had happened so far, and about my hate towards both my parents, especially my dad.

My state of culture shock was so obvious that whatever I said went back to Brooklyn. She sensed that I had hit extreme

317

homesickness with all the exposure to different mannerisms, lifestyles and people. When she asked how we could solve it, I told her there *was* no solution. My father didn't want to return, he wants to stay in *his* country. I was just going to rot in this country, run away and become a fugitive, or just kill myself. A tear shed while saying the last part. I loved life so much, but hated it right now. That's how I felt now. I was so lonely, filled with anger, and was tired of fighting all the time. I was totally detached from my current reality.

I told her I didn't want to speak with her again. She ended the session and started speaking to H$_2$O in whispers.

Since I had no interest in what she had to say, I peaced out and went downstairs to sit in the car and listen to my pop music. My mom returned teary-eyed.

Oh man, I couldn't take this anymore.

•••

I had made friends here, went through a horrible experience of a job, put a scarf on to cover my hair at all times, and dealt with leaving my life back home. Now, I felt like a depression storm was hovering over me. I *did* have so much ahead of me and knew this was not a phase I would overcome. There was no road ahead.

I started writing aggressively at home. Highly emotional stuff: love, sorrow, my deep sense of loss and sadness, anxiety and fear. The writing was trying to cure the bleeding, to give me some sort of solace and understanding.

Opening up to the pen and paper, I realized there was one element shining within me: passion. I could still smile and imagine I would be back home one day. Yes, I could smile at this situation. No one could rob me of my smile. I still refused to speak with my dad. I didn't have any desire. I ignored him and only spoke to answer my mom when she asked some questions, which normally ended in "yes," "no" or "I don't know."

Initially, I felt I had the energy and passion to fly through it. And that passion wasn't anywhere near dead, but something was killed along the way. What had died was being blown away, the ashy remains of an inflamed argument. The probing questions and guilt trips just exemplified how we saw life. Fine, even if I was thrown off the boat, I could still swim. But how? The answer to this was so unclear to me. How could I leave this country?

I knew my parents were concerned for my health, and they never wanted this to happen. But they also knew my nature was bound to preordain me to some trouble with the authorities here, the first being themselves! My instincts told me my dad had bluffed about the phone line being screened by him. We didn't have a caller ID and this was just part of his full house poker strategy. After a good week and a half one night I took out my secret phone and called Arash.

He picked up immediately. "Shaghayegh, where are you?" he asked impatiently. "It's been so long since you called me. What's going on with you?"

I felt bad for not calling him these last few days, but I needed to find myself again after the explosion. I didn't know whether he would answer, or act upset. Regardless, I had to call him. He was my only SOS backup, my support and immune system!

"Well, *salam* to you too!" I said giggling.

"*Salam* back," he said now feeling assured that I was alive but was half angry and half happy.

"I needed some time to myself. I had this massive argument with my dad and felt the world was going to crash down on me and then the whole job thing..." I said and suddenly I felt weak again but managed to tell him the whole story. He already knew and knew I was going through hell.

"I need your help and I have a plan. Can you please help me? I really need to get out of this stupid country before I commit suicide," I said. He knew I wouldn't actually commit suicide.

"What's up *azizam*?" he said trying to calm me.

"I need your help twofold: to buy me a ticket to the U.S., and to let me know how I can do this with all the rules in the airport," I said.

"Are you out of your mind?"

"Yes, I *am!* I hate it here and no one understands! My parents think it'll pass or I will get better by seeing a therapist or something. The only part I look forward to every day is you!" I said holding back my tears. "I feel like an alien that everyone looks at when they hear I'm from New York, I can't stand pretending and lying over and over and over again."

"I think you can talk to your dad about this. C'mon you are being a bit irrational, no?"

"Arash, just look at my situation and tell me what is irrational? My father has his ways and they will not change and my mother tries to be the glue when deep down she knows I'm right. There is no way to fight this and I'm tired. I want to go back."

"What will you do when you get back? You have no money, no place to stay."

"I will go to Christina's house until I get a job somewhere. There I have opportunities and know my way around. I can find my way there. Here I feel like I'm in a maze! You can meet me over there, in New York. We can be together on the other side without the bullshit I have to deal with here," I added in a pleading voice.

"*Azizam*…this is something big. Why are you running away?"

320

"It looks like I'm running away but I'm not. I'm just going home and will call them a bit after, when I get settled. I feel I am going insane here."

"But what's going to happen to us?" he questioned.

"I don't know, but Iran won't help our relationship either. We are a team and I need your help," I said. We had become part of one another's life. Spending so much time together, sharing so many thoughts and moments had brought us closer than even we thought. There was a deep silence and we both knew we were playing with fire, but I hated Iran.

"I care for you and know you are in a tough spot, but let me help you talk with him. Maybe if I introduce myself and he gets to know me it might be better," he said.

"Arash, I hate living in this country! There is nowhere to go from here, especially with all the limitations for females, and I don't like the belief system dictated. Why do I always have to watch if my scarf falls off and have a third eye for the *Komiteh*? Anyway, I don't want to get married now and if you come forward the Emperor won't just sit and watch us date!" I said miserably.

I felt awful doing this but I needed to breathe. Arash connected with me and surrendered to my request. We talked until the sun rose, until I started to pass out.

I wanted nothing more than to open up my eyes to the streets of New York.

•••

Within the two days of my talk with the TV therapist I could hear my parents having huge arguments. When I heard them arguing I would just put my headphones on. All I could think about was Arash helping me get out so I could live again. A couple of words I did hear were, "This is my country and it's my home!" Then H$_2$O would answer, "You are being selfish, because it's not her home!' Then some other stuff which I had no interest in hearing. The road to peace of mind was still *Home Alone* or *Tango & Cash*. I knew every line of these two movies by heart by now.

•••

That evening my mom knocked and in a pleading voice came into my room. Her eyes were red and I could smell the argument was over me.

"How are you?" she asked.

Obviously, I had lost more weight and was not looking like my Oscar red carpet finest! So what kind of question was that?

"I have been speaking to your dad, and we have come to a decision. I want you to hear me out," she said.

Okay, this was getting weird and scary. What more was there to hear? Oh there was one thing they could've done: take away my VHS tapes, which would leave me without oxygen and food. I felt the Emperor walking around and asked her to shut the door because I didn't want to see him. She listened without hesitation.

"Listen, I want you to know how much we both love you. Coming here was not an easy choice for us either. I mean, I had friends in Brooklyn, your dad had a great job, everything was so easy and fun," she continued. Why she was saying this I had no idea. Get to the juice, mom!

"We really made this decision so it would be a better life for you, you were turning so white and were forgetting you were Iranian and that you have Iranian roots. We thought this would be a great way for you to get in touch with your family and your culture. That's all *azizam*. We never wanted to hurt you," and with that she burst out crying. I handed her a tissue.

"Mom, what's your point?" I said, so not interested in any of this small talk.

"I just want you to know we love you and your dad adores you. He really wants to talk to you and is here," she said that pointing towards the door.

Wrong move.

"No interest. Mom, I get it. Could you please leave now? All of this was for you, not me. If I was involved the least, tiniest bit you would've asked for my opinion *before* the move!" I said raising my voice. "Just leave me alone!" I said partly screaming. Lord, I had no tolerance for this anymore.

"I will leave but wanted to tell you that we had no idea this would happen with all this culture shock and homesickness for you. We would do anything for you," she said.

Blah. Just the same repeats. I was so tired of listening and trying to understand. I thought it was the other way around. Parents were supposed to try and understand teens.

"I can't see you like this. I've talked to your father and the therapist and we have decided to return to New York."

Wait—did my ears hear the words right? We were going back home! No, I couldn't believe it. I just looked at her.

"When, like, my hair turns the color of my teeth?" I said sarcastically.

"No *azizam*. In three weeks. I have bought our ticket already and you and I are going," she said.

What? You and I? Were they getting a divorce? Was he going to stay and enjoy wimple land? I looked at her in surprise and she knew exactly what was on my mind.

"Your father doesn't like this either and believe me if he knew, he would never have made the move back. Financially it cost him a lot too, and seeing the family like this is not what he wanted. I think you should give him a chance to explain it," she continued.

"Is he staying here?" I asked, ignoring the other part of her question. I didn't want him to explain it. I was so over it.

"He is going to stay here, sell the house and wrap up our life here while we go and try to figure this whole thing out in New York," she answered looking straight at me.

"Mom, are you joking with me just to make me feel better, or have you guys really decided to move back?" I asked seriously.

"These are our plane tickets, all booked," she confirmed. She handed me two plane tickets. Was this true? Was my dream becoming reality? The tickets were real, physical and not fake!

She held my hand tight. "We are going back, and you can study whatever you want and work without having to pretend. This wasn't easy for me either or for your father, but we are used to this country and way of life. I mean, we were brought up here but never thought it would hit you this way," she continued.

"You are the most important thing to us and your happiness is number one for us. Listen, we are not perfect. We are trying to understand you and never thought the situation would end up like this," she said again.

Apology accepted! I was ready to dance all around the house and celebrate! My optimism toward life and the energy I once felt were slowly coming back. I couldn't believe it was true, but the plane tickets were sparkling in front of me! The moment was so real I wanted to capture and frame it so it wouldn't disappear, and then go and dance on top of the roof. That is, if no religious HR followed me around!

"Mom! Thank you so much! I truly hate it here. I've felt so lost," I said half happy and half crying. It was the first time I had opened up to her since I got fired.

"I love you guys but can't believe you did this," then I froze in my words, knowing they had no clue it was going to turn out like this either.

We hugged it out and I just wanted to sleep with the tickets under my pillow, thinking someone might come and steal them in the middle of the night. I didn't want to share the news with anyone either, in case someone jinxed it!

I later found out what had prompted all this: the therapist. After I had peaced out to the car that day, she had told my mom that I was in extreme culture shock and if we were to stay here I wouldn't make it. She knew some girls had committed suicide who were in somewhat the same situation as me in Iran. Someone got it.

Suddenly I thought about Arash. I had to take out the secret telephone and make a priority call tonight.

• • •

I spoke to Arash that night, and he had already bought me a ticket to leave the week after. I told him what had happened and he was shocked, but he could return the ticket.

Sometimes I wondered if the same sort of thing had happened to him when he returned from London, but was too mentally tired to ask. I just gave him the good news and went to bed with the tickets underneath my pillow!

I had no idea what would happen to us, but at least some part of this crazy piece of the puzzle was solved.

24

Look Up

June 1998

LIKE EVERYTHING ELSE, THIS COUNTRY had a catch even when you were leaving!

In addition to an exit fee that had to be paid, unmarried women must have permission from their father or male guardian before leaving the country! I was outraged when I heard that! So unmarried women were slaves…ugh! If the father decided to bring the child out of the country, permission wasn't required, but if the mother or the kid wanted to leave, the father needed to give permission! Ridiculous!

Oh and the best part was, married women in Iran always needed their husband's permission to be able to hold a passport. Husbands could ban their wives from leaving the country at any time! This mentality meant that women should have owners, are slaves. Arash told me the majority of the people not allowed to leave Iran were either women who didn't have the permission of their husbands, or tax evaders. Modern slavery.

So my father had to apply in person, then my passport was stamped to indicate the valid period I was to be out. Since the Emperor was fully on board, I didn't have any problems.

The next morning he had come in my room and we had hugged it out. The good part for him was that momma had done the talking for him the night before so he was safe and didn't need to do lots of explaining. The bad part was that it was awkward. He just whispered, "Everything is going to be all right. I will wrap things up here and you need to focus on college and taking care of your mom there," he said.

"This will be a hard time for all of us and your mom has always been dependent on me being there, but now you need to help her out and be a team until I wrap stuff up here," he said worried in a way.

The crappy part was that I was going to miss him. He kept telling me to be strong. Strong for what? It wasn't going to be tough because I knew my way around back home. But I knew we were headed for a brand-new life and every change comes with a difficult start, especially when it starts with your family being divided for some time.

How long was this so-called wrap-up going to take? I hope this didn't damage their marriage. It also scared the living hell out of me that I had to support my mom. She had never worked a day in her life and now that dad was going to be in Iran until he finished the wrap-up, god knows what would happen in between. I was happy and scared both at once.

"*Azizam*, I never wanted to hurt you," he said while looking into my eyes then kissing my forehead. "Let's go have some pancakes, I'm making them!" Pancakes? He was the pancake master in

Brooklyn on Sundays, so I wasn't surprised if he made the batter from scratch in Tehran.

•••

I started counting down the days until we officially left. I was beyond excited. I doubled my effort to help out in selling furniture, packing bags, wrapping up all the sculptures momma had in the living room and saying goodbye to everyone with a smile. I was in rush, rush, rush mode to get home. I felt there was so much to look forward to and I had completely accepted the fact that I was a full blood Iranian, but with a completely different set of beliefs and way of life. Yes, to repeat myself so I can recap my experience in this country, I had come to a full understanding of my American and Iranian sides and cherished both parts, but I had accepted that I was connected to them in different ways. It was a tough uphill battle.

Oh my gosh, now came another round of getting things right. Where were we going to stay in NYC? We had no house! How were we going to survive when all the money was here in Iran? But at this point, I wanted to leave the past behind and focus on the moment. My parents could figure it out. Mom told me we were going over her friend's house until we got a place of our own.

After putting all of my ducks in one row, the night finally arrived. I didn't want to miss any moment of my last night in Tehran, since I knew I would not come back. I had formed somewhat of an emotional connection here to my family and its people

I spent the whole last day with my parents and friends. Everyone came to Aziz Joon's house to send us off. I would definitely miss them. I loved them so much, but knew we were so different. My dad, the dearest man to my heart, and Aziz Joon,

Bahareh, Ghazaleh, all my girlfriends…but I was going back home. If they understood the differences between two places I call home for different reasons, it would be great. And if they didn't, I still had to move forward with my life.

As we reached the airport, the night was dark and I felt scared. Scared of what was ahead of me. I had no security waiting on the other side; only freedom. Part of my soul was being left behind because of the Emperor, but I was very happy at the same time. Why? Why did this have to happen this way?

The whole family had come to the airport to say goodbye. I'll admit I had already forgotten some of their names! So bad.

I hugged everyone goodbye and when it came to my dad, I was so sad. I didn't want my family to separate like this, but it was for the better. "It's going to be all right. You are a survivor and I will come in a couple months," he said while kissing my forehead. This was a new habit he had picked up.

I would never forget the good friendships I had made here. People were so special and kind. I just didn't fit in the system. And my beautiful grandmother, Aziz Joon. She understood and saw what was going on from the moment we arrived. I knew she was going to visit us in New York.

My mom and dad had a long goodbye hug and he whispered something in her ear then kissed her on the lips. Whoa! Mr. Emperor kissing in public! I wondered if the *Komiteh* opposed that even though they were married? I wanted to eavesdrop on what he whispered in her ear, but it was too loud. I could see my mom was a bit scared. I had no idea what the plan was but knew momma would fill me once she got ahold of her emotions and we were on the plane.

I wanted everyone to leave because I didn't want to burst out crying. I loved my parents, my cousins, and Arash…most of all

Arash. I had met up with Arash earlier and said goodbye, but I was so scared of getting caught by the *Komiteh* on the day I was leaving and jeopardizing my freedom, so I kept it super short between us. I realized then that I was also scared of breaking down in front of him about how much I was going to miss him. I promised to contact him once I was settled. That's all I *could* promise him then.

I left the group, grabbing my momma's arm and dragging her towards the security check-in after *another* round of sad goodbyes (Persian style), with my masculine side leading and my feminine side observing what was happening.

We finally passed security and passport control. Everything worked out fine since I had my American passport and my father's permission to leave the country.

We waited in silence until our flight was ready to board. Tears rolled from my eyes as I looked at my final moon in Tehran's sky.

I knew this freedom came at a hefty price.

Dear Reader,

I sincerely hope you enjoyed reading about my crazy journey of identity during some of the most formative years of my life. I want to thank you from the bottom of my heart for purchasing my book and reading through my crazy ups and downs. If you enjoyed the read (or even if you have some other words about the book you'd like to share!), it would be wonderful to see a review from you up on the book's page at Amazon.com. Your reviews help storytellers like me get ourselves out in front of more readers and help to spread word and awareness about the coming-of-age I experienced in a world where I feared my identity was being swallowed whole. If you think these kinds of stories are important to be told, then please become a part of the story by posting a review. Thank you!

Sincerely,

Shaghayegh "Poppy" Farsijani

About the Author

After returning to New York, Shaghayegh Farsijani became a poet and perfume entrepreneur. She has traveled extensively throughout the world and has finally permanently settled in her hometown of New York City. After publishing her collection of sensual poetry, she decided to share her story as a young woman during some of the most heated years in Iran's modern history--a story about her hardships as a westernized Brooklyn teenager in Iran that ultimately led to her self-discovery and strength. She is also the founder and CEO of Desert35, a fragrance company based in NYC in which you can create your own custom fragrance from scratch. She also has a signature collection of Eau De Parfums inspired by her memoir capturing the spirit of independence of a woman journeying to find her herself and fortifying one belief: staying true to your authentic self, every day, all day. She is also featured in *Shark Tank* original Shark Kevin Harrington's upcoming book on successful entrepreneurs and was endorsed by him for her unique business concept, rapid growth and fostering the sense of authenticity within her product.

SHAMING MY RED LIPS

67338448R00205

Made in the USA
Middletown, DE
10 September 2019